PRAISE FOR *REHUMANIZING THE W*

In *Rehumanizing the Workplace*, Rosie and Jon reinforce what every leader of today needs to know: people thrive in environments where they feel cared for, safe to create and innovate, and part of an organization's shared purpose. Let this book guide you in building a team or company through which people have the opportunity to become their best selves!

Bob Chapman, author of *Everybody Matters: The Extraordinary Power of Caring for Your People Like Family* and CEO of Barry-Wehmiller

Imagine a world in which you walk into work and feel safe. Imagine using words like *compassion*, *purpose*, and *belonging* to describe your culture. Imagine a workplace where you deeply trust the people around you. *Rehumanizing the Workplace* teaches us how to create this kind of world. It's practical, actionable, and timely, and it will hit you straight in your heart. If you want to learn how to transform a culture regardless of the position you hold, this is the book for you.

Kristen Hadeed, founder of Student Maid and author of *Permission to Screw Up*

Rehumanizing the Workplace is a tour de force. It pulls extensively from the lineage of leadership and organizational research, thought, and practice leadership. It then distills all that into a very readable and practical guide for creating an organization fit for purpose in highly complex environments. It compellingly makes the case for a radically human workplace and for a more conscious approach to capitalism. If you want to create a workplace where people thrive, bring their best, and create amazing results, this book is well worth a read.

Bob Anderson, chairman of The Leadership Circle and coauthor of *Mastering Leadership* and *Scaling Leadership*

Rehumanizing the Workplace is an important and engaging guide to building workplaces that work in the modern world. Its five rehumanizing principles are compelling and actionable. Managers, consultants, and anyone else who wants to help organizations thrive should read this book immediately!

Amy C. Edmondson, professor at Harvard Business School and author of *The Fearless Organization: Creating Psychological Safety in the Workplace for Learning, Innovation, and Growth*

Admit it. You've questioned (silently) whether a truly human workplace can be successful in the marketplace. Can kindness and capitalism coexist? Does purpose elevate profit? Can an entire organization of individuals—no bosses, no hierarchy—self-manage themselves into excellence? The answer: yes, yes, and yes. *Rehumanizing the Workplace* gives example after example of companies generating exceptional performance by prioritizing respect, trust, and meaning. Rich with ideas, richer with practical steps, it's a worthwhile read. But beware, you might run out of reasons to avoid bringing more humanity into your own business.

Wendy Lynch, PhD, cofounder of *The Heart of Human Capital* blog and coauthor of *Get to What Matters: Tools to Transform Conversations at Work*

We know that work plays an increasingly vital role in our lives at the same time that the vast majority of people are unfulfilled and removed from their full potential at work. We are in need of new disruptive models that challenge our conventional thinking and instill a sense of humanity at work. *Rehumanizing the Workplace* is just that—a powerful blend of research, inspiration, and actionable steps for the changes our workforce needs. In their book, Rosie and Jon leave us without an excuse to make measurable progress in the movement to humanize work.

Arthur Woods, cofounder of Mathison

This book is the real stuff, written by real people doing the work on multiple levels. *Rehumanizing the Workplace* is the culmination of genius and experience of two of the most inspiring leadership authors and practitioners today. I've worked with the authors, taken their certification training, and experienced them firsthand teaching and applying successfully what is shared in this book.

Craig Neal, lead author of *The Art of Convening: Authentic Engagements in Meetings, Gatherings, and Conversations* and cofounder of the Center for Purposeful Leadership and the Convening Institute

The bad news for employee health is that the workplace was recently declared the fifth leading cause of death in America. There is no question that the health of most working people across the globe has been declining at a steady pace for years, and there is no end in sight to this unfortunate trend. Traditional worksite wellness programs have not proven to be the solution. So what's next? Rosie and Jon lay a foundation for creating workplaces that help people thrive, not just survive. *Rehumanizing the Workplace* takes the reader on a guided journey that, if followed correctly, will create an employee experience that can improve the thriving of people *and* organizations.

Ryan Picarella, president of WELCOA (Wellness Councils of America)

REHUMANIZING THE WORKPLACE

REHUMANIZING THE WORKPLACE

Future-Proofing Your Organization While Restoring Hope, Well-Being, and Performance

ROSIE WARD | JON ROBISON

Foreword by RAJ SISODIA

Conscious Capitalism Press
www.consciouscapitalism.org/press

Round Table Companies
Packaging, production, and distribution services
www.roundtablecompanies.com

Editorial Review *Agata Antonow*
Design *Sunny DiMartino*
Proofreading *Adam Lawrence, Carly Cohen*
Project Management *Keli McNeill*

Printed in the United States of America

First Edition: March 2020
10 9 8 7 6 5 4 3 2 1

Library of Congress Cataloging-in-Publication Data
Rehumanizing the workplace: future-proofing your organization while restoring hope, well-being, and performance / Rosie Ward and Jon Robison.—1st ed. p. cm.
ISBN Hardcover: 978-1-950466-13-9
ISBN Paperback: 978-1-950466-14-6
ISBN Digital: 978-1-950466-15-3
Library of Congress Control Number: 2019918885

CONTENTS

FOREWORD
BY RAJ SISODIA

This is a timely and important book. I can think of no greater imperative for the world of business than to bring full humanity to the workplace.

This shift has been a long time coming. In the 1920s, US President Calvin Coolidge made a speech in which he said, "The business of America is business." In many ways, this was a true statement. The United States is a uniquely entrepreneurial nation. It was founded on the idea that ordinary people could rise from nothing to great heights by dint of their vision and hard work. But it does beg the question, "What is the business of business?" For too long, we have answered this question in the way that Alfred P. Sloan did. He built General Motors into the largest corporation in the world, and pioneered many aspects of modern management. Sloan said, "The business of business is business." In other words, business should focus purely on making money and leave the rest to other sectors of society, including the government and civil society.

But there is, we believe, a better way to think about business. This was articulated by Herb Kelleher, the person who built Southwest Airlines into the most successful airline in the history of the world and one of the greatest companies. Over its nearly fifty-year history, Southwest Airlines has never had a single strike, despite being the most heavily unionized of the major airlines. It has only had one passenger casualty, the result of a freak accident a couple of years ago. It has been consistently growing and profitable over all those decades. It has never laid off a single employee, even after 9/11, when most airlines had massive layoffs. The company stock market symbol is LUV, and it operates with love toward all of its stakeholders. Herb Kelleher articulated the company's philosophy in the way that all of us can understand: "The business of business is people—yesterday, today, and tomorrow."

This is a fundamental truth that we must keep in the forefront of our consciousness at all times. We need a Copernican revolution in our thinking; after decades, if not centuries, in which profits were at the center of the corporate universe, we must restore people to their rightful position at the center. Everything else, including profits, must serve human flourishing.

Instead, we have a world in which many human beings are subject to enormous suffering in the pursuit of profit.

What does it mean to be human? We are divine beings, worthy of being treated as such by each other. We are the only creatures with imagination, a moral compass, and free will. Each one of us has such extraordinary potential that it is hard to conceive of any limits on what we can achieve. Businesses refer to human beings as a resource, but we are not a resource. Human beings are the *source*, capable of unlimited amounts of caring, creativity, and innovation. But if people are treated as resources, they become that. They get depleted and they burn out, just like lumps of coal.

The human seed has never been more potent; people today are more intelligent, more educated, better informed, better connected, and more caring than ever before. But the soil around the human seed remains toxic. Most workplaces do not enable human beings to operate at their peak potential and deliver the gifts they were born to bring to the rest of us. To take the analogy further, we can use seeds in different ways. A seed can simply be used as birdfeed, or it can be used to start a whole new forest. Too many of us are being used as birdfeed.

Why is humanizing the workplace the greatest imperative of our times? The fact is that our work is literally killing us. Heart attacks are significantly higher on Mondays. In his book *Dying for a Paycheck*, Jeffrey Pfeffer estimates that one hundred and twenty thousand Americans die every year due to stress connected to work. It is not the work itself but the ways in which we lead, manage, and organize companies that results in all the suffering. An estimated seventeen thousand Chinese die every day from overwork.

It doesn't have to be this way. We don't have to hurt people or kill them in order to make money. As we show in our book *The Healing Organization*, quite the contrary: workplaces where people physically, mentally, emotionally, spiritually, and socially thrive are far more successful workplaces by every measure.

How did the workplace become so dehumanized in the first place? It has to do with how we think about business. Many people think of business as a jungle in which "survival of the fittest" is the cardinal rule. "Kill or be killed." Some treat business as a dehumanized machine with inputs like physical capital, human capital, and financial capital and outputs like profits and products. Some have reduced business to a math problem, seeking to maximize one thing—shareholder value—while treating everything else as a means to that end. Still others treat business as a game in which you make multiple bets, hoping that some would pay off. The fact is that business is one of the most human things that we do, and it impacts our lives as human beings in so many different ways.

I attribute these harmful ways of thinking to an excess of masculine energy in the world of business. Adam Smith wrote *An Inquiry into the Nature and Causes of the Wealth of Nations*, which laid out the foundational principles for how free markets operate and how individuals pursuing their self-interest will result in many, if not most, of our needs being met through businesses. But Smith also wrote *The Theory of Moral Sentiments* seventeen years prior to *The Wealth of Nations*. In that book, he elaborated our need to care for each other, without regard to self-interest. In a sense, capitalism had a mother and a father, and both were Adam Smith. Unfortunately, we ignored the mother energy—his message about caring—and focused only on the father energy—his message about pursuing self-interest.

Today, they are two things hidden away in the corporate closet. The first is unexpressed love. Human beings have a deep need to express their caring for each other, and most workplaces do not allow for that. People are expected to put on their mask and armor and go to battle in the marketplace. The second thing that is hidden in the corporate closet is silent suffering. Life is difficult; people are carrying around enormous burdens as they go through their workday. We need to allow both of these things to come out of the corporate closet. Our innate need to care can help alleviate much of the suffering that people are experiencing in life and in the workplace. By allowing this to happen, we can greatly enhance the amount of joy that people experience at work, which to me is the ultimate expression of what it means to have a fully humanized workplace.

INTRODUCTION

Businesses have long operated like ships at sea. A single captain is responsible (in name) for everything that happens on the ship; and a small handful of officers oversees key functional areas like navigation, cargo, or propulsion. Meanwhile, a large number of sailors labor away at the day-to-day tasks required to make the ship actually work.

However, the seas are volatile, uncertain, complex, and ambiguous (also known as VUCA). Some days, sailing is smooth; but many days, crew and cargo are tossed about the ship as humans work against the awesome power of nature. Sometimes, the VUCA sea even triumphs over the ship, and the sailors are thrown to the mercy of the elements—their only hope is to find a path toward calmer waters or an island that might offer shelter and sustenance.

Imagine that the VUCA sea caused a shipwreck, and the survivors landed on such an island. Many of the crew, and a few of the officers, knew very little aside from life at sea. Their solution to being shipwrecked was to revert to the familiar and try to maintain the shipboard chain of command. They reasoned that doing things the way they'd always done them would keep them orderly and safe until help arrived. Operating according to this familiar, "tried-and-true" manner (i.e., an old paradigm) was all they knew, so they clung tightly to it, hoping that eventually someone would come along to rescue them.

While some of the crew were happy to follow the old system, others knew that life stranded on a forgotten island would not be anything like life onboard a ship. This diverse group of individuals knew they needed to shift their paradigm to survive—and even thrive—in their new surroundings. While their old-paradigm shipmates looked to the officers to figure out what to do next, this group of forward-thinking sailors got into action. They quickly aligned on their purpose and vision: to ensure survival, a hopeful rescue, and finding a way to thrive despite the unknowns and challenges of this new environment. With that shared clarity, these new-paradigm sailors realized that building a fire was a primary requirement for their survival; the light from the fire would help rescuers find them on the beach and perhaps signal their presence to any passing ships. They were *building a lighthouse* to illuminate their purpose and guide their actions.

Then the new-paradigm sailors recognized the need for fresh water, so a smaller group moved inland in search of a freshwater source. After a while, through the trees and underbrush, they spotted a group of the old-paradigm sailors. Some members of this new-paradigm group initially felt a sense of competition with the old-paradigm sailors, wanting to prove them wrong and look in a different place. But one member of the new-paradigm group stepped forward and called out to the other sailors, suggesting they all work together. After all, everyone shared the same vision of surviving and thriving. Even though she knew that some of her new-paradigm peers might disagree with her reaching out to collaborate, the new-paradigm sailors had worked to *create a fearless environment* where she could take a risk and where candor was embraced—and expected. This wasn't about being right; it was about working toward a collective vision to ensure that everyone could thrive in their new surroundings.

The new and old-paradigm sailors set aside their differences and, together, moved deeper into the jungle on the island, skirting a mountain along the way. One new-paradigm sailor, inspired by the fearless example of his colleague, risked the unsteady terrain and climbed partway up the mountain to get a better view. "It looks like there's water up ahead," he called down, "but there's a wicked-looking swamp between us and the water." The group debated whether they should look for a way around the swamp or go back to the beach and approach it from a different direction. Then one woman spoke up and said, "Surely there's uncertainty and risk going through the swamp, but we can't waste time. Sometimes we must do the uncomfortable things that move us toward our goal. We can't be afraid to *wade in the messy middle*."

On the far side of the swamp, one of the new-paradigm survivors suggested electing a leader. The survivors began to discuss priorities and goals, and after discussing among themselves for a while, they self-organized into groups focused on a variety of necessary tasks. They weren't posturing or trying to look good; everyone showed up authentically human, spoke their minds, and collaborated on identifying what needed to happen and how they each fit into the bigger picture. They were all *showing up as leaders*.

So they braved the unknowns and discomfort of the swamp and eventually brought water back to the beach. After the journey through the swamp, the survivors knew that the rules were completely different. This diverse group of individuals challenged the status quo, spoke candidly with one another, and *found their tribe* amongst the survivors who also imagined a new, and better, way of doing things. They didn't always agree on how they'd achieve this vision of thriving, but they appreciated one another's input and supported each other.

The members of the tribe discussed what to do next. One of them said, "We can't just wait for someone to accidentally sail past this island. We need to use our skills to help people see us—and to also help other ships not crash here like we did. We all agreed the first thing to do was build a fire, and that was important. I think it's time to take that to the next level and really *build a lighthouse*." As the tribe planned their work and gathered supplies, one member began to write down the steps the group was taking to serve as a guide in case the tribe ever had to do work like this again.

What Shipwrecked Sailors Can Teach Us about Rehumanizing Workplaces

Imagine a world where workplaces operate more like the new-paradigm tribe on the shipwrecked island—where everyone can show up as their authentically human, best selves. They can adapt to align with a shared vision. They feel fulfilled, supported, and cared for, and have meaningful, purposeful work. At the end of the workday, they are able to bring their best selves home, be fully present with their loved ones, tend to their well-being, and replenish their wells. We believe—and know—that this vision is possible. And it is desperately needed!

Our world is rapidly changing and becoming increasingly complex. Just as with the seas in our opening story, there is an acronym used to describe this reality—VUCA (volatile, uncertain, complex, and ambiguous). Although VUCA originated from the US Army War College, it is widely used today in the business world.

While at first blush it might seem odd that this now widely used business term originated in the military, it actually makes a lot of sense. Shortly after the creation of the concept in the mid-1990s following the end of the Cold War, I (Jon) had the amazing privilege of speaking to the graduating class at the War College in Carlisle, Pennsylvania. These leaders were about to graduate and take over their commands in the army. I was brought in to talk about thinking outside the box relating to health, motivation, and behavior.

If you can picture a mid-forties man with hair down to his shoulders and a full beard, perhaps looking a bit more like Jesus than like a PhD, dressed in an African dashiki and speaking to a room full of soon-to-be generals, you might be as curious as I was about why I was invited to present the graduation keynote. It turns out the person who invited me had seen me speak at the combined Army/Air Force Health Promotion Conference some months earlier. When I asked him why he had chosen me, he did not hesitate for even a moment. He said, "Jon, these leaders are going to have the lives of thousands of men under their purview. Where else could it possibly be more important for them to be able to think outside the box?" Needless to say, it was an experience I have never forgotten!

In a VUCA world, disruption is the new norm, and thinking outside the box in business, as in the military, is critical. To assure this happens, the rules of business need to evolve. Yet many organizations are stuck in outdated practices and are not equipping people to thrive in this new reality. Strategies that may have worked a few years ago have quickly become irrelevant due to changes in technology, our environment, and demographic shifts and demands in the workforce. For example, in December 2017 a McKinsey Global Institute report stated that nearly 375 million jobs worldwide will vanish by 2030 due to automation.[1] Yet, not all technological advances and process improvement efforts are actually improvements when it comes to *people.*

The Bad News: How the VUCA World Has Increased Dehumanized Workplaces

In the 2009 movie *Up in the Air*, George Clooney plays the role of Ryan Bingham, a corporate downsizer. He flies into various companies and breaks the news to the employees being let go. Anna Kendrick plays Natalie Keener, his new, young MBA graduate coworker who is about to disrupt Ryan's world. She proposes cutting costs by changing to virtual downsizing—firing people via videoconference rather than in person. Of course, Ryan is appalled at this "know-it-all" and wants to preserve the life he loves—being a constant traveler.

Ryan ends up needing to cramp his style by bringing Natalie along with him to show her the ropes so she can try out her virtual firing approach. They set up shop in a conference room at the client site near another conference room where the soon-to-be-fired employees will be so they can test Natalie's approach. Ryan is hoping she can see how important it is to be human, by being in person, during a difficult process of losing one's job. At one point during the movie, one of the people Natalie fired ends up killing herself. Not surprising, this really shakes up Natalie. She comes to the realization that technology isn't always a viable replacement for humans; and the company ends up putting the remote layoff program on hold.

Sadly, trying to replace humans with technology doesn't just happen in the movies. Donna took a break from the workforce for a few years to raise her children. As her kids entered school, Donna also went back to school to finish her economics degree. Last year she graduated and began searching for work. As she applied to several different organizations, she expressed frustration over how much things have changed. The companies that wanted to interview her expected her to leave a video recording; she didn't even get to talk to a real person. "What in the world has work come to when you don't even get to talk to a person to determine if a job or the organization is a fit?" she lamented. And she started to second-guess whether it was worth going back into the workforce if this is how people are treated before they even start a job.

This technology-based interviewing process is being used with increased frequency at many large companies; it is promoted as being more efficient and saving money when there are many candidates to screen. What kind of message does it send to people when we think technology can replace human reasoning and our ability to connect with others? Of course, technological advances are a cornerstone of this VUCA world and have been great for many things; however, when they are used to the point where they dehumanize the workplace, we have a serious problem. Technology can't take the place of humanity. We need to rethink what it takes for organizations and people to thrive today and in the future.

In his 2017 TED Talk, David Lee, VP of Innovation and UPS Ventures at UPS, discusses the role of technology and how it is replacing jobs at a rapid pace. He makes a bold assertion for how we can avoid a jobless future. He suggests we need to take steps now to change the nature of work—to create environments where people love coming to work, and to foster the innovation needed to replace the millions of jobs that will inherently be lost to technology. David believes that the key to doing that is to "rediscover what makes us human and to create a new generation of human-centered jobs that allow us to unlock our hidden talents and passions that we carry with us every day." He argues that we need to move away from machine-like, task-focused jobs to focus on the skills that *people* bring to work.[2]

What Ryan, Natalie, Donna, and David show us is VUCA in action—and, at the same time, how misusing technology perpetuates and invites more dehumanization. However, this new reality can also bring great opportunities. For example, by leveraging technological advances for more machine-like tasks, we can free people to grow, create, and innovate. We need to create the conditions to leverage the creativity and capability that only humans can provide to solve challenges that a VUCA world brings.

Besides, the tolerance for dehumanized workplaces is shrinking. People are craving better work–life harmony, meaningful and purposeful work, and the ability to show up authentically human. As Erica Keswin writes in her book *Bring Your Human to Work*, "People are no longer willing to accept work as a soul-crushing, Dilbertesque, cubicled nightmare."[3]

We don't want to be treated like machines; we want to feel valued as *human beings*. Unfortunately, *stuck* businesses neglect to acknowledge the VUCA reality and have become increasingly dehumanized; just like the old-paradigm sailors, they cling tightly to what is familiar and end up treating employees more like controllable, predictable machines, lab rats, or small children. As a result, engagement, performance, and well-being continue to erode. An estimated 88 percent of the workforce in the United States go home each day feeling like they work for an organization that doesn't listen to or care about them.[4] According to Jeffrey Pfeffer's research from his 2018 book *Dying for a Paycheck*, these dehumanized workplaces account for an additional one hundred and twenty thousand deaths per year—making them the fifth leading cause of death in the United States.[5] We have a humanity crisis on our hands!

We also know that human beings are complex and messy; we frequently get in our own way, preventing us from showing up as our best, authentic selves. We don't start each day wanting to look stupid, disconnected, or ineffective. Most of us want to be smart, capable, and helpful. However, we also don't like to be vulnerable where we face risk, uncertainty, and emotional exposure. In fact, we learn relatively early in life how to manage and avoid interpersonal risks where we might look ignorant, incompetent, or disruptive.[6] Researcher and bestselling author Brené Brown describes this as "armoring up"; much like medieval soldiers would put on armor to protect themselves during a battle, we put on invisible armor to protect ourselves and avoid looking bad. The problem is that it leads to disconnection and silos, and keeps us (and organizations) from thriving. Add in the disruption of living and working in a VUCA world, and our instinct to *armor up* only gets worse.

Given this, it is critical that organizations intentionally create human, psychologically safe environments where people can lay down their armor, take risks, and be comfortable expressing and being themselves; where they can share concerns and make mistakes without fear of embarrassment or retribution. In her book *The Fearless Organization*, Amy Edmondson defines psychological safety as "the belief that the work environment is safe for interpersonal risk taking . . . Psychological safety is present when colleagues trust and respect each other and feel able—even obligated—to be candid."[7] And these environments are not only more human, they are more responsive and resilient[8]—something we need in a VUCA world.

The Good News: The Humanity Business Revolution

The good news is that there is a revolution already underway where organizations are operating more like the new-paradigm sailors and breaking the mold of "business as usual." They are creating psychologically safe work environments and finding success by honoring what it means to be human and putting people first. We are at a tipping point where the old, dehumanized model is rapidly collapsing. A large contributor to this revolution is Conscious Capitalism.

Conscious Capitalism is "part of a growing movement that recognizes the tremendous value and potential of capitalism" and seeks to "elevate this powerful force for potential good to a new level."[9] Conscious Capitalism's purpose is to *elevate humanity through business*, recognizing that businesses and their leaders have the potential to do more than just simply make money. In fact, when conducted with a higher level of consciousness, business has an extraordinary potential to create value that does not come at the expense of our own health or the health of our planet.

Conscious Capitalism is a rethinking of what business can and should be. It is changing the narrative of business by anchoring on four key tenets that all work together and reinforce each other:

- **Higher Purpose:** Every business should have a higher purpose that transcends making money. In his book *Start with WHY*, Simon Sinek asserts the importance of clarifying and anchoring our work on a higher purpose. It not only creates clarity, but it fuels energy and passion.[10] Yes, businesses need to be profitable in order to exist, but profit is not the purpose.

- **Stakeholder Orientation:** Shareholders are only one stakeholder for an organization. Businesses need to consciously create value with and for *all* its stakeholders (employees, customers, suppliers, shareholders/investors, communities, the environment, etc.). Instead of a binary approach where one stakeholder wins at the expense of another (e.g., conducting mass layoffs to balance the books so the quarterly returns are favorable for shareholders), organizations look for synergies to create win-win relationships among stakeholders.

- **Conscious Leadership:** Conscious leaders operate from a place of purpose and service to others rather than power and self-interest. They are self-aware and intentional so they can effectively mentor, develop, and inspire people; consequently, they are able to call others to greatness and foster high levels of engagement, creativity, alignment with the higher purpose, and performance.

- **Conscious Culture:** Rather than operating on fear and unhealthy levels of stress, conscious organizations intentionally foster cultures with high levels of trust, authenticity, transparency, and genuine caring. They create environments where people feel valued as human beings and are nurtured to continue to grow. And it doesn't just start with the C-suite. We need more courageous leaders—at all levels within organizations—to join this revolution!

Businesses large and small are leveraging these tenets to become more conscious about the impact they have on people's lives and the planet.[11] And, these conscious, human-focused organizations can even be a source of healing—restoring hope and well-being while being financially successful at the same time. Research conducted on some of these publicly-traded businesses shows they consistently outperform their competitors; over a fifteen-year period, they have outperformed the S&P 500 by fourteen times![12] We have been so encouraged and inspired by the growing revolution of these conscious businesses; they are paving the way and showing what is possible—and sustainable—for us to thrive in a VUCA world.

We've also had a bit of an awakening in the past few years—thanks to being fortunate enough to do some incredible work with organizations that stretched us out of our comfort zones. What we've realized is that, while support at the C-suite is important, it's not a deal-breaker or completely necessary. Really! We have seen firsthand that you can transform and rehumanize workplaces at the grassroots level by working with one team at a time and building momentum from there—and it is profound!

If you think about it, given that culture and psychological safety ultimately reside at the team level, it makes sense that organizational transformation can happen team-by-team. It just takes one person to choose to be courageous, *show up as a leader*, and make a positive impact. We hope to bust the myth that change has to start at the C-suite level, and energize and equip you with examples and tools to be part of the rehumanization revolution.

Who We Are and the Journey That Led Us Here

As you will learn throughout this book, rehumanizing the workplace is not without its bumps and bruises. While it should seem like a "no-brainer," being intentional to put humanity back at the forefront of business takes incredible effort and can be challenging at times. Every organization we feature in this book humbly shared their own challenges. Yet, with the challenges also comes great learning and reward—for all stakeholders. Our journey is no exception.

We both started our careers in the health and wellness industry, focusing on employee wellness. I (Jon) graduated from the University of Michigan in 1974 with a degree in music literature. Once I had satisfied my parents' desire that their good Jewish boy attend college, I followed my own passion and went on the road for fifteen years playing in a rock 'n' roll band. Although I enjoyed it, playing six nights a week in smoky bars until two a.m. was certainly not the healthiest of occupations. To keep myself from succumbing to the unhealthy circumstances surrounding me, I took up running and eventually graduated to long distances and triathlons.

When I got off the road, I went to Michigan State University to pursue graduate health degrees in nutrition, exercise physiology, and health education. While working on my PhD, I was asked to help create the first employee wellness program (Healthy U) at the university. When I graduated, I was recruited as a consultant to help with program implementation. I gained some good experiences putting my newfound education to use.

But I also gained some experiences of another kind. There were two other people on my team that were helping to implement the Healthy U program. Both of these individuals were my juniors in terms of age and education; however, they had been in their positions longer than me, and they clearly felt that I as the newcomer was somehow getting in their way. To make a long and very painful story short, they were often openly hostile, which made for a less than desirable work environment.

One day, I walked into the bathroom next to our offices and found a cartoon in the stall depicting a man with a beard (not unlike mine) in a tub of water with my name on it and words that had a definite German flavor, suggesting that it would be appropriate to include me in some kind of an experiment. Being Jewish (which they knew), I was blown away, as it was clear that the reference was to Hitler's Nazi Germany. I confronted them with the cartoon, and, although they apologized and said they were "just joking," it was clear that this was not a place I wanted to be any longer. I suppose I could have made things very uncomfortable for these people and perhaps for the university as well. However, I chose to just let it go—probably out of some fear of potential retribution and partially because I knew I was going to leave anyway. It has, however, remained indelibly etched in my memory as a vivid reminder of the impact dehumanized workplaces can have.

From that day forward, I decided that I would always be my own boss, a decision I have stuck to now for more than three decades. I moved on from there and, together with a physician friend, started the Michigan Center for Preventive Medicine, where we worked with people referred from insurance companies for issues related to weight, stress, smoking, and substance abuse. More on that experience later.

As I was attending various health promotion conferences, I became really interested in speaking; after all, being on stage was something I had been doing for decades. As I pursued this desire, I met an amazing woman—Karen Carrier. We became instant friends and decided to write a book together. *The Spirit and Science of Holistic Health: More Than Broccoli, Jogging, and Bottled Water . . . More Than Yoga, Herbs, and Meditation* (2004) was conceived as a college textbook and a guidebook to help practitioners incorporate holistic principles and practices into their work.

This book provided the foundation for the creation of Kailo in 1997, one of the first truly holistic employee wellness programs. The program was developed at Mercy Hospital in Mason City, Iowa, (of Buddy Holly fame) after its creator, Kelly Putnam, heard me speak at the National Wellness Conference. Way ahead of its time, Kailo focused less on the traditional goals of reducing biomedical risk factors for illness, and more on bolstering physical, psychological, and spiritual factors for health. The focus was well reflected in its motto: "Caring for ourselves as well as we care for our patients." Kailo won prestigious awards in both Canada and the United States, and the creators lovingly claim me as its father.

In the late 1990s through early 2000s, I (Rosie) was working as a contractor for Target, running their on-site wellness center while finishing my master's degree in public health. I was also a new manager with no clue what I was doing. With no one to develop me, I started getting my hands on every business and leadership book I could to try to not screw up this opportunity. It should have been a sign that I was getting the wrong master's degree when I loathed epidemiology but lit up for a management and leadership in health care class!

I tried to follow published "best practices" for employee wellness programs at Target, but something felt *off*. I couldn't understand how these published reports were achieving the results they claimed when every practitioner I spoke to faced incredible challenges with being able to implement "best practice" programming. I remember having this sinking feeling as I thought, "I just raked up $80,000 in student loan debt, and this crap doesn't work. What the hell am I going to do now?"

In 2002, I eventually took a job working for a local public health department. This was a pivotal turning point; I found myself in a dysfunctional, toxic work environment for the first time. It was everything I had read about: poor leadership, poor morale, high turnover, apathy, and people taking advantage of the system. And even though I was still teaching group fitness classes on the side and cared about my health and well-being, it was literally being eroded in front of my eyes. Barely four months into the job I found myself having gained ten to fifteen pounds, getting sick all the time, arguing with my husband, watching the clock, and shifting from a ridiculous overachiever to doing the minimum to get by; and the worst was when my friends would say to me, "Rosie, what's wrong? You just don't seem like **you** anymore."

This was my wake-up call. I remember thinking to myself, "No wonder what we're doing in worksite wellness doesn't work. If you can take someone who's knowledgeable and who cares, and still have the work environment literally suck the wellness out of a person, we have a problem." I realized that the industry wasn't pointless, it was just off-course. Then I remember having this conversation with myself: "Rosie, are you seriously about to take on an industry? Are you going to take on these cronies and the good old white boys of wellness? Damn straight, I am!"

In that moment, I knew I needed to expand my knowledge beyond health. So I pursued my PhD in organization and management and began immersing myself in the research on organizational culture, leadership, followship, coaching, and motivation. I started to see the incredible interconnectedness between effective organizations and individual health and well-being.

While pursuing my doctorate, I was working as the Health and Wellness Director for a natural health care university. I came across Jon's book and knew this was a perfect environment to leverage a holistic approach to health and wellness. During my tenure at the university, there were two different presidents. Both regularly spoke of the need to diversify revenue to balance the dips in enrollment that occur. I was a regular speaker at national conferences, and, as people began to know me and learn about the work I did, I would receive requests as to whether our program was exportable or not and if I could help them; I started to see the possibility for consulting with other organizations. However, each time I brought forward the idea, both presidents would shoot it down and say, "We just can't keep up with you, Rosie!"

I also was regularly in disagreement with our CFO about the purpose of my role and what "health and wellness" meant for the employees and the university. One July day in 2006, the CFO got some sort of bug up his butt and decided to freeze my budget until we could get on the same page about the direction for my department. I was livid and thought to myself, "Screw you!" I retreated to my office, shut the door, and started brainstorming what kind of business I'd have since the university just didn't get it. I didn't really have a plan other than what I knew how to do well: coach, consult, and speak; however, I figured that could be a viable business somehow.

Then I started trying to figure out a name. I googled Latin and Italian words (mainly because I figured there would be something that sounded cool). I came across *Salveo*, the Latin word meaning to be well or in good health. I liked it! I searched for existing trademarks and web domains; the only Salveo in existence was a pet food company. Since salveo.com was already taken, I came up with adding *Partners* because when you coach, consult, and speak, it's really about a partnership between people. I purchased web domains and started creating text for the website. When I met my husband, Dave, for dinner that night and said, "Look what I did today, honey!" he probably thought I was crazy.

Other than a website, I didn't really have a business plan. Additionally, I was just finishing my PhD and didn't have the financial risk appetite to just quit my job and try to make Salveo Partners a viable business. So it became a side gig; I would use my paid time off and take small projects, hoping momentum would build and I could eventually be a full-time business owner. Then, in the spring of 2007, an insurance brokerage and consulting firm reached out to me. I ended up accepting a position there (more on that later in the book) and put Salveo Partners on hold; I figured someday I'd come back to it.

Jon and I met in 2008 or 2009. There was so much alignment with us in terms of the researchers and thought leaders we follow, what we both spoke about in our presentations, and more. We started toying around with the idea of writing a book together in 2013 to share our insights from our work. Then, when things started going south at my job (more on that later), we got more serious about it. By the fall of 2013, we had a publishing agreement in place and began writing. We also started thinking more seriously about going into business with each other. I suggested resurrecting Salveo Partners; and so our current journey began.

Our initial focus with writing our first book, *How to Build a Thriving Culture at Work*, was to essentially respond to requests from people who heard us speak and followed our work; they were asking for more tips and resources to help them "do what we do" and to have a blueprint for transforming workplaces so that the people and the organization can thrive. *How to Build a Thriving Culture at Work* is based on the approach we've taken in consulting with organizations to help them improve their workplace culture and the well-being of their people. It details a step-by-step blueprint for moving past an outdated, mechanistic paradigm to a new, humanistic paradigm to transform workplace cultures.

We call the blueprint *The 7 Points of Transformation* (POTs). We use the analogy that building a thriving workplace is similar to building a structurally sound and aesthetically pleasing house; if you skip important steps or use outdated materials, that house won't withstand the test of time—and, in many cases, may be about as stable as building it on quicksand. But it also takes another level of attention and intention to turn that house into a home—one where people feel safe, loved, and connected, and where they are nurtured to grow and become the full expression of themselves. For context, here is a brief summary:

- **POT 1: Survey the Land (data collection and analysis).** This includes taking a holistic view of data (both qualitative and quantitative) and using it more as a source of feedback than measurement. It's about understanding the good, bad, and ugly of the current state and looking for trends and patterns that incorporate the inextricable interconnectedness of organizational and employee well-being within our organizations; this is to avoid the whack-a-mole approach that typically occurs when using data in a silo to deploy an intervention, only to have other issues pop up elsewhere. This is the first thing the shipwrecked sailors from our opening story did when they arrived on the island; they had to know what they were dealing with before they could create any sort of strategy or plan.

- POT 2: Create the Blueprint (strategic and annual planning). Margaret Wheatley has said that "people only support what they've helped to create." Therefore, it's critical to include everyone in the process of creating a shared vision of the desired culture and then what we need to start, stop, and continue doing in order to get there. A shared vision creates passion and energy and leverages the collective wisdom of people to guide transformation efforts. The new-paradigm tribe on the shipwrecked island collectively created a shared vision that helped guide their next steps; and everyone knew how they fit into that vision.

- POT 3: Pour a Solid Foundation (develop quality leaders). The quality of leaders is **everything**; they set the tone for the culture and the entire employee experience. But we need to rethink how we define leaders, who we develop as leaders, and how we develop people; we need to take an inside-out approach rather than a typical outside-in approach. The new-paradigm tribe on the shipwrecked island created an environment where everyone could *show up as a leader*, learn, and grow.

- POT 4: Frame the House (create a supportive climate). It is important to create a structure that supports your organization's purpose and desired culture in being realized. Much like a garden, culture must be tended to and nurtured while also "hard-wiring" it into daily operations. By documenting the steps they took as they *built the lighthouse*, and self-organizing to create a structure that aligned with their new environment, the new-paradigm tribe was able to support their shared vision of thriving.

- **POT 5: Wire the House (rethink change).** We must realize the critical difference between technical challenges (i.e., those that have a straightforward solution where we can use our existing thinking, knowledge, and skills to solve) and adaptive challenges (i.e., those that have no known solution and require us to get uncomfortable, step into the unknown, and generate new thinking to solve). Since most challenges have largely adaptive components, we need to support people in being more self-aware, shifting their mindset, and then leveraging more effective thinking and narratives to guide and lead change. The new-paradigm tribe quickly recognized they were dealing with incredible adaptive challenges. They had no choice but to embrace the discomfort and support one another to operate in a way that allowed everyone in the tribe to do their best work.

- **POT 6: Decorate the House (deploy QUALITY, evidence-based programs and resources).** Once the house is built, we can implement programs and services that support people in all areas of their well-being so that they can thrive and be the best versions of themselves. And we must offer them in a way that honors what it means to be self-authoring human beings, not controllable machines. For the new-paradigm tribe, they leveraged the collective wisdom of everyone to do their best to make their new surroundings feel like "home," support the tribe's culture, and be the most healthy and helpful to the group.

- **POT 7: Maintain the House (continuous quality improvement).** Culture is an ongoing journey, not a destination. However, this doesn't mean metrics don't matter. When we select the metrics that are meaningful to let us know how we're doing, we are better equipped to either keep nurturing the path that is working or course correct to a more effective path. With the VUCA sea and storms still raging for the shipwrecked sailors, setting the stage for surviving and thriving couldn't be a one-time project. The new-paradigm tribe had to consider how to constantly manage and improve things in both a proactive and a flexible, adaptable way.

In the past five years, we've had hundreds of people reach out to us saying how helpful *How to Build a Thriving Culture at Work* has been in giving them language for what they'd been experiencing, and saying that it has become their "workplace Bible." Yet, at the same time, these "new-paradigm tribe" members experienced great frustration with clashing with countless "old-paradigm sailors" who insisted on doing things the same old way. They also kept trying to decorate the house (POT 6) because they didn't feel they had the knowledge, skills, or influence in the other POTs. But then they'd be frustrated because their efforts were met with resistance or lack of enthusiasm, or they just weren't working or having the impact they desired. We knew we needed to find a way to help people find a productive path out of being stuck.

From Identity Crisis to Building Community

The first couple of years of our company were anchored on *How to Build a Thriving Culture at Work*, leveraging the *7 Points of Transformation* blueprint in our consulting work with organizations and equipping others to do the same. It wasn't even until after our book was published that we came up with language to more succinctly describe our work (i.e., recognizing and supporting the inextricable interconnectedness of organizational and employee well-being): *The Fusion*.

In the fall of 2015, we created an eleven-week, in-depth development program called the Thriving Workplace Culture Certificate™ (TWCC) training program. It started out as an experiment in response to our readers asking for more to help them do the work outlined in our book. We honestly didn't even know if there would be a legitimate interest or business opportunity but figured it couldn't hurt to try. We intentionally limited the group size to twenty-five people but weren't certain we'd get any registrations. We were shocked—and thrilled—when our first group sold out! The original intent was simply to support people in building additional skills to apply the blueprint and leverage *The Fusion* to build thriving workplace cultures. Since our first cohort, we have used the TWCC as our anchor program, building on *How to Build a Thriving Culture at Work* to add in new insights, research, and tools so people can help workplaces thrive in a VUCA world and address the humanity crisis. We have over two hundred TWCC graduates so far, and this community continues to grow.

What's funny is that many years ago, I (Rosie) got into a debate with the

CEO of my company at the time about how to grow the consulting practice to improve culture with our employer groups. He said to me, "Rosie, the problem with your model is that it isn't scalable; **you** can't be everywhere." My response was simple and clear: "the model is absolutely scalable when you develop *other* people to do this; and it provides them meaning and fulfillment in their work." I wanted to help develop my counterparts in other offices throughout the country, but he didn't think there was a need or market for it. Given our growing TWCC community, I have to admit there's a bit of "I told you so" glee on my part to show how completely misguided that CEO was. We are creating scalability by developing others and building community to rehumanize workplaces.

Even though we firmly believe in the value of the tenets of Conscious Capitalism and regularly assert the importance of starting with a Higher Purpose, we were primarily focused on our products and services and trying to find ways to have our business be financially viable. That said, every product and service we created was done with intention—and usually in response to requests from our stakeholders. When our TWCC graduates said they wanted ongoing support, we created our Annual Licensing program. It was important to us that we didn't just collect a fee for people to keep their TWCC license current; we wanted to be intentional and truly build community and support them. As part of the Annual Licensing program, we started having monthly group consulting sessions to bring people together, increase their knowledge and skills, and strengthen community. It was also important for us to provide them with additional tools, templates, and resources to support them in building thriving workplaces.

During this time when we were being very intentional about some aspects of our business, we also had to face the fact that we had an identity crisis. We consulted with organizations to help them improve their culture and leadership and had our TWCC training and community. However, we really didn't have a strong business plan or strategy; and we didn't have a clue who we were or where we were headed. Basically, we had not been walking our talk. We didn't really have clarity about **WHY** we do what we do; we didn't have a clear sense of purpose. People would say to us, "I love your book, white papers, webinars, and workshops, but what the heck do you do? We don't get it."

Then we took a risk with a business development contract with a company that was supposed to essentially do "matchmaking" services between us and companies who need and would value our services. As part of their discovery process to understand us and our products and services, it became clear we didn't really know who we were. Were we a training company? A consulting firm? A coaching firm? Something else? How do we convey our value and why workplaces should care about *The Fusion* (the inextricable interconnectedness of organizational and employee well-being)? That was our wake-up call to stop just "doing stuff" and figure out who we were as a company first and then realign our services, strategy, operations, and messaging. So we dove into the work to figure out our purpose, core values, and behavioral anchors.

We realized that what we're ultimately called to do is to not just build thriving workplace cultures; that's an important start. We are called to advocate for humanity. Our purpose is *to rehumanize the workplace so that people can bring their best selves to work—and home—each day.* Our *7 Points of Transformation* blueprint is still an important ingredient for rehumanizing workplaces; and there are so many other facets necessary to have, and advocate for, workplaces that nurture humanity.

Being able to activate and live our purpose also required us to get clear about our core values—how our behavior helps our purpose be realized. Here is what we created:

- **Embrace your humanity.** Honor the complexity and messiness of being human. Strive for excellence, not perfection; give yourself and others grace.
- **We are stronger together.** This is not a solo journey. There is power and energy in building community. Operate with an abundance mindset to build and grow relationships and support others' success.
- **Choose courage over comfort.** Be deliberate and intentional in your actions. Embrace the discomfort of challenging the status quo; growth never happens in our comfort zone.
- **Sound science is your friend.** Every solution and recommendation must be rooted in sound science appropriate for human beings.
- **Pave a path for others to thrive.** Help others see what's possible. If you're going to suggest stopping something or moving away from an approach, always provide a more effective, more human alternative.

Never in a million years would we pretend to be perfect. But once we gained clarity of why we're here and of the behavioral anchors that make Salveo Partners what it is, it became so much easier to refine and focus our energy in an intentional way and have a clear filter for how to make decisions. That requires sometimes saying "no" to revenue and growth opportunities. As a small example, on more than one occasion we have turned down speaking engagements because the host didn't want us to mention the science or talk about what isn't working (even though we'd share what to do instead). We know that we cannot be in integrity with who we are at our core and ignore the science; so even though it meant forgoing the revenue and being able to educate, enlighten, and inspire others, it was easy to say "no" to these opportunities.

Clarifying our purpose and core values also helped us refine our strategy and guide our operations. We've always asserted that rehumanizing workplaces is not a solo journey; and there is more than enough work to be done for our vision of truly human workplaces to be realized. As we've continued to support our community of Thriving Workplace Culture Certificate (TWCC) grads ("Paradigm Pioneers"), we've been blown away by their courage, generosity, and humanity! They are phenomenal people who put themselves out there to challenge old-school paradigms and advocate for more human workplaces.

As this community has grown, it has become even clearer to us that fulfilling our purpose of rehumanizing the workplace requires a village of kick-ass leaders. With that, our focus shifted to being even more intentional about building and nurturing community. So we started creating more thoughtful structures for people to build relationships and learn from the collective wisdom from each other. And we continue to share what we're learning along the way so that, together, we can create thriving, human workplaces. We also started training and mentoring some of our TWCC grads to help with our consulting work and create more opportunities for them to have meaning and fulfillment.

Given the vast need for more human workplaces, we want to see more amazing leaders step up so that work can be a source for energy, caring, and good and help create a better world for our children. With that, we realized that if we want to grow the village of kick-ass leaders who can help rehumanize workplaces, we must share our lessons learned and tools beyond our Paradigm Pioneer community. So here we are hoping to equip more people to *show up as leaders* and put humanity back at the forefront of business.

LEGEND
1 Build a Lighthouse
2 Create a Fearless Environment
3 Wade In the Messy Middle
4 Show Up as a Leader
5 Find Your Tribe
1
2
3
4
5

Five Key Rehumanizing Principles

The VUCA world is anything but simple and easy; it presents many opportunities and also brings many challenges that can easily lead to dehumanization, including inviting us to self-protect (which increases silos and disconnection and hinders growth and collaboration). From our research and experience, we've learned that future-ready, successful organizations are conscious, **human** businesses. They recognize the nature of living and working in a VUCA world; and they respond by supporting people in showing up as their whole, authentic selves and engaging in ongoing, meaningful growth and development.

Just like the lessons learned by the new-paradigm tribe on the shipwrecked island, we have found five key principles that are interconnected and essential to creating thriving, future-ready human workplaces:

1. *Build a lighthouse.* Much like a lighthouse can help cut through the fog and provide clarity for where to go, having a clear purpose and core values can help to do the same. People can't be successful unless they know what's expected of them, feel connected to a shared vision, know how they fit into that vision, and know how they need to show up and behave in order to realize that purpose and shared vision. *Building a lighthouse* can provide calm and clarity in the VUCA storm, and passion and energy to keep forging ahead. (The new-paradigm tribe rallied around a shared vision of a thriving future and then built a lighthouse and a playbook to help guide the path forward.)

2. *Create fearless environments.* The VUCA world inherently brings some discomfort, as it demands we do things differently. However, we can only adapt and grow when people feel safe taking the risks required to do transformative work. Intentionally creating psychologically safe teams supports people in taking off their masks and armor so they can show up as their full, authentic selves and be vulnerable to take risks and grow. (The new-paradigm tribe created a fearless environment for people to speak up and take risks—which was essential for their survival.)

3. *Wade in the messy middle.* Change involving humans is complex and evokes discomfort (which is why we must *create fearless environments*). We need to do the work to move from self-protection to

self-reflection and then rewrite our inner narratives; we can't hit fast-forward. Growth happens at the edge of our comfort zone, so there is tremendous value in letting ourselves embrace the discomfort and be in the middle of the mess; it's the only way to transform and be equipped to thrive in a VUCA world. (Remember how the shipwrecked tribe needed to wade through the uncertainty of the messy swamp in the middle of the mountain in order to get to the water on the other side?)

4. *Show up as a leader.* Leadership is a **behavior**, not a title or role. *Everyone* can learn how to, and then choose to, show up as a leader and make a positive difference. And it is impossible to show up as a leader unless we've *waded in the messy middle* to do the necessary transformative, adaptive change work. Once we've done the inner work necessary to show up as leaders, we are better able to advocate for the common purpose and vision provided from *building the lighthouse*. (The new-paradigm tribe self-organized around a common vision, and everyone showed up as a leader.)

5. *Find your tribe.* You don't have to go it alone; this is not a solo journey, nor should it be. We're hardwired for connection. And people only tend to support what they've helped to create. So build diverse relationships and leverage the energy to remove silos and build community. (The shipwrecked sailors leveraged their community to build the new-paradigm tribe and find ways to survive—and thrive.)

These serve as guiding principles and an overarching roadmap for any work designed to build thriving, human workplaces. And building on the fifth principle—*find your tribe*—the starting point is developing relationships and engaging others in a dialogue about why rehumanizing workplaces matters and about key considerations; enter the Thriving Organization Pyramid™.

THE THRIVING ORGANIZATION PYRAMID™

How to create a high-performing organization where employees are freed, fueled, and inspired to bring their best selves to work—and home—each day.

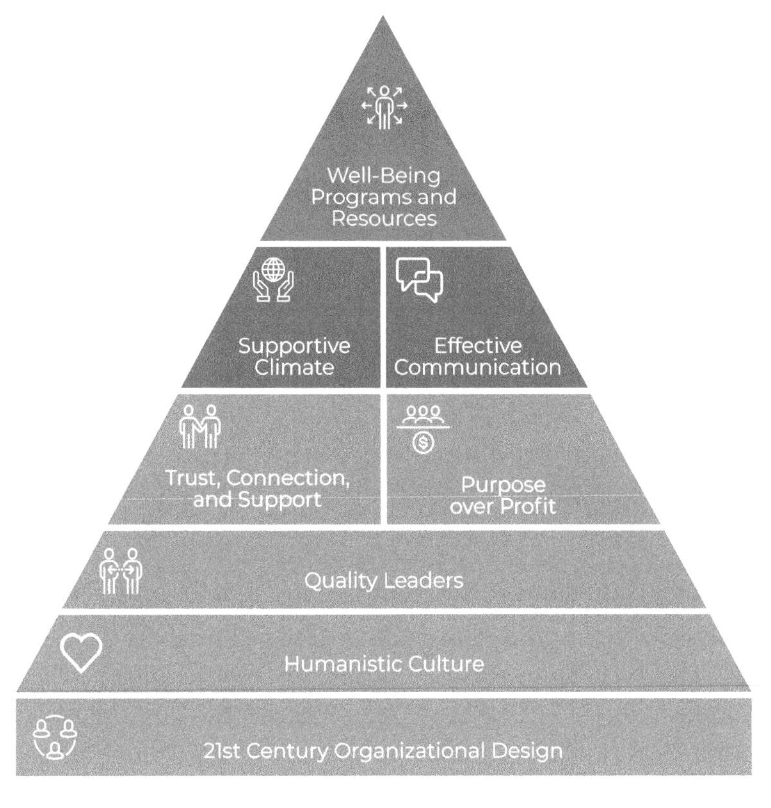

Sources: Peter Senge, Margaret Wheatley, Edward Deci, Edgar Schein, Patrick Lencioni, Robert Greenleaf, Simon Sinek, Bob Kegan and Lisa Lahey, Amy Edmondson, Brené Brown, Aaron Hurst, Raj Sisodia, Bob Chapman, Tony Hsieh, Tom Rath and Jim Hartner, Frederic Laloux, Ron Friedman, Heart, and Common Sense

The Thriving Organization Pyramid

A couple of years ago, we were speaking with a prospective client and trying to describe *The Fusion* (the inextricable interconnectedness of organizational and employee well-being). We were using the *7 Points of Transformation* blueprint and the house metaphor to try to help them understand why they were struggling with their efforts to support employee well-being. In that conversation, we ended up using the analogy of a pyramid. We figured that most people could understand that the base represents the essential foundation; without a solid base, it's nearly impossible to have any impact further up the pyramid. This resonated with them and allowed for rich discussions about where their organization was stuck and where to start.

We also had an aha moment that this might be really helpful for others who are trying to engage people in paradigm-shifting conversations. So we took that experience and created the Thriving Organization Pyramid based on the work of great leaders who have inspired us. It is designed to be a guide to foster conversations so people can gauge where they are and create a roadmap for where and how they can begin to build a more human, thriving workplace that can handle whatever the VUCA world brings.

The pyramid is basically a visual of what *thriving* looks like in an organization (and what leveraging the *7 Points of Transformation* blueprint can help build), and how *The Fusion* is critical in a thriving, human workplace. The base includes the critical factors determining organizational well-being, and the top supports individual employee well-being. The middle is where more of the overlap and interconnectedness emerges within workplaces. And at every stage of the pyramid, the Five Rehumanizing Principles come into play. We have had countless people say that they have this visual hanging as a poster on their wall and that they've used it to facilitate discussions within their organizations and guide their transformation journey. (You can download your free copy at salveopartners.com/pyramid.)

How to Use This Book

We leverage the Five Rehumanizing Principles and the Thriving Organization Pyramid to provide key insights, lessons learned, and a framework to help you rehumanize and future-proof your workplace, so you can thrive regardless of what the VUCA world throws at you. We believe in blending quality research with real-life application. Although advocating for a more human workplace seems like it should be common sense, it is going against the grain of "business as usual"; so it is important to have a solid foundation on which to build. We build on the research by sharing stories from our own lives and work, stories and examples from companies we've worked with over the years, and people we've interviewed.

With the Five Rehumanizing Principles serving as the overarching guide, this book is organized by each section of the Thriving Organization Pyramid to help you rehumanize your own workplace. The first three chapters set the stage for why rehumanizing the workplace is necessary. The remaining chapters detail key considerations for strengthening each component of the pyramid—starting from the base and working to the top.

As we learned in our own work, transforming workplace culture takes a community of people rallying around a common vision and collaborating to influence and lead positive change. In fact, Ronald Heifetz and Marty Linsky assert in their book *Leadership on the Line* that going it alone is a mistake. "Creating change requires you to move beyond your own cohort, beyond your own constituents, your 'true believers.'"[13] With that, as you think about your own workplace, start putting the *find your tribe* principle into play; keep in mind your potential partners and the diverse relationships you might want—and need—to build at each stage of the journey.

Additionally, for each section of the pyramid, we provide tips for how to leverage the *show up as a leader* principle so you can lead and influence positive change, regardless of your role. As we speak with hundreds of professionals who are trying to support humanistic change at their workplace, we regularly hear self-limiting dialogue and frustration of being able to actually do the work needed to build a thriving workplace. We hear them say things like, "But I'm just a ______ [wellness, HR, safety/risk management, etc.] person." Then they express frustration about not having the relationship or buy-in at the CEO level they need to gain momentum. First of all, we need to remove the "just" limitation from our narrative. Second, CEO buy-in *helps*, but it is not a deal-breaker.

We are hoping everyone reading this book can move past self-limiting dialogue and apply the principles so, together, we build a critical mass of thriving, human workplaces that can transform people's lives and their communities. Regardless of your title or role, *everyone* has the opportunity to show up as a leader and influence change. So let's get this party started . . .

Chapter 1

THE DEHUMANIZED REALITY

We as a nation must undergo a radical revolution of values. We must rapidly begin the shift from a thing-oriented society to a person-oriented society. When machines and computers, profit motives and property rights, are considered more important than people, the giant triplets of racism, extreme materialism and militarism are incapable of being conquered.
—MARTIN LUTHER KING JR., "Beyond Vietnam—A Time to Break Silence" (1967)[14]

Every time you turn around these days, there is bleak news—about the state of our political system, health care, violence, and increasingly dehumanized workplaces where people are treated more like replaceable machines than human beings. Employees are constantly being asked to do more with less and, in many organizations, feel like nothing more than a number. As the saying goes, *it's always darkest before the dawn*. Well, if the current data is any indication, we've hopefully hit the darkest. We have a humanity crisis on our hands.

- The American Institute of Stress reports that work is a major source of stress for working adults; in fact, 80 percent of people report feeling stress on the job, and job stress has increased significantly over the past few years.[15]

- The 2017 American Psychological Association's *Stress in America*™ survey reports that 59 percent of Americans, regardless of their age, believe that this is the lowest point they can remember in the history of the United States.[16]

- A 2014 study by the National Bureau of Economic Research found that approximately 30 percent of US employees are working on weekends, with approximately 25 percent working at night—which is a significantly higher proportion than any other countries included in the study.[17]

- We are painfully connected. A TechTalk survey reported that 81 percent of people check emails on weekends; 55 percent log in to work after eleven p.m. and 59 percent check email while on vacation.[18]

Steve (not his real name) worked for a large Fortune 100 company. Leadership appreciated him because he was highly knowledgeable and emotionally intelligent, and he knew how to work with people to move business initiatives forward to successful outcomes. However, they relied on him too much. The company was horrible about effectively onboarding and training new people, and stress and burnout were rampant throughout Steve's coworkers. Sales would sign a new account and expect implementation within a timeline that could only happen with a small miracle. IT resources and systems were clunky, making it nearly impossible to be ready to implement new accounts effectively by the deadlines. And they consistently underestimated staffing needs to have the systems function properly and onboard new accounts; yet when requests for more people were made, they were ignored.

Steve took pride in doing a good job. However, with over-stressed coworkers, broken systems, and unrealistic deadlines, he found himself frustrated. At every turn there were roadblocks. People were so overscheduled with meetings that they barely had time to take a short break to go to the bathroom, let alone a lunch break. People worked long hours—both at the office and at home. And every time Steve tried to take a vacation, he found himself logging into WebEx calls and putting out fires. He literally could not unplug for even a day. At the same time, company communications would regularly boast about record profits, while employees (including Steve) were finding their raises dwindling and bonuses being dramatically cut—despite having stellar performance reviews and working harder and harder each year. A clear message was sent to employees that they didn't matter and were essentially expendable.

This business-as-usual approach to do more with less took its toll. Apathy set in all around Steve—making it difficult for him to rally people to meet business goals. And the stress took its toll on Steve; he found his physical and emotional health declining. When he was home with his family, he was distracted by or complaining about work. Every good intention he had to exercise or go do something fun was undermined by his emotional exhaustion and lack of energy. He was starting to not sleep well at night and even had what he presumed were anxiety and panic attacks. As much as he wanted to leave, he didn't even have the time or energy needed to look for a new job. One day, Steve just decided it was enough and that he couldn't take it anymore. He knew that his only solution was to quit, let himself emotionally recover, and then eventually search for a new job; that's how much damage this dehumanized workplace had done to him.

Unfortunately, Steve's experience is far too common. Stanford Graduate School of Business professor Jeffrey Pfeffer argues in his book *Dying for a Paycheck* that our "business as usual" way of operating in organizations is literally killing people, and not just in the United States.

- The Japanese even have a word for death from overwork: *Karoshi*. In fact, the Workers Compensation Bureau in the Ministry of Labor compensated 812 families in 2012 who were able to show a link between overwork, illness, and death—including 93 suicides; by 2015 the claims rose to 2,310.

- China also has a word for death from overwork: *Guolaosi*. According to the China Youth Daily, about six hundred thousand people a year (sixteen thousand every day!) die from working too hard.

- And it has gotten so bad that, in 2016, France recognized that work intrudes on nonwork time and passed a law that embodies a "right to disconnect."[19]

How sad is it that words are being created to describe this phenomenon?! However, it is not surprising; we have been headed in this direction for decades. Despite considerable research and effort focusing on employee engagement, it has not improved much in more than thirty years; 70 percent of people are not engaged at work. Additionally, in 2017 Gallup reported that 51 percent of the American workforce were actively looking for a new job or searching job openings.[20]

Steve is one of millions of people suffering the effects of a toxic work environment and negative job conditions. A meta-analysis of 228 studies conducted by Harvard and Stanford researchers found that workplace stress and bad bosses have negative health effects as bad as what are seen in people exposed to significant amounts of second-hand smoke.[21] Pfeffer's research concludes that such workplaces are associated with increased behaviors related to drinking, smoking, drug abuse, and overeating. And not only do these toxic workplaces result in excess of one hundred and twenty thousand deaths per year, but they account for approximately $180 billion in excess health care costs (approximately 8 percent of the total health care spend).[22]

According to Margaret Wheatley, we shouldn't be surprised. In her book *Who Do We Choose to Be?*, she describes the pattern of collapse of complex civilizations and suggests that our current dehumanized state is completely predictable. She cites the work of Sir John Glubb who studied thirteen empires all experiencing their decline and fall in the same stages over a two-hundred-and-fifty-year period (ten generations). With each stage, there is an increase of materialism; as this happens, morality erodes and the civilization declines into decadence, exhibiting the following characteristics:

- Money replaces service as the core motivator.
- Hierarchical leaders focus on maintaining power at all costs.
- The future disappears from decision-making.
- The status quo is preserved by the few elites who prosper from it.
- Relationships disintegrate into distrust, self-protection, and opposition.[23]

Wheatley suggests that our current civilization is in a state of decline. Just look at what is happening in our society with our politics and me-focused celebrity climate. Consequently, we see these characteristics reflected in our workplaces as well; it's no wonder that we are seeing the ill effects of these dehumanized workplaces. Bob Chapman is the CEO of Barry-Wehmiller, a multi-billion-dollar manufacturing company headquartered in St. Louis, Missouri (and named the number three CEO in the world in 2017 by *Inc.* magazine). He argues that we have a leadership and humanity crisis: "7 out of 8 people in the American workforce work for an organization that doesn't care for them, contributing to broken marriages, broken families and broken lives."[24]

About two years ago, Rosanna left a well-paying financial services job and decided to switch careers. She couldn't quite put her finger on it; all she knew at the time was that she was constantly stressed and didn't feel like herself. So she reinvested in herself, becoming trained as a leadership coach, engaging in meditation and reflective practices, and reconnecting with who she is at her core. Anyone who meets Rosanna now can tell she cares deeply for people; she is very intentional and thoughtful in how she approaches every interaction with everyone she meets. Having time and space away from her previous work environment, Rosanna was finally able to realize why she needed to leave her previous job.

The high-pressure, numbers-focused nature of her previous employer started to influence Rosanna. She became completely task-focused and controlling as she tried to manage the pressure, meet goals, and please her boss and company leadership. She realized that she was constantly in a reactive mode, essentially running in circles yet feeling like she was getting nowhere; yet at the time she couldn't see it, as she was just trying to get through the day. She didn't realize what she was doing to her team either (we rarely do when we're in self-protective mode). Rosanna suddenly had this insight as she was reflecting on her previous job: she burst into tears and said, "Oh my God! I was literally fighting for my life in that job; it was all I could do to survive! I so want to go back and apologize to each and every one of the people on my team for how I treated them. That was not me."

No one should—ever!—have to feel like Rosanna, where they're fighting for their lives just to survive when they go to work. Shifting this trajectory requires understanding the critical differences between machines and humans. People are not machines; we are living systems. Forward-thinking biologists believe that there are two biological imperatives of life:

1. **Life must be free to create itself.** Something is considered to be "alive" if it has the capacity to create itself (otherwise known as *autopoiesis*).
2. **Life is systems-seeking.** Living beings need to be in, and are in continual search of, relationships.[25]

The science of living systems teaches us that we strive to be self-authoring and self-organizing. Self-determination is part of our DNA; we want to charter our own destiny. Just like the new-paradigm tribe in our opening story, we are very capable of organizing ourselves and creating relationships that allow us to adapt to our surroundings. In fact, the ability to organize around an identity or boundary is what distinguishes a living being from everything else. Human beings are living systems; and, unlike machines, we are able to exchange information with our environment and use our cognition to learn and then adapt and change.[26]

Rosanna wanted to be in relationship with others and her team, but her organization's hyper-focus on tasks and numbers didn't support it. However, once she was able to step back and gain clarity about who she was and what mattered to her, she was able to create a new path full of joy and fulfillment. She leveraged what Kevin Cashman refers to as *The Pause Principle*, a universal principle that is inherent in living systems: "The Pause Principle" is the conscious, intentional process of stepping back, within ourselves and outside of ourselves, to lead forward with greater authenticity, purpose and contribution."[27]

In this VUCA world, we are unhealthily busy, overscheduled, and constantly connected via our phones and other devices. Cashman suggests that we need to step back to find clarity in order to step forward to be able to deal with complexity. Basically, we need to build our internal "muscle" to pause before we act. It seems counterintuitive, but pausing helps us regain our balance and feel grounded and centered. Machines may be able to keep going and going; however, humans need to rest and regenerate. We need to shift from environments focused on doing more to *reflecting* more; pausing powers performance.

When we ignore that people are living systems and instead operate from a paradigm idealizing machine-like qualities, dehumanization emerges.[28] We forget that people want (and demand) to charter their own destiny, learn, grow, and create meaning. We assume people are predictable and replicable, and we employ machine-like logic in how we run businesses and try to foster change. Not only do we end up with casualties like Rosanna, we end up with organizations that are slow, rigid, and unresponsive. Margaret Wheatley describes this predicament perfectly:

> The accumulating failures at organizational change can be traced to a fundamental but mistaken assumption that organizations are machines. Organizations-as-machines is a seventeenth-century notion, from a time when philosophers began to describe the universe as a great clock. Our modern belief in prediction and control originated in these clockwork images. . . .
>
> But why would we want an organization to behave like a machine? Machines have no intelligence; they follow the instructions given to them. They only work in the specific conditions predicted by their engineers. Changes in their environment wreak havoc because they have no capacity to adapt.
>
> These days, a different ideal for organizations is surfacing. We want organizations to be adaptive, flexible, self-renewing, resilient, learning, intelligent—attributes found only in living systems. The tension of our times is that we want our organizations to behave as living systems, but we only know how to treat them as machines.[29]

"Wellness or Else": A Dehumanized Approach to Supporting Health and Well-Being

The dehumanization trajectory also ignores the large role workplaces play in influencing our individual health and well-being. Not surprisingly, another area where we have a humanity crisis is with supporting people in their health and well-being at work. Once upon a time, companies that offered wellness programs for employees did so because it was "the right thing to do" and an employment perk; many programs were fairly holistic in terms of supporting multiple areas of well-being. However, over the course of time, the need for a concrete business case for investing in the health and well-being of employees grew, and wellness programs took a very mechanistic turn as a supposed health insurance cost-savings strategy.

In the United States, the practice of manipulating health insurance premiums based on employee health behaviors is widespread and became even more popular after 2010 due to the Wellness Provisions in the Affordable Care Act; these provisions increased the amount of additional health insurance premiums companies can charge their people for not participating in wellness programs or not meeting certain health outcomes—what we call "wellness or else." The thought process behind it is that if people reduce their health risks, companies will save money on their health insurance. However, it is a flawed strategy that is not supported by the research:

- The Wellness Provisions in the Affordable Care Act were largely based on claims from Safeway about their program and the money it supposedly saved them—which turned out to be untrue.[30] Interestingly, most major health organizations (including the American Heart Association, American Diabetes Association, American Lung Association, American Cancer Society, and the Prevention Institute) were opposed to the amendment, because they believed it would disproportionately impact those who could least afford it. Unfortunately, their concerns were ignored.[31]

- Even if we ignore the Safeway issue and examine the research about this program design in general, the data doesn't support its effectiveness. A study published in the *New England Journal of Medicine* by behavioral economist Dr. Kevin Volpp and colleagues concluded, "Although it may seem obvious that charging higher premiums for smoking (body mass index, cholesterol, or blood pressure) would encourage people to modify their habits to lower their premiums, evidence that differential premiums change health-related behavior is scant. Indeed, we're unaware of any insurance data that convincingly demonstrate such effects."[32]

- Regardless of claims made by vendors whose livelihood depends on the numbers working in their favor (and frequently using flawed research methodologies), these "wellness or else" programs do not result in a return on investment (ROI) when it comes to health care costs. In fact, they don't even pay for themselves.[33]

- Employees hate these programs! A recent Willis Towers Watson study examined the Net Promoter Scores (NPS) for various industries. The NPS is an alternative to traditional customer satisfaction research that is used by more than two-thirds of Fortune 1000 companies. It is based on a response to a single question: "How likely is it that you would recommend our company/product/service to a friend or colleague?" The average NPS for wellness programs is −52 in the United States (yes, that's negative 52) and negative in multiple other countries; that's lower than any other industry—including utilities and cable companies.[34] And it's no wonder; these programs go completely against what it means to be a self-authoring living being.

In the spring of 2018, West Virginia teachers went on strike for nine days, largely due to health care benefits. They also demanded an end to the coercive measures involved in their proposed "wellness or else" initiatives.[35] And they are not alone. Employees from all over the country have been speaking up on blogs and social media about these programs. As one angry employee put it, **"The whole idea of these wellness programs is that if you are ill, you must be stupid, irresponsible, or both. It's all about blaming people who are sick. I absolutely hate the people who made me go through all that humiliation when I was so sick. If I could punch them in the face, I would."**

What are we doing to people with these types of programs? This is hardly humane!

Now, just because the typical approach to wellness is flawed, it does not mean that organizations should ignore well-being all together. In fact, when it comes to organizational effectiveness and performance, employee well-being profoundly matters; the key is how companies are viewing and supporting it. Gallup's research has provided great insight into just how important well-being is; and it's much more than physical health and biomedical risk factors. There are five universal areas of well-being:

- Career/Purpose: liking what you do each day and having meaning and fulfillment in how you spend your time
- Social: having good, strong relationships and love in your life
- Financial: managing your economic life well
- Physical: having enough energy each day to get things done that are important to you
- Community: feeling connected to the community where you live

All areas are inextricably interconnected. Focusing too much on any one area can lead to frustration—and is about as effective as a game of whack-a-mole. That said, career well-being (a.k.a. purpose) plays a particularly important role. It has the largest impact on overall well-being. If people are thriving in their career well-being, they are 50 percent more likely to be thriving overall.[36]

The problem is that employee engagement rates have remained consistently low for the past three decades; a mere 30 percent of workers are engaged. Even if people are engaged, they can be working so much that they're stressed and impeding their own well-being. But when people are *both* engaged and thriving in their well-being (compared to those who are engaged but not thriving in their well-being), they:

- miss fewer days of work;
- are 45 percent more likely to report high levels of adaptability in the presence of change;
- are 37 percent more likely to report always recovering "fully" after an illness, injury, or hardship; and
- are 59 percent less likely to be looking for a job with another organization within the next twelve months.[37]

We need to stop focusing primarily on physical health and forcing people into these "wellness or else" programs thinking this will solve our health care crisis. Although properly implemented well-being initiatives can have positive benefits, the research is clear that they are not an effective health care cost-savings strategy. Encouragingly, there are real solutions for addressing health care costs that employers can implement (which we'll discuss in chapter 12).

Instead, we need to better support all areas of well-being. Organizational and employee well-being are inextricably interconnected. And, although we have employee well-being at the top of the Thriving Organization Pyramid, it really starts at the base; our individual health and well-being is profoundly impacted by the well-being of the organizations in which we work. This is why rehumanizing workplaces by putting people back at the forefront is so critical to addressing the crisis of disengagement, eroding health and well-being, and fractured communities. We've got to do better than this! The answer to our dehumanized reality is to be courageous; we must step out of our comfort zones to adapt our leadership and how we operate so we can enable people to do their best work rather than forcing them. As Jeffrey Pfeffer says, what we need to do is, **"First, Do No Harm . . . stop doing the things that create toxic work environments."**[38]

It's one thing to simply aim to do no harm; that's a pretty low bar. But just what is a humanized workplace? In his book *The Human Workplace*, Andy Swann suggests that a human workplace is one that adapts, innovates quickly, involves everyone, communicates, and acts in perpetuity. It focuses on developing its people and *creates relationships* rather than transactions.[39] This makes sense since we know that all living systems crave relationship.

We suggest taking it a step further. A humanized workplace also supports people in being able to show up as their whole, armor-free, authentic selves. It is a place where we can be vulnerable and strive for growth and excellence, not perfection; and we can give ourselves and others grace when we make mistakes. And this is becoming even more important given the realities of living and working within a VUCA world.

Take-Home Points about Our Dehumanized Reality

- Our workplaces have become dehumanized—treating people more like machines. Unfortunately, this toxic "business-as-usual" approach is literally killing people worldwide. In the United States, this makes workplaces the fifth leading cause of death and accounts for 8 percent of our health care spend.

- These "business-as-usual" practices ignore the biology of what it means to be human. As humans, self-determination is part of our DNA; we are hardwired to be self-authoring and in relationships with others. We need to be able to show up as our whole, authentic selves, yet we end up "armoring up" and showing up guarded rather than open and collaborative.

- Machines may be able to keep going; humans cannot. With the pace and flux of a VUCA world, we need to leverage *The Pause Principle* so that we can step back to find clarity in order to step forward to be able to deal with complexity. We need to move from doing more to *reflecting* more.

- Our well-being profoundly matters. But we can't effectively nurture it with punitive "wellness or else" programs. We must focus on not doing harm with toxic work environments and creating the conditions where people can be fully human and thrive.

Chapter 2

THE FUTURE OF WORK

Don't wait for a return to simpler times; they are over. —CY WAKEMAN[40]

We can learn a lot about the future of work from the shipwrecked sailors. The VUCA seas and the unknowns of the island required them to rethink how they organized themselves and operated. Life on the island was not anything like their life onboard the ship. And in the face of new, unfamiliar circumstances, we saw the old-paradigm sailors clinging desperately to what felt familiar and comfortable to them; and they ended up struggling. However, the new-paradigm tribe recognized they were dealing with new circumstances that required them to let go of the familiar structure they had aboard the ship. It required them to reorganize, show up differently, and stretch themselves outside of their comfort zones to find new ways of thinking and operating in order to have a thriving future.

We know that the world we live in is not certain, simple, static, or easy. In fact, the inherent characteristics of living in a VUCA world can disrupt the sense of psychological safety and trigger people to operate from a place of scarcity and self-protection rather than from openness and collaboration. Consequently, people are frequently holding back—reluctant to ask or say something that might make them somehow look bad.

Why is this? Well, we can understand this by distinguishing between the two main types of challenges we face as human beings: technical and adaptive.

- **Technical challenges** are those for which there is a known solution. We can use our existing knowledge and skills (or easily obtain or find the necessary resources) to solve them. This is where using standard operating procedures and checklists and looking back at what has been done before can be helpful.

- **Adaptive challenges**, on the other hand, are more complex and have us venturing into uncharted territory; there is no known solution. In fact, relying on our existing knowledge and resources and past experiences won't work. They require experiments, new discoveries, and

> adjustments. We also can't just will ourselves to the solution; we can only solve them by reframing how we think and operate.[41]

A common request we receive is to do some sort of communication training for a team or group of leaders so that they can be better at having difficult conversations. We have come to realize that such a request has a lot behind it; there are usually many underlying cultural issues at play—making it much more than a simple training solution. But let's set that aside for a moment and just look at training. Let's say we were going to provide such a training for a team within your organization.

There are several available models that provide a structure and framework (including scripts and conversation starters) for how to have a difficult conversation. If the training was done well and included lots of practice and application, and this was a technical challenge for your team, the structure, checklists, and conversation starters would be all they need. They should be able to leverage the tools to effectively navigate difficult conversations. However, if the thought of having to actually *use* the resources elicits anxiety and has your team members wanting to throw up in a garbage can at the thought of having the conversation (or perhaps they will spend countless hours or days ruminating and second-guessing themselves after the conversation), what you are dealing with is an adaptive challenge. Until you support your team in doing the necessary adaptive change work, they won't be able to effectively *apply* the technical aspects of the solution.

With adaptive challenges, we are faced with a sense of loss. We have to let go of what is familiar and predictable, and many times what has allowed us to be successful up until this point. Consequently, it causes great discomfort. Essentially, we are forced to let go of part of our identity; we have to change the way we see and do things—including our values, attitude, and habits. When the familiar personal and organizational equilibrium is disturbed, not only do people push back, but they seek out what is familiar and try to use technical fixes to solve problems that are actually adaptive.[42] This is why we tend to seek out "quick fixes" or "magic bullets" rather than acknowledging the complexity and uncertainty that accompanies adaptive challenges. It's uncomfortable to *wade in the messy middle*—yet absolutely necessary. Welcome to being human!

There is a hilarious video clip of a Comedy Central skit where Bob Newhart plays the role of a therapist, Dr. Switzer. His client, Catherine, proceeds to describe her issue; she has a fear of being buried alive in a box.

DR. SWITZER: Has anyone ever tried to bury you alive in a box?

CATHERINE: No . . . but truly thinking about it does make my life horrible. . . .

DR. SWITZER: I'm going to say two words to you right now. I want you to listen to them very, very carefully. Then I want you to take them out of the office with you and incorporate them into your life. . . . Are you ready?

CATHERINE: Yes.

DR. SWITZER: Okay, here they are: **Stop it**!

CATHERINE: I'm sorry?

DR. SWITZER: **Stop it**!

CATHERINE: Stop it?

DR. SWITZER: Yes! S-T-O-P, new word: I-T! . . . This is not Yiddish, Catherine. . . . Just stop it! . . .

The skit progresses with Dr. Switzer continuing to tell her to just "stop it!" with lots of laughs along the way. If only life was that simple and we could will ourselves to just "stop it!"—or be like Nike's slogan suggests and "Just Do It!" We can if what we're dealing with is a technical challenge. However, all the willpower in the world won't help us when what we're dealing with is an adaptive challenge.

The deeper the change and the greater amount of new learning that is required, the more resistance there will be, and the more people will gravitate toward the "just stop it" or "just do it" approach. It's hard for people to see that the new situation will be any better than the current one; what they do see clearly is the potential for loss, and that feels very immediate and real. Part of the human condition is to avoid making painful adjustments if we can postpone them.

This is problematic because the rate of change in a VUCA world is exponential. It demands that we are able to effectively navigate adaptive change.

In their book *Leadership on the Line*, Ronald Heifetz and Marty Linsky state why understanding and being able to navigate adaptive challenges is so critical to our future success: **"Without learning new ways—changing attitudes, values and behaviors—people cannot make the adaptive leap necessary to thrive in the new environment."**[43]

Additionally, given that today's employees spend 50 percent more time collaborating then they did twenty years ago,[44] we need to create environments that foster their ability to navigate adaptive challenges and effectively work together. We must provide the tools to enable people to learn new ways and show up fully rather than showing up armored and clinging tightly to what is familiar.

The Value of Showing Up Authentically Human

Showing up fully means showing up authentically human. Brené Brown defines authenticity as "the daily practice of letting go of who we think we're supposed to be and embracing who we are."[45] However, being able to show up authentically puts most of us into a space of adaptive change; it requires us to have the courage to embrace our humanity, be imperfect, and allow ourselves to be vulnerable—to be seen fully as we are (as opposed to who others think we are or how we want others to see us).

Carley Kammerer is an amazing young leader and force for good in this world. She is the founder of Wildflyer Coffee based in Minneapolis, Minnesota. Carley grew up in Milwaukee, Wisconsin. Her parents owned a local coffee shop. For a long time, she didn't see coffee as having value beyond just being a good beverage. Then, when she was nineteen years old, Carley's mom passed away. At the funeral, everyone's stories revolved around the coffee shop; they described the simplest moments that really stuck with them and how they felt part of the community and cared for by the coffee shop. Carley had this realization that coffee can bring people together and serve as a vehicle for providing a moment or experience that can have an impact and stick with people for years.

She started to see that she wanted to do something with coffee but have more than just a coffee shop. Carley studied social work in college and started volunteering at a homeless shelter for adults. At the shelter was a group of neighborhood kids hanging out who didn't really seem to have much to do. They were unstably housed; some were sleeping in cars, and some were couch-hopping or on the verge of homelessness. Carley felt like their needs were different and that it could be potentially dangerous for some of the really young girls to be hanging out around older adults; she thought they needed some special programming. She approached the directors with her idea, thinking they would do something about it. Instead, they told her to create programming. So she started some informal programming and mentoring with the kids.

Carley realized these youth were lacking in job skills. A lot of them would frequently start new jobs but then couldn't keep one long enough to actually gain some traction in life. So she started forming an idea of a coffee shop that also served as a training ground for youth.

After college, Carley moved to Denver to do some street outreach and ended up interning with a coffee shop that existed to help employ people experiencing homelessness. She was able to experience work in that environment—the struggles and how to do it well. In 2014, she moved to Minneapolis to work as a case manager and street outreach worker with youth experiencing homelessness; she continued to see the same struggles as her days working with youth in the shelter. These youth could get jobs, but they typically could only find entry-level positions in fast food and retail where they weren't really respected. They struggled to keep the jobs and get ahead in life. Carley saw that many of her youth wanted to work; they were just struggling because of a lack of employment skills, housing barriers, and everything that goes with being unstably housed.

She had this dream of starting something that would allow these youth to learn tangible skills so they could leave homelessness and become self-sufficient. Carley met her business partner, Ben Griswold, in 2016 after friends suggested they meet. Ben had a background in finance and had been focused on channeling community development and social entrepreneurship to empower marginalized groups of people; one of his biggest passions was creating sustainable models to provide opportunities in critical areas such as employment, food, and housing.

In 2017, Wildflyer Coffee was born (called Gutter Punk Coffee until 2019). Wildflyer Coffee is a nonprofit company that exists to create employment opportunities for youth experiencing homelessness. They work with youth ages sixteen to twenty-four who represent the entire spectrum of homelessness (couch-hopping, living on the streets or in shelters, sleeping in cars, etc.). They began roasting and serving coffee at farmers markets and are now working toward opening a storefront. Wildflyer employs these youth for nine months, during which they focus on skill development to help them with independent living and employment. They have monthly workshops which are part of the employment agreement that address topics like building relationships, effective communication, self-care, budgeting, cooking, knowing your rental rights, and how to be successful in a rental situation. These youth are full employees who get paid and receive their tips. They have the same expectations as if they were just an employee, so they're developing critical on-the-job employment skills. The idea is that when these youth leave Wildflyer's program, they'll have the knowledge base to actually maintain independence.

Carley is working to *create a fearless environment* for these youth to show up authentically as they are and develop and grow so they can *show up as leaders* in their lives rather than victims. Along the way, she has had to find her own voice and self-acceptance to show up as her authentic self. Carley never saw herself as a leader; as a child she was labeled as a super shy bookworm. She never considered herself to be a strong person, or someone who would inspire people or who would take these kinds of risks. She struggled with calling herself a *leader.*

Anytime the "real" Carley would shine through—the visionary, dreamer, nonconformist—people would make her feel bad about it. They labeled her a "dreamer" like it was a bad thing; they would say she had her head in the clouds and was seen as flighty and noncommittal. Carley started to see those aspects of herself as a liability rather than an asset. And venturing from the social work world into the business world prompted her to hide even more of her authentic self. She said,

> Being a young (twenty-seven-year-old) female who looks like a baby in a male-dominated business world of sharks is hard. Half of my board are men, including the president and vice-president; they're very matter-of-fact, statistics-, facts-driven. It's just a lot less emotional and empathetic than social work and can be intimidating for me. I started feeling like I'm just this girl who likes homeless youth and doesn't know much about anything. So the first year I didn't really speak up and went with whatever the board said; I was eaten alive a little bit.
>
> And I feel like this leadership thing is tricky. There's this extra weight on me as a woman, feeling like I can't show emotion and can't let anyone think I'm weak or struggling because I have so much working against me being so young and not a typical business person. But I don't want to do that either. The precedent shouldn't be that

> you have to become a bitch to successfully do anything. I don't even like that word, anyway; we're called that all the time when we're just trying to get stuff done. I want to be able to show emotion and empathy and still be considered tough.

Whenever Carley hides her authentic self, she struggles. As an example, in November 2018, she was invited to speak as part of a panel for a launch for the Twin Cities Chapter of Conscious Capitalism. Carley describes herself as never being mainstream and adopting more of the grunge look. At the time of this event, she had dreadlocks, multiple facial piercings, and tattoos. She was nervous knowing she'd be in a room full of business people and thought to herself, "I've got to be one of them."

> I bought what I thought was this professional-looking suit that didn't even look good on me; it was just not good. I think I felt this pressure of having to show up to these things looking like everyone else. And the added pressure of being young tipped me over the edge. The thing is that I was so uncomfortable. I felt like I was a little kid playing dress-up, trying to be someone I wasn't or trying to fit into this world that I didn't think I could fit into; I felt ridiculous and didn't feel like I could totally be me and therefore wasn't fully present or showing up as my best. Of course, afterwards I realized that people aren't going to invest in my company because I wear a stupid suit to an event.

Carley's experience is not uncommon. How often do we wear our own type of mask (or suit, in her case) to try to look the part or fit in? When we are hiding the parts of ourselves that make us uniquely us, it's challenging to feel equipped to handle situations, much less *show up as leaders*; and it's emotionally exhausting. However, there's something liberating about being able to show up as we are and be enough—flaws and all—while we also work to grow and improve. **We can only experience true connection when we let ourselves be fully seen.**

In the movie *Pretty Woman*, Edward (played by Richard Gere) hired Vivian (played by Julia Roberts) to be his "beck-and-call girl" (a.k.a. prostitute) for the week. Vivian purchased all of these expensive, conservative clothes so she could fit in at the various business social events Edward had that week. In one scene, the couple are at a business polo match. Edward's lawyer, Stuckey, starts getting on his case about where Vivian came from and questioning whether she might be a spy for the opposing side of a business deal. Edward finally calms Stuckey down by assuring him that Vivian is no threat; she's a hooker he hired.

Stuckey finds this amusing and then proceeds to come onto Vivian, letting her know he knows she's a prostitute and then treating her poorly. Later, Vivian and Edward fight. She asks him why she had to dress up in these fancy clothes if he was just going to tell everyone she's a hooker and says, "At least in my own clothes I'm me and feel prepared to deal with someone like Stuckey."

It's exhausting to pretend to be something we're not. We free up so much emotional energy when we can show up as our authentic selves. I (Rosie) always say that my favorite color is sparkle (oh, I assure you sparkle is a color!). Wearing bright colors, sparkle, and a little pizazz is part of who I am. When I worked for a conservative consulting firm, I suddenly added several boring suits to my wardrobe. Then somehow I decided that in order to be taken seriously, I had to wear these suits when I'd present keynotes and workshops. There's nothing wrong with them, but I would feel like I was posturing and playing a role while on stage. Recently, I went through my closet and removed all of my suits and donated them to charity; it felt amazing! I also used to worry about swearing in any of my presentations (yet my friends will tell you I can keep up with most sailors or truckers in terms of profanity); but sometimes there are no better descriptors than "bullshit" or "asshole." It may sound silly, but these simple moves allow me to be more and more of who I am and less of some story I've created about who I think others think I should be; and it's energizing!

Now, let's be real for a moment. Showing up authentically may seem like it should be easy or not a big deal. However, it's asking people to step into the realm of adaptive change—big time. **It's familiar and comfortable to go with the flow and fit in, do what we've always done, and hide our inadequacies by operating from a place of self-protection.** Carley has been doing a lot of work to be able to show up more as her authentic self, as have I (Rosie). And that's only been possible by *wading in the messy middle* and embracing the discomfort of transformation. When we show up trying to hide our own inadequacies and are guarded, it keeps us from experiencing true connection and growth and stifles creativity and innovation. If people within organizations aren't showing up with authenticity, it only increases barriers to being able to thrive in a VUCA world.

So just what does it mean to show up authentically? Being truly authentic includes being honest and vulnerable; but that's only part of the equation. In his book *Bring Your Whole Self to Work*, Mike Robbins suggests a formula for authenticity:

Authenticity = Honesty – Self-Righteousness + Vulnerability[46]

Typically, we think of authenticity as simply being real and honest. But how many times have you experienced people being honest in a manner where others respond by shutting down or getting defensive? We can be honest about how we feel or see a situation; however, when we're attached to being *right* about our perspective, it hinders connection and collaboration. Besides, most of the time our filters that guide how we see ourselves, others, and situations stem from our ego—our inner voice that craves acceptance and approval and leads us to please, perform, pretend, and self-protect. So, without removing self-righteousness, our ego takes over, and it's impossible to show up authentically.

This is why honesty is only part of the authenticity formula. We must also remove self-righteousness; we must let go of being attached to our own narrative and interpretation of situations as being "right" and true and instead get curious. We must realize that we make up our own stories in order to make sense out of our experiences; and many times those stories are misinformed by our ego. In other words, we need to be honest about how we see or feel about something while also being open to other perspectives.

Once we are being honest about our own experience and are remaining open and curious (i.e., letting go of our attachment to being right), we need to add in the final component of the authenticity formula—which is frequently the most challenging. We need to add in vulnerability; this means we need to let ourselves be fully seen as we are. However, doing so inherently opens us up to risk, uncertainty, and emotional exposure. Take Carley, for example. In order for her to show up as her authentic self, she has to be honest about her perspective and her passion. At the same time, she remains open and curious (rather than being attached to being right) about how she sees things. And she also needs to embrace the qualities about herself that make her unique rather than trying to play a role of what she thinks others want her to be; but that requires her to be vulnerable and risk potentially being judged or not taken seriously. Yet, when she lets herself be vulnerable enough to show up as her full, authentic self, she doesn't have to hide, posture, or pretend. Her authenticity helps her continue to be a stronger leader.

Showing up as our full, authentic selves is freeing and energizing; yet it is also a risk. We don't know how people will react when we take off our masks and armor; we are exposed. Additionally, given that our sense of what is familiar is completely disrupted in this VUCA world full of adaptive change, we tend to become more self-righteous and stuck instead of being more open and vulnerable. It can feel too risky to *wade in the messy middle* and embrace the discomfort of being vulnerable. But putting on a mask, pretending to have it all together, look the part, or be someone we're not to fit in and be accepted gets in our way of connection and collaboration.

If we are going to thrive in our VUCA world and be able to grow, innovate, and adapt, we need to intentionally create the conditions where people can move from being righteous to curious, from holding back to honest communication, and from armored and guarded to fully seen. Creating these *fearless environments* creates a space for true authenticity and supports people in being able to bring their best selves to work—and home—each day. Author and leading psychological safety researcher Amy Edmondson describes the importance of creating these *fearless environments*: "A fearless organization is one in which interpersonal fear is minimized so that team and organizational performance can be maximized."[47]

When interpersonal fear is present, we armor up; we put on our masks and hide our authentic selves because it feels too risky. On teams, interpersonal fear inhibits people from speaking up and sharing ideas or concerns. Not only does this prevent innovation, creativity, and the thinking needed to address adaptive challenges, but it increases everything from ethical to safety issues because people fear backlash, retribution, or being *not enough* if they risk speaking up. People don't want to be the ones to stick their neck out, so they fall back on what is familiar, known, and comfortable. However, when we *create fearless environments* that remove interpersonal fear, incredible results can happen.

Removing Interpersonal Fear and *Creating Fearless Environments* at BTM Global

BTM Global is a one-hundred-and-thirty-person consulting firm with locations in Minneapolis, MN, and Vietnam that specializes in retail system implementations. Andy Huynh founded BTM in 2004. He grew up in

Vietnam as one of eight kids. In 1981, massive amounts of people were escaping the country due to war and violence. So, at age twelve, Andy's parents decided to send their children out of Vietnam in phases to escape the volatile conditions and ensure a safer future. Andy, his older sister, and his younger handicapped brother had to go down to the beach in the middle of the night to get on a boat with 137 other people. The Coast Guard chased them off the coast of Saigon.

By the time they reached international waters, the water pump stopped working on the boat. So they ended up drifting, knowing there were only three possible outcomes: 1) they float out to sea—and would most likely die; 2) they float back to Vietnam—and would get arrested and thrown in jail; or 3) they luck out and catch the right current to float into Thailand. Luckily, option 3 prevailed, and the boat landed in Thailand.

Before they left, Andy's dad told him that when they arrived at a refugee camp and were able to select which countries to apply for asylum to pick the United States. Within a month of being at the camp, Switzerland offered asylum to Andy and his siblings due to his brother being handicapped. But Andy remembered his father's guidance and turned down the offer. Later, the Australian government offered to move them to the top of the list due to his brother's condition; again, Andy turned down the offer. He was twelve years old and making life-or-death decisions for himself and his siblings. After fourteen months of waiting, a Catholic church in Rochester, Minnesota, sponsored Andy and his siblings; they were able to honor their father's request and make it to the United States.

Keep in mind that Andy and his siblings didn't speak English and had to relearn everything. In high school, a physician working at the Mayo Clinic became Andy's guardian. Andy took a variety of odd jobs, worked really hard, and eventually graduated from the University of Minnesota with an electrical engineering degree. About twenty years ago, Andy was hired by Tom Schoen. Tom had only been working for their mutual employer for two months and was leading a software development team, a group known to be inherently challenging to lead. The second week Andy had been working for Tom, he came up to him and said, "Tom, what's the biggest problem on your plate, and how can I help you solve it?" Tom almost reached over and kissed Andy because, at that point, he really needed that kind of stability. And that began their relationship.

Andy worked for Tom for three or four years and then moved on to other opportunities. He had this incredible desire to give back—to the United

States, Minnesota, and the people who gave him an opportunity to get out of Vietnam and have a better life. Years later, when Andy told Tom about his idea to start his own firm that did some work in the United States and some in Vietnam, Tom told him that he was nuts. But because they were friends, Tom agreed to help him. Andy knew his strengths were more on the technological side of things. So, in 2006, he asked Tom to run the company. Tom agreed to give it one year to see if they could get BTM off the ground; and the rest is history.

One of the hallmarks to BTM's success is *creating a fearless environment*. Tom and Andy are an odd couple, kind of like Arnold Schwarzenegger and Danny DeVito in the movie *Twins*. Tom describes himself as a six-foot-two, slightly overweight white guy; Andy is a short, bald Vietnamese guy. They truly love each other and use humor to tease each other relentlessly and set the tone for their team members to able to say anything.

One day, Andy approached Tom and said, "The guys in Vietnam want to do something for the kids at the local orphanage; they want to take Friday off and bring blankets and gifts to the kids. But don't worry, they're all gonna make up their time on Saturday." Tom and Andy had never talked about charity or giving back to the community, so Andy didn't know how Tom would react. Tom wanted to learn more about what they wanted to do. Then he said, "This is great. First, how can we help them? And, second, they don't have to work on Saturday; we'll give them the day." This started their focus on giving back to communities (more on this in a later chapter).

BTM is successful because they listen to their employees and enable them to take initiative and share ideas—even if initially the ideas seem far-fetched. They encourage people to communicate. Tom tells everyone he interviews who wants to work at BTM, "There's one hard-and-fast rule here that's not negotiable . . . we pay you for your experience and expertise, so I expect to hear it." They encourage a place where everyone feels safe to enter into "ferocious debate." They want everyone to feel comfortable to say anything about anything; and they also teach them how to listen.

As an example, BTM needed to hire a new VP of finance. They narrowed the candidates down to three people—two men and one woman. During the second round of interviews, Tom asked each person, "Why should I trust you?" In his mind, that's a big deal for the finance person. He interviewed the men first. They were literally squirming in their seats and didn't know how to answer the question and fumbled. Judy Wright answered without skipping a beat and said, "You shouldn't trust me right me away because you don't know me well enough. But I'll tell you why the guy that I work for now trusts me." At that moment, Judy became Tom's top choice due to her honesty and directness. He said, "I don't need somebody to fumble in their chair on why I should trust them. I mean, that's a basic question—especially someone working with our finances."

At BTM, there is open debate amongst Tom, Andy, and the other leaders to show others that it's okay—and expected. They also ask a lot of questions and intentionally push back on people. Sometimes Tom admits to testing the waters by pushing back on things that are insignificant just to see how far he has to go before people will finally push back on him; he forces their hand to push back to show how important open debate is.

Unlike in many organizations, where the comfort level and vibe suddenly changes when the CEO or COO shows up in a meeting, when Tom shows up in a meeting, people aren't on edge. They know he's just there to listen. However, one time Tom showed up at a meeting around lunchtime and everyone stopped and looked at him. He responded, "Okay, what the hell is going on because your reaction is kind of weird. So, unless you're doing dope in the corner or something, I don't know what you guys are doing." It turned out they had a mustache-growing contest and were judging it over lunch. Tom replied, "Well now I'm mad; you didn't even ask me to help judge!"

Through leading by example, Tom and Andy have created an environment where people are at ease. As a result, they speak up, share ideas, and aren't worried about retribution or feeling embarrassed. And BTM continues to grow and thrive as a result of *creating a fearless environment* where interpersonal fear is minimized.

They also have a holistic perspective of how they measure the success of their company. In addition to top- and bottom-line measures, they also look at the project level. When Tom or any of the key leaders have to spend less time on some of the projects, they know they've created greater enablement and people are stretching themselves and taking ownership of the work. Here's a great example of how BTM *creating a fearless environment* enables their people to *show up as leaders*.

In Vietnam, the vast majority of the population is below the age of thirty-five. There's a transition happening in terms of mindset. A lot of the men thought they were entitled as soon as they were working at BTM for a certain amount of time. However, the women (especially younger women) were working harder; so they were being promoted ahead of the men. About five or six years ago, there was a woman working for BTM. She approached the lead of the Vietnam office and said, "I have to resign." He replied, "Why? You've been here a long time, you're an extremely good person, you're in an important position, why are you resigning?" She said, "Because I'm pregnant." You see, she rides a motorbike to work every day. But doing so would jeopardize her pregnancy.

Without hesitation, and without having a conversation with Tom first, he turned down the resignation and worked with this employee so that she could work from home for the rest of her pregnancy. This was a big deal because it is so different than the typical workplace cultural norms. He told Tom what he did after the fact. And Tom was so proud because it was exactly the right thing to do; he knew he had successfully enabled this man in the right way to think about things differently. And this woman still works for BTM today.

What BTM has done to *create a fearless environment* is powerful. Now, let's be real. Creating an environment that minimizes interpersonal fear is one thing; equipping people to be able to be courageous enough to show up without their self-protective armor requires a different level of intentionality. It requires rethinking how we approach developing ourselves and others. In order to thrive in this increasingly complex world, we need to develop our capacity to effectively adapt to a new, disruptive reality; and it starts from the inside out.

Developing Greater Mental Complexity to Thrive in a VUCA World

> *If I continue to believe as I have always believed, I will continue to act as I have always acted. If I continue to act as I have always acted, I will continue to get what I have always gotten.* —MARILYN FURGUSON[48]

The future of work demands that we are able to effectively navigate adaptive challenges. Therefore, a key component of creating workplaces where people can thrive within the VUCA realities is supporting their development—so they can *wade in the messy middle* to stretch and grow and make the adaptive leaps required to be successful. In particular, we need to focus on fostering people's ability to operate with greater mental complexity. What do we mean by greater mental complexity? Robert Kegan, PhD, is renowned for his theories of adult development. Of the five stages of development, three are primarily found in adulthood; with each one, the level of mental complexity increases:[49]

- Stage 3: Socialized Mind. This is a very outside-in way of viewing the world. We are shaped by the definitions and expectations of our personal environment and seek external validation for ourselves. And when we're defined from the outside in, our ideas and work become our identity. So if someone challenges our ideas or our work, we feel like **we** are being attacked; it's an attack on our identity. Consequently, we end up in this space of playing to not lose. It's a very ego-centric, armored, and guarded place from which to operate. Carley's descriptions of not showing up authentically out of worry of what others think is a classic example of operating from this developmental stage.

- Stage 4: Self-Authoring Mind. This is a more inside-out way of viewing the world. We are able to self-direct, take stands, and set limits and boundaries on behalf of our own voice and what matters to us. We see that we are more than our ideas or work. So if someone challenges us, we are able to take a perspective about it, filter the challenge, and determine what is helpful and what is not. It's a more intentional, open place from which to operate. As Carley continues to do her own self-development work, she describes being able to more comfortably speak up with her board and others and wear clothes that are professional but still let her feel like herself. This is her self-authoring mind starting to emerge more; and, as it does, her confidence and energy grow.

- Stage 5: Self-Transforming Mind. When we reach this stage, we are able to step back and recognize the stories and constructs we've created about ourselves, others, and our experiences; and we can even start to see the irony and humor of it. We can see that any one system by itself is incomplete and can embrace contradiction and opposites. Very few of us actually reach this stage. (Gandhi is an example of someone at this stage.)

Why does this matter? Because in our increasingly complex, adaptive world, we need people to be able to understand themselves and respond with higher levels of mental complexity. We need to be able to bring new thinking to solve adaptive challenges. And we need more people to be able to move from operating from their ego (our inner voice that craves acceptance and approval and leads us to please, perform, pretend, and self-protect) and being reactive (i.e., our socialized mind) so they can be more intentional; we need to be able to hear and leverage our own voice and be able to balance the complexities necessary to thrive in a VUCA world.

Unfortunately, there is a large gap between where we are as a population and where the complexity of the world needs us to be. We expect people to be able to innovate, act intentionally on behalf of their own voice, and take initiative (all characteristics of a self-authoring mind). Yet only 20 percent of the population is estimated to be in this stage of development. The majority (75 percent) are operating from the socialized mind (or somewhere in between socialized and self-authoring), showing up as faithful followers seeking external direction. And when things get hard, we tend to revert to this stage. We're also expecting leaders to be able to move toward self-transforming—where they can embrace a compelling vision and hold multiple perspectives at once; yet only 5 percent of the population is actually in this developmental stage.[50]

In this VUCA world, we are essentially asking for a quantum shift in individual mental complexity across the board. As Robert Kegan and Lisa Lahey write in their book *Immunity to Change*, "When we experience the world as 'too complex' we are not just experiencing the complexity of the world. We are experiencing a mismatch between the world's complexity and our own at this moment . . . there are only two logical ways to mend this mismatch—reduce the world's complexity or increase our own."[51]

Since we know that the world's complexity is never going to decrease, we must find a way to increase our own mental complexity. Kegan and Lahey have found a way to do that through their Immunity to Change (ITC) work. ITC helps people systematically overcome their unconscious, psychological immunity to change behaviors and also develop to a higher level—like self-authoring or self-transforming (we will discuss in more detail the value of leveraging their work in chapter 7). For now, it's important to understand that the process of developing greater mental complexity and fostering meaningful, sustainable change starts with being aware of our internal stories and assumptions.

The Stories We Tell Ourselves

We all have stories we hold—about ourselves, others, and how things work. The question is whether these stories serve us well. Much of the time, these stories are self-limiting and stem from our ego. How much our ego is in the driver's seat depends on our mindset, what Robert Anderson and William Adams call our *Inner Operating System* (IOS), or how we relate to the world. The IOS operates beneath the surface and consists of our conscious and unconscious meaning and decision-making system, mental models, beliefs, values, assumptions, self-awareness, identity, and emotional intelligence.[52]

Given that 75 percent of us are operating from the socialized-mind developmental stage, this means that the majority of us are operating from very self-limiting stories. At the root of most of these self-limiting stories is usually something about not being *enough*: not smart enough, lovable enough, thin enough, pretty enough, strong enough, or good enough. And when *not enough* is in the driver's seat, we show up guarded, in self-protection mode, and limited in being able to navigate through adaptive challenges.

Michael (not his real name) is a highly renowned and skilled surgeon. He has a great track record with his surgical outcomes and patient satisfaction. At the same time, Michael kept taking on more and more work and was becoming burned out. Even his colleagues expressed concern for him. He recognized his own sense of burnout, yet couldn't quite seem to do anything differently. As his stress and anxiety increased, he became reactive; he would blow up at different people or just withdraw completely.

When we started working with Michael to help him uncover his underlying assumptions and stories, his current behaviors started to become clearer. Michael had several instances growing up that, at the time, seemed minor but profoundly shaped his internal scripts that he was less than others (a.k.a. *not enough*). He was homeschooled through high school. Around the age of five, he realized that all of his friends could read; but he had not yet learned how to read. He was sad and embarrassed; the story he told himself was "I'm dumb and not as smart as my friends," which quickly turned into "I need to figure out how to read fast." He developed an assumption or self-imposed rule that he could never be seen as weak and needed to prove that he's as smart as others.

Around the age of eight, Michael was caught stealing change from a jar at home. Feeling ashamed, he told himself, "I'm a bad person and am not trustworthy." From that moment on, he vowed to never again let people down. That's quite a burden to carry (not to mention unrealistic)! When Michael was twelve, a kid in his class called him ugly in front of others, and the kids laughed. Again embarrassed, he told himself, "I'm ugly," and then mentally beat himself up, wondering why he didn't stand up for himself. Consequently, he developed another assumption and self-imposed rule that he needed to prove himself in other areas of his life and show that this kid was wrong. Additionally, for many years, Michael's mom would intermittently threaten to leave the family. So he regularly had this inner story playing that he was going to be abandoned and that she didn't care. He then took it upon himself to learn to be 100 percent self-sufficient so he didn't have to be dependent on anyone.

All of these instances started to script Michael's inner narrative of not being *enough* and that he must always prevail, have it all together, and be perfect. Anytime he was in the operating room with someone he perceived as having more clout or credibility, he'd be triggered; his narrative of needing to be perfect and not letting anyone see him struggle would kick into high gear. If the operation didn't go as quickly or smoothly as he imagined it should, he'd get frustrated, beat himself up, start yelling and swearing (thus creating an uncomfortable environment for those around him), and then wouldn't take the time to debrief residents and fellows afterwards so they could benefit from the learning experience. He'd "armor up" by withdrawing (so he didn't need to show his weakness to others) and would then push himself harder the next time he was in surgery to overcompensate for any previous less-than-perfect operation. This created a vicious cycle that only perpetuated his burnout.

Christine Miller (not her real name) is a highly regarded and successful leader. She had a pivotal turning point in her personal and leadership journey. Christine had an overly humble, self-deprecating quality that led her to constantly apologize for herself (even when she didn't need to), work exceedingly long hours, bend over backwards to please people in an effort to help the organization, and work through vacations. After several major stressful life events occurred, these behaviors became even more pronounced to a fault; it got to the point that some members of her team started losing confidence in her abilities.

Luckily, Christine embraced the opportunity to take advantage of this juncture in her leadership journey and engage in work to develop herself. We began working with her and examined where she was getting in her own way and the underlying stories that shaped her behaviors. When Christine was six years old, her mom gave birth to twins—a baby girl and a baby boy. The baby boy (who we'll call Max) died two days after he was born. Christine accompanied her mom on countless errands as she made arrangements for Max's funeral and trips to the hospital to visit her newborn sister (who we'll call Angie), who was still in the nursery. Christine watched as her mom literally slept under Angie's crib each night to tend to her in case she stopped breathing. This was confusing and hard for Christine to process at such a young age. She decided to become her mom's helper; she thought if she could free up her mom to tend to Angie, she could somehow help ensure that her sister would live.

Fast-forward a few years, and Christine's other brother was diagnosed with juvenile diabetes. Christine watched him have several "low blood sugar" episodes and was determined to help. She even used to stuff her cheerleading uniform with candies just in case he needed them during basketball games in high school. Christine began to put an incredible burden on herself; she felt that the world rested on her shoulders and that she needed to be a good girl and do the right thing or the world would basically fall apart. And, in the case of her family, her young brain literally was running a life-or-death script.

Christine found her value in helping others and putting others first. The problem is that this narrative didn't evolve as she became an adult; she was operating with an underlying assumption that her sole value came from being helpful—and anything not in service to others meant she was selfish and *not enough*. In her mind, this meant that she couldn't advocate for her own needs and be of service to others; they couldn't coexist. So she was constantly apologizing anytime she felt she might come across as advocating for herself (which actually led to others interpreting her actions as weak) and was becoming increasingly stressed and burned out.

Our *Not Enough* Stories

When we are running an IOS of being *not enough*, we end up operating from what Anderson and Adams refer to as the Reactive Mind.[53] The structure of our Reactive Mind is very similar to that of a socialized mind; we let forces outside of ourselves define and shape us and cling tightly to familiarity and predictability. Therefore, we tend to be problem-focused and driven by fears rooted in externally organized beliefs and assumptions.

Structure of the Reactive Mind

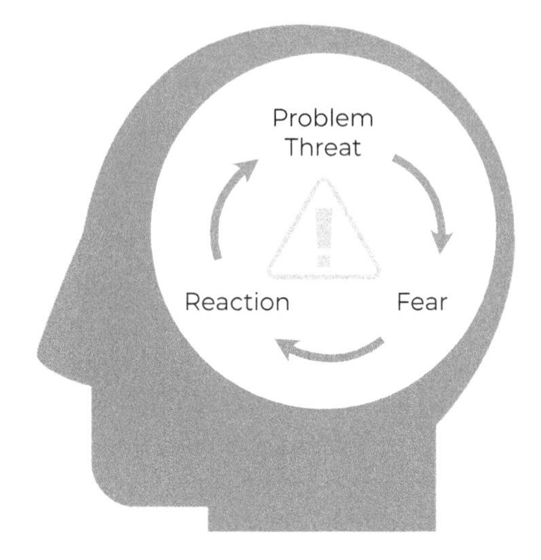

Reactive Structure of the Mind (adapted from Mastering Leadership)

When this structure is running our IOS, we end up in reactionary, "armored up" mode—responding out of fear related to a perceived problem or threat. And we get a very predictable pattern of performance—that rarely serves us well. Let's look at Michael as an example. Any time he's in the operating room with someone who he perceives as having more clout, his Reactive Mind is triggered. That person with clout is the perceived threat that elicits anxiety—fear of looking weak, having others see him struggle, and not being perfect. So he reacts by getting flustered in the operating room if anything doesn't go perfectly, shutting down, avoiding any debrief with the residents, and then beating himself up for days afterwards. The internal narrative he's created during this time then makes it even worse the next time he's in the operating room under similar circumstances; so he'll put even more pressure on himself to be perfect . . . and the vicious cycle continues.

In Christine's case, advocating for herself was a trigger for feeling guilty. As an example, any time she tried to take a vacation, people would put appointments on her calendar (even though it was blocked); this sparked guilt and a fear of disappointing people, and then she'd cancel or work during her vacation. Then she'd feel trapped, resentful, overworked, frustrated, and weak; as a result, she was unable to show up effectively under times of stress.

What triggers this Reactive Mind? Neuroscientist and researcher David

Rock describes how our brains are hardwired to maximize reward and minimize threats. When we perceive a threat, our brains are triggered to respond automatically in a fight-or-flight mode (often referred to as the "amygdala hijack"), resulting in us putting on our armor to prepare for a fight and behaving in all kinds of unproductive ways out of an innate need for self-protection. The problem is that our brains don't know the difference between an actual physical threat and a perceived social threat. Rock developed the SCARF model to describe the five domains of human social experience that activate reward or threat signals in the brain:[54]

- Status: how we stack up against other people
- Certainty: our ability to predict the future for ourselves
- Autonomy: our power to control our own destiny
- Relatedness: our sense of trust in the people around us
- Fairness: our trust that we are being treated as well as others

When we perceive a threat to any one of these domains, we move from making thoughtful, intentional choices to an automated threat response where our ego takes over, and our instinct is to protect ourselves by pleasing, performing, and pretending. We end up operating from a Reactive Mind structure. As a result, our prefrontal cortex functioning (responsible for higher-level brain functioning and mental complexity) is diminished. So we are unable to think clearly or process thoughts effectively; we are unable to learn or solve problems. Consequently, any hope of being able to effectively navigate adaptive challenges goes out the window because, cognitively, we are unable to function in a productive manner.

At the same time, our amygdala hijack kicks in and we start to generalize more, make connections that don't exist, and avoid taking risks. When any one of our SCARF elements are threatened, it's a threat to our ego. Our *not enough* script kicks into high gear, and we end up quickly in a downward spiral with our thinking and start assembling our armor.[55] And when our thinking is operating from this reactive place, our behaviors quickly follow. Here are some examples of how we might show up when amygdala hijack takes over, self-protection is in the driver's seat, and our IOS is run by the Reactive Mind:

- Avoiding speaking up or giving feedback
- Protecting our turf rather than collaborating
- Judging others or throwing them under the bus

- Clinging tightly to the way we've always done things
- Being inflexible and unwilling to consider change
- Trying to control others
- Perfectionism and intolerance for error
- Hoarding information
- Overly skeptical and assuming people have poor intentions
- Focusing on all that is wrong
- Acting like a victim and blaming others

These are also the types of behaviors that show up in dehumanized, toxic work environments. It makes sense because these environments breed all sorts of threat triggers. And even in healthy, thriving workplaces, the very nature of living in a VUCA world signals some level of threat to each one of these domains and can trigger the Reactive Mind; so the risk of self-protective behaviors showing up will only continue to increase in the future.

This is where *creating fearless environments* comes into play. Our remedy is to ensure that we create a psychologically safe context. We need to help minimize the threats people perceive so they can show up authentically and collaboratively rather than reactively and self-protectively. Then we can help people *wade in the messy middle* so they are able to leverage a more effective IOS where they can engage in their lives from a place of worthiness—where we can all tell ourselves, *I am enough and have value—just as I am. No matter what mistakes I made or what didn't get done today, I am worthy of love and belonging.*

It's incredibly liberating to be able to show up recognizing we are *enough*. Carley Kammerer has had people tell her she intimidates them because they're not used to people actually going after their dreams and taking risks. The irony is that, as she was running her own *not enough* script, she was intimidated by these same people. She said, "If we're all intimidated by each other and we are all secretly self-conscious, we should just start owning our own stories and who we are and let go of all the other crap; it's nonsense. We need to own our strengths as much as our weaknesses and not apologize for it. Especially for me as we start expanding operations and move into fundraising for our storefront. If I think I'm an idiot, then why would anyone want to give me $30,000?"

Here's the thing: it's part of the human condition to be triggered to self-protect and have our ego take over. So trying to fight it or pretend we're immune to it doesn't make any sense. What we need is to get to know ourselves on a more intimate level so we know the signs and signals we are triggered by and what triggers us to self-protect. Then we need to be curious and move to a space of self-reflection. Otherwise, the merry-go-round of our Reactive Mind will continue to take over and we'll be in a never-ending, vicious cycle that will keep us from thriving and having the impact we want to have in the world.

Moving from Self-Protection to Self-Reflection

The reason why consciousness exists, and why there is an urge to widen and deepen it, is very simple, without consciousness things go less well.
—CARL JUNG[56]

Just because it may be our innate instinct to operate from a place of self-protection doesn't mean we can't choose a better path—so we can *show up as leaders*. Luckily, there is another IOS we can leverage that allows us to thrive in this VUCA world and navigate the waters of adaptive change. The structure of the Creative Mind is similar to a self-authoring mind. It starts from purpose and vision rather than a problem. So rather than operating from fear, we operate from passion, love, and commitment. Anderson and Adams say that the "focus on vision, fueled by passion, results in **action**, not reaction."[57]

Structure of the Creative Mind

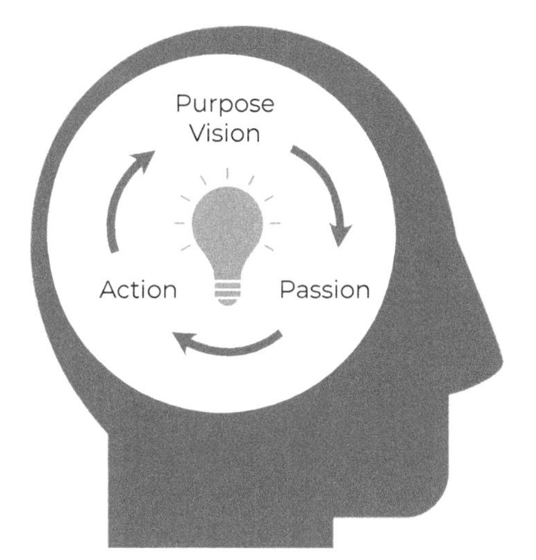

Creative Structure of the Mind (adapted from Mastering Leadership)

It doesn't mean we don't have any fear in the Creative Mind; but the passion, love, and commitment generated from the vision are bigger than the fear. So we are more willing to embrace the discomfort and *wade in the messy middle* to move from fear to *vision*. This is also why *building a lighthouse* is so important; it helps fuel our Creative Mind, allowing us to *show up as leaders* and make a positive impact on those around us. And this is also why building our muscle to pause is so critical.

In his book *Man's Search for Meaning*, Viktor Frankl put it well when he wrote, "Between stimulus and response is a space. In that space is our power to choose our response. In our response lies our growth and freedom."[58] With our world becoming increasingly fast-paced and complex, and demanding us to come up with new, adaptive solutions, we need to equip people to pause and embrace the space; so we can move from a Reactive to a Creative Mind. We need to develop people to be more self-aware, reflective, and intentional. In other words, we need to *create fearless environments* that foster cognitive development so we can progress toward operating more with a self-authoring or self-transforming mind.

When Christine Miller hit a pivotal point in her leadership journey, her organization *created a fearless environment* for her to do the transformative work she needed to step back into her greatness as a leader. While some leaders might hide their heads when receiving difficult feedback, Christine did not. At first, she did repeatedly apologize for herself; but then she decided to *wade in the messy middle*. She did the work to become more aware of her self-limiting stories, what triggers her Reactive Mind, and rewrite her inner narrative.

Christine started to challenge the assumptions she was holding that she couldn't recover if she let people down and that she couldn't help others and tend to her own needs. Through coaching sessions and the hard work she did, she stopped apologizing for herself at every turn. She owned her mistakes and started embracing gratitude for the opportunity to upgrade her IOS. She reported feeling calmer and more poised and said, "My gut reaction to self-protect and shut down is gone; leaning into the discomfort of my old assumptions actually makes me stronger."

As Christine laid down her self-protective armor, she started to re-step into her greatness—at work and at home. And as her confidence grew, she knew she was ready for the next step and has taken on a new role to become the chief nursing officer for two hospitals in the Midwest. Christine describes the value of *wading in the messy middle* to do the work to upgrade her IOS:

> It was my great fortune to have the type of fearless environment where thinking through why feelings and behaviors appear under times of stress, and then being able to *wade into that messy middle*, allowed me to gain the clarity I needed to show up again as the leader I knew I was. I asked others (found my tribe) for insight into how I was showing up in meetings and other situations I was leading through, and then dissected that valuable feedback to serve as my lighthouse while moving forward. I believe there is truth in all feedback, and I search for those nuggets. Working with Rosie was a gift I will never be able to repay but will pay it forward!

Upgrading from a Reactive to Creative Mind benefits teams as well as individuals. Susan is a leader who was struggling with her team. They had significant issues with adopting the various organizational changes, communicating poorly, and negativity and blame. She tried bringing in people to lead workshops on change management and effective communication, but they never seemed to work. When we began working with her team and introduced the concept of VUCA and how the very nature of work can trigger us to go into self-protection mode, things finally started to make sense; they were relieved to have language to use to describe what they were experiencing.

The organization had been in a constant state of flux—including significant changes in leadership and organizational structure, acquisitions, and expanding their products and services. Her team's status was threatened because they weren't sure where they fit given all of the changes. There was little certainty; they didn't yet know the new leaders, and they felt like they had no say in how these changes impacted their work. Everyone on Susan's team was showing up in full armor ready to battle, and they didn't even realize it.

Once they started to become more aware of their triggers, and how they each were showing up guarded rather than collaborative, we were able to teach them skills and techniques to pause, self-reflect, and then try on new stories that served them better. They were able to have more empathy for each other and see how they all were showing up in full self-protective mode. As they each laid down their armor, they were able to make the collective purpose more important than any one individual being "right." Being able to equip people to move beyond their triggered, self-protective, and Reactive Mind is becoming even more essential given the ever-changing landscape of work.

The Changing Landscape of Work

The changing landscape of work only adds to the demands that we evolve and adopt better ways of leading and operating within our organizations. By now the millennial generation (people born between 1981 and 1996) is likely the most studied generation in history. This is due to the fact that, as of 2017, they are the largest generation in the US workforce (35 percent)[59] and will comprise 50 percent of workforce by 2020 and 75 percent of the workforce by 2025.[60] In fact, some companies already report that millennials make up over two-thirds of their workforce base. And the changes they are seeking are those that ultimately make workplaces more human:

- They don't want to just collect a paycheck; they want meaning, purpose, and fulfillment in their work.
- They have great reverence for the environment and place an emphasis on corporate responsibility.
- They seek to build communities around shared interests.
- They want meaningful feedback to learn and grow.[61]

Then there's the newest generation starting to enter the workforce, Generation Z (people born in 1997 and later). They will account for 36 percent of the workforce by 2020.[62] They tend to be more realistic and pragmatic than millennials and view financial stability as critically important. The good news is that workplaces that focus on fostering a thriving, purposeful culture tend to perform better financially and provide better pay and benefits for their people; so it's a win-win for all generations.

While millennials and Gen Zs are sparking the need to have more human workplaces, it's not just these younger generations who are seeking a different employment experience. As Rasmus Hougaard and Jacqueline Carter write in their book *The Mind of a Leader*, which studied more than thirty thousand leaders, "Today's workforce is increasingly looking for meaning, human connectedness, true happiness, and a desire to contribute positively to the world."[63]

I (Jon) taught college for twenty-five years, engaging with hundreds, if not thousands, of millennials over that time. My experiences with them support what the research says. As much as you can generalize about any one group, I found that they care much less about the differences between people—ethnic, racial, religious, gender, etc. What they do care about is having their lives have a larger meaning—over and above just receiving a paycheck. And though they are often accused (perhaps accurately) of being a bit impatient, they are simply not willing to settle for less. As Joshua, my millennial son, said to me recently after three months in his latest job working for a recruiting firm, "It is a little frustrating, Dad, because I have not gotten a promotion yet [after three months]; but I love the fact that I am able to help people get jobs to be able to improve their lives!"

It takes great courage to create future-ready workplaces where people can thrive, grow, and develop so they can leverage greater mental complexity and navigate adaptive change, and find purpose and fulfillment. We need to shift our mindset and paradigms about work and break away from dehumanized business-as-usual practices; it's a strategic imperative—for all generations.

According to the 2017 Deloitte Human Capital Trends Report, "business and HR leaders can no longer continue to operate according to old paradigms. They must now embrace new ways of thinking about their companies, their talent and their role in global social issues."[64] And in 2018 Deloitte added that organizations are also being judged for more than just their success as a business; "they're now being held responsible for their impact on society at large."[65]

Quite simply, organizations that can't adapt to the demands of the world today and tomorrow will become obsolete, a warning echoed by the authors of the book *Firms of Endearment*: **"Join capitalism's radical social transformation—or fall by the wayside."**[66]

Take-Home Points about the Future of Work

- Our VUCA world inherently invites more adaptive challenges that require us to let go of how we've always done things and adopt new ways of thinking; and this sparks incredible discomfort in our brains. This discomfort can trigger us to fall back on familiar solutions and self-protect; however, we cannot effectively solve adaptive challenges using technical solutions.

- People need to be able to show up fully, authentically human, and leverage new, more complex thinking in order to make the adaptive leaps necessary to thrive in a VUCA world. This requires that we intentionally *create fearless environments* to support them.

- We have a fundamental developmental gap between where we are as a society with our level of mental complexity and what the world is demanding of us. Closing the developmental gap can help us move from a Reactive Mind, where we are triggered and react from fear in a self-protective way, to a Creative Mind fueled by purpose and passion. We cannot close the developmental gap without *building a lighthouse* and *wading in the messy middle.*

- The changing landscape of work demands more human workplaces that foster meaning and connection and that make a positive contribution in the world.

Chapter 3

HOW WE GOT SO STUCK

That "change makes us uncomfortable" is now one of the most widely promoted, widely accepted, and under-considered half-truths around. [I]t is not change by itself that makes us uncomfortable; it is not even change that involves taking on something very difficult. Rather, it is change that leaves us feeling defenseless before the dangers we "know" to be present that causes us anxiety. —ROBERT KEGAN[67]

Imagine that the shipwrecked sailors from our opening story continued to cling to the familiarity of what they always did onboard the ship. If they stayed rigid with the command-and-control structure and day-to-day operations they had aboard the ship, stayed in their comfort zone, and waited to be saved, the story could have had a very different, unpleasant outcome. They likely never would have found the fresh water, as that required them to get uncomfortable, take risks, and venture into unknown territory. As stress grew, they would have probably start fighting rather than collaborating. Rather than order, what they would ultimately experience would be more chaotic.

We don't have to be shipwrecked on an island to experience chaos, stress, and disconnection. The very nature of a VUCA world invites us to grasp even tighter to how we've done things in the past and become even more attached to the rightness of our perspective and stories; we do this instinctively to protect ourselves from the discomfort of the unknown. It's part of the human condition. And our perspectives and experiences are largely shaped by paradigms we hold.

The Power of Paradigms

Folk singer David Roth's song "Five Blind Men" tells a version of an old Indian fable about five blind men walking in the woods who encounter an elephant resting in a glade. Each man grabs ahold of a different part of the animal and, since none of them has ever seen an elephant, promptly concludes that it must be a tree (leg), a spear (tusk), a hose (nose), a fan (ear), or a rope (tail).

The elephant gets up and turns around; the men now find themselves holding on to a different part of the animal, resulting in an immediate re-evaluation of its nature. Roth sums up the reality of the lesson learned by saying, "Whatever you might think you see depends on where you stand and how you feel."[68]

Like the five blind men, our beliefs, feelings, and behaviors are powerfully shaped by our life experiences. The sum total of these life experiences creates what is often referred to as our worldview or paradigm. A paradigm is defined as "A frame of reference from which we determine how we feel about and interact with our surroundings. A set of rules and regulations that defines boundaries and tells us what to do to be successful within those boundaries."[69]

The frame of reference and rules and regulations that make up our worldview (or paradigm) are actually a composite of many, many layers of life experiences related to our ethnicity, religious affiliations, geography, family upbringing, and gender experiences, to name a few. Paradigms are helpful in that they act as filters of the otherwise overwhelming influx of data that come into our brain every second of our waking lives. They help us to focus on the things that matter most to us at any given time. Similarly, paradigms provide scientists with a governing framework as an important starting point to guide and focus their inquiry and research.

The problem is that when they become too deeply entrenched, paradigms create a "stuckness" that can inhibit innovation and limit our ability to adapt to change. As Dr. Thomas S. Kuhn writes in his seminal work *The Structure of Scientific Revolutions*, "The proponents of different paradigms . . . see different things when they look from the same point in the same direction . . . [W]hat cannot even be demonstrated to one group of scientists may seem intuitively obvious to another."[70]

The term for this is "paradigm paralysis,"[71] and history is strewn with examples of how the *stuckness* it creates can have devastating consequences. Although we reference this story in *How to Build a Thriving Culture at Work*, it is such a powerful example of paradigms that it is worth repeating.

Around the turn of the seventeenth century, the dominant paradigm with respect to the structure of our solar system was that the sun and all the planets revolved around the earth. Soon thereafter, Galileo claimed that, in fact, all the planets, including the earth, actually revolved around the sun. The blasphemy of contradicting the prevailing paradigm was met harshly by experts of his time. Galileo was forced to publicly recant his claim and spend the rest of his life under house arrest. So powerful was the existing paradigm that the experts refused to even look through the telescope he had invented to support his conclusion!

However, this reaction to Galileo's findings is not surprising; it is unsettling to have our paradigms challenged. Consequently, we tend to behave in a fairly predictable, Reactive Mind manner. As Margaret Wheatley writes in *Who Do We Choose to Be?*, "As a paradigm exhausts its sense-making capacities, people always grasp onto it more desperately, insisting that it still works, that it can and will answer all questions."[72]

As the VUCA world continues to disrupt how we do things and sparks discomfort, we see people acting like some of the sailors in our opening story: they cling for dear life to the paradigms that are familiar to them. The good news in this regard is that if people become aware of their *stuckness*, and then embrace the discomfort and *wade in the messy middle*, it can actually provide the impetus to break free and learn and grow.

As M. Scott Peck tells us in *The Road Less Traveled*, "The truth is that our finest moments are most likely to occur when we are feeling deeply uncomfortable . . . For it is only in such moments, propelled by our discomfort, that we are likely to step out of our ruts and start searching for different ways or truer answers."[73]

It is only when we embrace the discomfort that we can let go of our *stuckness* to outdated paradigms and begin to transform and make the adaptive leaps necessary to thrive in this disruptive, VUCA world.

Our *Stuckness* to a Four-Hundred-Year-Old, Outdated Paradigm

We believe that most people are well-intended when it comes to trying to build thriving, human workplaces. However, just as with the experts in Galileo's time, our approaches to organizational and employee well-being and our understanding of behavior change remain stuck in an outdated paradigm that is over four hundred years old. The "mechanistic worldview" or paradigm of the seventeenth-century Scientific Revolution envisioned the universe as a great machine. Everything within that universe, including all living things, were considered to be machines as well. As Renes Descartes, one of the architects of the mechanistic paradigm, declared, "There is no difference between the machines built by artisans and the diverse bodies that nature alone composes,"[74] and "I consider the body as a machine . . .

my thought . . . compares a sick man and an ill-made clock with my idea of healthy man and a well-made clock."[75]

The prevailing wisdom of the time separated the universe into two nonintersecting halves, one containing all the things that could be seen, touched, and measured (in relation to health—blood pressure, weight, cholesterol, etc.), and the other made up of everything else (thoughts, feelings, emotions, spirituality, etc.). The assumption was that the latter could have no impact on the former and therefore was not worthy of scientific study.

The overarching approach to science within this mechanistic paradigm was just as you might expect. Whereas medieval scientists queried about the purpose of science might respond by saying something like "to understand and live in harmony with nature," Sir Francis Bacon, another architect of the seventeenth-century worldview, had quite a different recommendation for how the secrets of nature might best be revealed: "When by art and the hand of man she is forced out of her natural state, and squeezed and moulded."[76]

Given the dominance of patriarchy in this mechanistic paradigm, it is hardly surprising to see the control of a feminine nature at the hands of men become the fundamental approach to science! Sadly, this mechanistic, patriarchal paradigm is still very prevalent today. And although the desire for and illusion of control may have brought some peace to the seventeenth-century world (and may have bestowed some initial benefit in the scientific management of the twentieth century), in the long run, trying to control living systems to navigate the chaos of the VUCA world is doomed to fail.

Our *stuckness* to this outdated, mechanistic paradigm has us stuck in three critical areas that lead to dehumanization: organizational well-being, employee well-being, and behavior change. We believe it is critical to understand and identify the *stuckness* in order to rehumanize workplaces and allow people and businesses to thrive in this new disruptive normal.

The *Stuckness* of Organizational Well-Being

We've already established the devastating consequences of workplaces and business practices that treat people more like machines than living beings. But where did these practices originate? They emerged largely from the work of Frederick W. Taylor and scientific management in the early 1900s. He believed it was human nature for people to "goof off" (what he referred to as *soldiering*) and that men were motivated purely by economic self-interest.

The pitfall of "Taylorism" was that thinking was essentially engineered out of work. As a result, supervisors had to micro-manage workers to ensure they didn't get away with goofing off (and, unfortunately, this type of management is still very prevalent today). In his book *From the Neck Up: The Recovery and Sustaining of the Human Element in Modern Organizations*, Steve Byrum describes Taylor's view of the management/employee relationship: "Each man must give up his own particular way of doing things, adapt his methods to the many new standards, and grow accustomed to receiving and obeying instructions, covering details large and small, which in the past had been left to individual judgment. The workmen are to do as they are told."[77]

Perhaps this was helpful at the time, but our world is far more complex today. We need people to be able to think, leverage more of a self-authoring mind, and make the adaptive leaps necessary to successfully usher organizations into a thriving future. The legacy of the old paradigm and Taylorism still shows up in many business-as-usual practices today, where the desire to "control the machine" prevents workplaces from honoring what it means to be human.

For example, think of all of the business initiatives that have evolved to get more work done in the name of "progress": LEAN manufacturing, Six Sigma, automation, and twelve-hour shifts, to name a few. Many of these seem like great solutions on paper. However, in too many cases these processes actually dehumanize the workplace and do not account for the reality that humans are not machines; unlike machines, we are deeply affected by stress, fatigue, injuries, and disengagement. When employees are treated like machines, not only does the workplace culture erode, but individual well-being and productivity suffer as well. We're not saying efforts and processes to streamline work and create efficiencies aren't important; but when they are implemented without consideration for the human impact, that's when problems with organizational well-being emerge.

Additionally, when we don't equip people to navigate the adaptive nature of a VUCA world, more *stuckness* emerges. Organizations clinging to tenants of this old paradigm tend to value hypermasculine traits of money, power, and control. They reward people for working themselves to a point of exhaustion (hence the dismal stats on how workplaces are literally killing us). What we need are some more feminine traits of nurturing, empathy, flexibility, and receptivity.

Many years ago, I (Rosie) led the well-being/culture consulting practice for an organization. I was initially drawn to them because they had won awards for being a fast-growing company and a great place to work. Like many companies, they also were heavily focused on revenue and ran very lean. For longer than is humanly sustainable, I was working sixty- to eighty-hour work weeks. You see, when they first hired me, it was to build a team. But for two years, it was just me. I was being spread thin and having sales leaders fight over who got access to me.

I love getting my butt kicked in a painfully, sweaty workout with Shaun T. One of his favorite lines is to "Dig deep!" He uses it when we're tired, swearing at him, and wondering if we're more insane than he is for actually doing his workouts. "Dig deep" became the mantra I used to keep pushing through and keep working harder, because that's what my company expected and rewarded. But we can only push past the exhaustion point for so long before something's gotta give. We can't "dig deep" forever.

One day, we were having what I saw as another pointless meeting about "rationing" my services. In this meeting were my leader, his leader (the COO), the president, the CEO, and two of the sales leads. I remember feeling like a *Peanuts* episode as they were talking; I stopped hearing what they were saying and just heard "wha-wha-wha-wha wha wha-whaaaa" (like the mumbling adults were portrayed). The CEO looked at me at one point and said, "Rosie, we've been sitting here talking about the vision for your area; what's your vision?" There was nothing left for me to dig deep; my Reactive Mind was running the show. I didn't even blink and had absolutely no filter when I blurted out, "It's really quite simple; you hired me two years ago to build a team. I can't keep working these insane hours! Build my f^*%#ing team or I'm gone!" Yikes!

Luckily my outburst didn't count against me; within two days they had a position posted. It shouldn't have to get to a point of exhaustion for people to pay attention and act humanely—and with common sense. Additionally, when I looked back at that time, I was not producing the quality of work I was capable of. We can't unleash the best in people when they are being pushed to keep going and going until their breaking point.

In his book *Management Rewired*, Charles Jacobs urges why we need to shift our paradigms about business: "When it comes to how we approach business, we need to rethink everything we thought we knew about management. This isn't just about a new model for measuring a business, reengineering its operations, or motivating its people. This is about the nature of the world being different than we thought it was and about the need for a fundamentally different paradigm to drive the way we think and act."[78]

Does your organization balance valuing masculine (results, money, growth) and feminine (nurturing, compassion, connection) traits? Are people supported in having autonomy and bringing forward ideas? Are you considering the *human* impact of process changes? Are you doing the necessary work to bring forward adaptive solutions to challenges (instead of continuing to rely on "tried-and-true" technical solutions)? If you answered "no" to any of these questions, don't fret; this just shows how incredibly powerful and prevalent the *stuckness* to the old paradigm can be.

The *Stuckness* of Employee Well-Being

The way we've gone about trying to support people in improving their individual health is also rooted in this illusion and desire to "control the machine" and apply technical fixes rather than honoring what it means to be human and what is needed for adaptive change. How else can you explain how "wellness or else" programs ever came to be or why we keep focusing on turning the workplace into a doctor's office or laboratory? The notion that shuffling people into behavior change programs focused on reducing biomedical health risks will help reduce health care costs is without scientific support. Yet it provides a sense of relief, convincing us that we can actually control another person's health behavior. After all, accepting the complexity and adaptive nature of well-being is far too unsettling.

We fervently believe that most people designing and implementing wellness programs are doing so out of a hope and desire to help. We often say the problem is "about paradigms and not people!" Almost every health professional has a story about an approach in the past in which they were highly invested, only to come to the realization later that what they were doing was not really helping and in fact was causing harm. We are no exception.

Back in the late 1980s and early 1990s, I (Jon) ran an Optifast weight-loss program (remember when Oprah wheeled out a wagon representing the weight she lost on this program?). My physician partner and I recruited a staff of psychologists, nutritionists, and exercise physiologists to help very large people reduce their weight in hopes of improving their health. All participants were required to engage in a protein-sparing modified fast. Real food was replaced by "milkshake" type meals of varying calories—usually around seven hundred to nine hundred a day.

Of course, this "starvation" diet resulted in substantial weight loss, often over one hundred pounds. Unfortunately, as with every other studied dietary weight-loss intervention, people began regaining the weight as soon as the program was over. Six months later, I saw some of the same people crossing to the other side of the street as a result of the shame they felt of having "failed" at another attempt to make and keep themselves smaller. At that moment, I swore that I would never again do this to people and, as we will discuss further in chapter 12, began to explore safer and more effective approaches for helping people with weight-related concerns.

Early in my career, I (Rosie) recall people hiding from me as I walked down the hall and saying things like, "Quick, hide your cookie so Rosie doesn't see it!" Or I would walk into someone's office and they'd immediately feel the need to prove they were engaging in "healthy choices" by showing me their carrots and saying, "See, I'm eating healthy." I remember thinking to myself, "Why in the world do people think I care or view me as the 'food police'?" And I remember being horrified that my intentions to help people were likely resulting in them feeling ashamed instead.

Fast-forward a few years to when I moved into a consulting role. I was trying to guide my clients in implementing what I believed to be "best practice" wellness programs. I attended every ROI workshop I could at conferences to try to help make the business case that wellness programs helped mitigate health care costs. I even advised clients on how to design "wellness or else" programs and advocated for vendors that overscreened employees. At the time, I thought I was being helpful and guiding them to be credible and on the leading edge of where the wellness industry was headed. My clients listened to me, trusted me, and thought they were truly helping their employees.

I was not coming from a place of malintent; I was basing my guidance on what we knew at the time, and wanted to follow industry best practices. I was so focused on trying to make the numbers work and prove the success of our programs that I never considered what they were doing to the end users. I didn't realize just how stuck I was and how stuck the wellness industry was; that came later. Thank goodness I eventually had enough sense to set down my pride, look at what the experience was for the people who were the ultimate recipients of my efforts, and let go of what was comfortable and my own *stuckness* to this powerful old paradigm.

Our point in sharing our stories is to show how powerful the *stuckness* to paradigms can be—and provide some comfort that there is hope for humanity when we release our vice grip on the familiar and comfortable. Any time you see an organization or well-being professional advocating for programs and strategies that oversimplify behavior change, treat people more like machines or rodents than humans, and reflect this desire for and illusion of control, it's a sign of a powerful and prevalent *stuckness* to this outdated paradigm. Rest assured, we will share humanistic alternatives in chapter 12.

The *Stuckness* of Behavior Change

The single biggest failure of leadership is to treat adaptive challenges like technical problems. —RONALD HEIFETZ AND MARTY LINSKY[79]

The overwhelming *stuckness* to the old paradigm when it comes to behavior change stems from our misunderstanding of adaptive and technical challenges. Most of the challenges we face within organizations and with our own well-being certainly have some technical components, but the overwhelming majority are adaptive challenges. Heifetz and Linsky describe four signs that what you're dealing with is actually an adaptive challenge:

1. When people's hearts and minds need to change, not just their preferences or routine behaviors
2. By a process of exclusion; when you've thrown all the technical fixes imaginable at the problem and it still persists
3. The presence of conflict; this indicates people haven't yet made the adjustments and accepted the losses that accompany adaptive changes
4. Crisis; this reflects adaptive issues that have festered[80]

Unfortunately, we keep trying to apply technical solutions to what are largely adaptive challenges; and our desire for and illusion of control (and wanting to avoid discomfort) has us engaging in strategies that forget the biology of being human and treat others like machines. Despite decades and hundreds of research studies on incentives showing they, at best, result in short-term compliance—while reducing cognition and creativity[81]—we still see them used everywhere in the name of trying to foster behavior change. It's continuing to try to use a technical fix and ignoring the largely adaptive nature of the changes people are being asked to make.

I (Jon) completed my PhD in health education and human performance in 1992. For my dissertation, I worked with a group of tenured health professionals to develop the Worksite Health Promotion Program for faculty and staff at Michigan State University. Ironically, perhaps, our team leaders were two psychiatrists and a psychologist who were Skinnerian behaviorists, believing in the supremacy of extrinsic motivation. It was a great learning experience for me as I got to see firsthand the damage these kinds of programs can do.

Thanks to recent advances in technology, we now know how extrinsic motivation (carrots and sticks) and intrinsic motivation differ in terms of the impact they have on the brain. The prefrontal cortex is the part of the brain that is responsible for taking in and assessing new information, creativity, verbal fluency, executive reasoning, and more. The basal ganglia act as a storage center for our memories and habits.

Extrinsic motivation signals the basal ganglia (our long-term memory storage area or habit center) that we need to go against what we have always done (signaling a threat), and the amygdala stimulates our fight-or-flight response (i.e., the "amygdala hijack" we referred to earlier). At the same time, the prefrontal cortex activity is minimized. Essentially the message being sent to our brains is *we don't need thinking and creativity—we need muscle!*

The Brain on Incentives

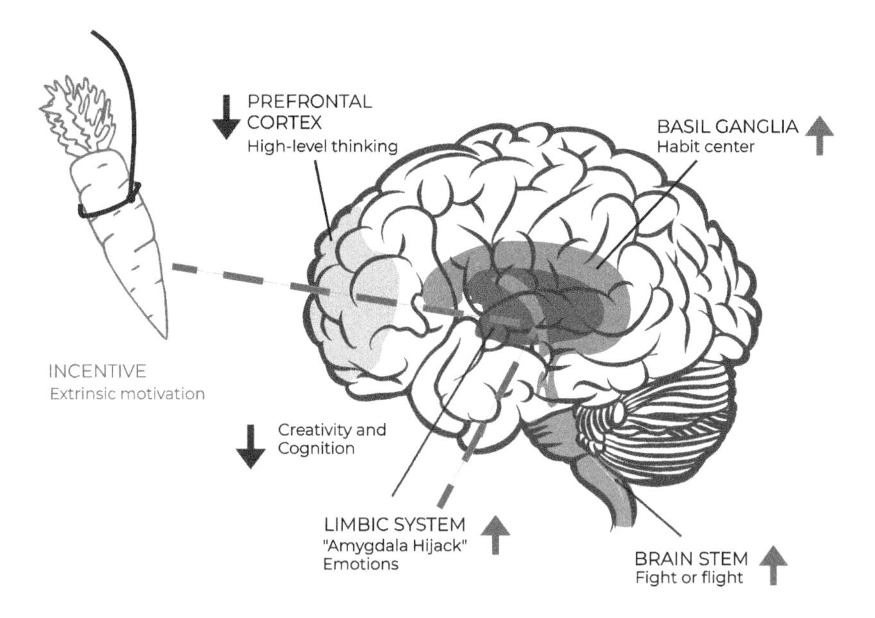

In the case of intrinsic motivation, the pathways are reversed. Signals are sent to dampen input to the amygdala, signaling "all is well here; no need to fight or flight." At the same time, neural input increases to the prefrontal cortex; so we have energy for thinking and creativity. Additionally, the nucleus accumbens releases dopamine, the "feel-good" chemical.

The Brain OFF Incentives

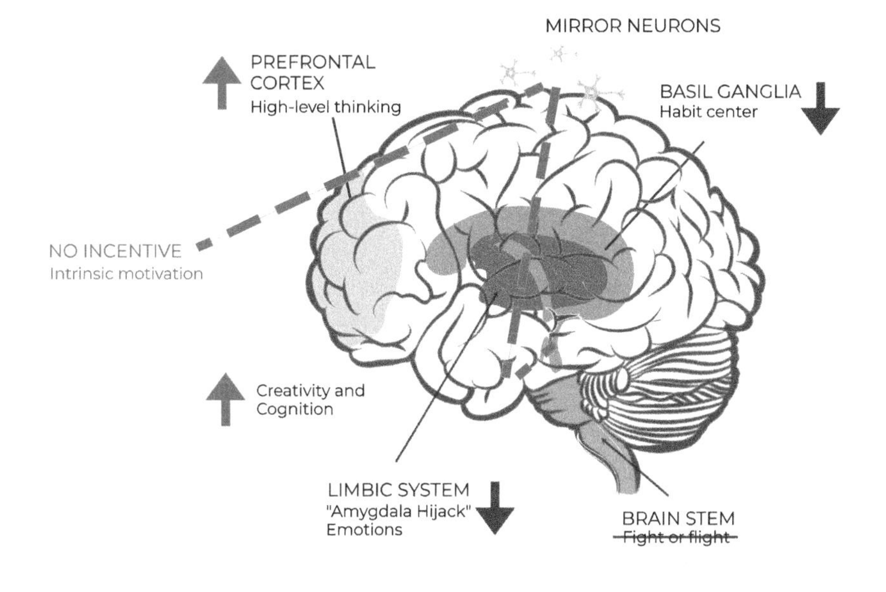

Think about it: the more we cling tightly to an old paradigm and try to control other people's behavior, the more we trigger the amygdala hijack and shut down higher-level brain functioning. This means we are inviting more of the Reactive Mind and self-protective part of people to show up, when what we need is more of the Creative Mind. **We end up inviting less thinking when what we need is *more* complex thinking.** Hardly a remedy for making the adaptive leaps the VUCA world demands! And if you want to break it down to simple common sense, try using carrots and sticks on your family and see how well it works.

As much as we know about the damage of incentives (particularly the contingency factor—"if you do this, then you'll get that"), even we get sucked back into the old paradigm from time to time. In our (Rosie's) house, the Avengers and all Marvel superheroes are a pretty big deal. When my son, Peyton, was five years old, I took him to see Marvel's Superheroes Live in downtown Minneapolis. It was on a Wednesday night, and he was super excited to be going to an arena event.

During the event, there were vendors selling a bunch of overpriced plastic crap that I had to keep talking Peyton out of getting. Once our favorite superheroes took the stage, Peyton set his sights on Wolverine. He started begging me to get him a Wolverine claw. I tried telling him that the vendors weren't selling them, but all night long he kept asking for it. The event ran later than I thought; by the time we got home, it was after ten p.m. and way past Peyton's bedtime. By this point, he was now asking for a full Wolverine costume.

I knew the next morning was going to be rough. I needed to get Peyton to his Montessori preschool and get to a doctor's appointment before I headed into the office. Not surprisingly, he was not wanting to get up and was not cooperating. I tried all of my usual appeals to his good-hearted nature. "Peyton, come on; it would be **super** helpful to mommy if you would get up and get dressed." Then it progressed to "Peyton, please get up now; we're going to be late, and I need you to cooperate." He mumbled something again about that damn Wolverine costume. I didn't even blink and said, "Fine; if you get up, cooperate, and I'm able to get to my doctor's appointment on time, we'll **look** to see what costumes they have online" (I was trying to not commit to buying one).

Peyton flew out of bed and got ready in record time. I wasn't going to have time to drop him off at school before my appointment, so he had to come to the doctor with me. When my appointment was done, we weren't even two steps in the lobby when he said, "Come on, mommy, pull up your phone and let's look for a Wolverine costume." Looking at them quickly turned into buying one because I didn't have the time to argue.

Then, as I was driving him to preschool, I started wondering how I was going to backtrack and undo the damage I had just done; I knew I was crossing a line of moving from appealing to Peyton's desire to be helpful to expecting something for cooperating, and I did not want to end up on that horrific path. So when we got to his school, I said, "Thank you for cooperating this morning. It really helps out mommy when you do that, and I appreciate it" (I'm desperately hoping he'll have amnesia about me dangling the "if-then" incentive over his head at this point). He looks at me and says, "I only cooperated because you promised me a Wolverine costume!" Ugh! It happens to the best of us.

Now, granted, this was a relatively simple task. But I knew that if I kept resorting to bribing him, I would start to create a sense of expectation and entitlement; and that would lead to increased frustration on my part (and decrease my bank account). I knew this wasn't sustainable. And I want my son to be able to think for himself and figure out how to be successful within the parameters of a schedule.

Just think of how many times you hear yourself or others say something like "How do we *get* people to ______ ?" Anytime we're trying to *get* people to do something, we're operating from the old paradigm and that illusion of and desire for control. Instead, we need to realize that our role is not to try to *get* or *motivate* others to act; our role is to create the conditions (i.e., *fearless environments*) that are safe enough and increase the likelihood that people will find their own motivation to act in a way that honors humanity and supports growth.

To Nudge or Not to Nudge?

Speaking of environments, it's also important to mention the increasing use of "nudges" in the workplace environment as a conduit for behavior change. Nudges at the workplace probably are most strongly associated with their use regarding 401(k) retirement plans. Companies have found that when enrollment in these retirement plans is done using an opt-out (i.e., a nudge) rather than opt-in strategy, the result is far more employees signing up to save money for their retirement.

Behavioral economics (particularly the use of nudges) has also become the darling of employee well-being efforts at the workplace, promoting everything from encouraging people to take the stairs, give themselves breaks from sitting, regularly move away from their computers to stretch, choose more healthful snacks, and the like. One of the major arguments in favor of nudges is that unlike the highly incentivized behavior modification approaches of "wellness or else," nudges are far less prescriptive and restrictive. Employees can still make their own choices without the pressure of rewards and the fear of punishment. However, behavioral economics and nudges are not without their limitations, problems, and critics.

The argument that nudges do not eliminate an individual's right to choose is, technically speaking, true. However, there is also no question that nudges often involve some degree of "trickery" used to move people in a desired direction—usually the direction that those in positions of authority (politicians, policy makers, business leaders) believe will result in more positive outcomes. The creator of the nudge, economist Richard H. Thaler insists that all nudges:

- Must be transparent and never misleading
- Must be easy to opt out of, preferably with as little as one mouse click
- Must be implemented with good reason to believe that the behavior being encouraged will improve the welfare of those being nudged[82]

Research supporting the use of nudges in the workplace is minimal.[83] When the challenges are technical ones, manipulation of the choices is done in a way that is acceptable (and hopefully fully transparent) to employees, and the behaviors being nudged are without question in their best interest, these tactics may result in beneficial changes, at least in the short term. However, when the problems are "wicked"—demanding adaptive change work—nudges will rarely be enough and can have unwanted consequences, including ignoring employees' needs and desires, focusing primarily on individual rather than bigger context solutions, and leading employees down paths that they would not have chosen had they been given all the information and choices, transparently and up front. Additionally, as we will see in chapter 6, sometimes these nudges can have unintended consequences of dehumanizing and excluding people, therefore doing the *opposite* of *creating a fearless environment.*

The reality is that there are no shortcuts when it comes to doing the work to navigate adaptive change—on an individual and organizational level. We must be courageous enough to embrace the discomfort and *wade in the messy middle.*

Take-Home Points about How We Got So Stuck

- Our *stuckness* that leads to dehumanization is about *paradigms*, not people. Paradigms powerfully shape how we see the world and provide a sense of familiarity and comfort. Consequently, people tend to cling even tighter to them in the face of the disruption a VUCA world brings.

- The most pervasive result from the old paradigm is a desire for and illusion of control. This leads to applying strategies that might work fine for machines and rodents (which are controllable and somewhat predictable) but not so well for humans. It also leads us to continue to try to apply technical solutions to what are predominantly adaptive challenges.

- Our brain responds to pressure and coercion (extrinsic motivation) by minimizing cognitive function and creativity and maximizing physical responses of fight and flight (amygdala hijack). When we are intrinsically motivated, the opposite is true. So, in order to be able to physiologically navigate the adaptive challenges inherent in a VUCA world, we must embrace discomfort, *wade in the messy middle*, and adopt a new paradigm so we can adapt, grow, and thrive today and in the future.

Chapter 4

THE FUSION: THE KEY TO REHUMANIZING ORGANIZATIONS

The future of great workplaces lies in helping employees fuse their personal and professional lives in ways that position them to deliver their best work.
—RON FRIEDMAN, *The Best Place to Work*[84]

Sailors need to adapt to whatever the seas might bring. Some days the waters in the ocean are calm; on those days, they can relax a little and rely on their tried-and-true expertise. On other days, the waters are fierce and dangerous. It requires them to be alert to their surroundings, yet not overreact. They must pause, reflect on what they're experiencing, and then find a path forward to navigate the VUCA waters. And when the waters become unmanageable, they can hopefully find a bright, clear lighthouse to guide the way to a safer destination.

The VUCA seas inherently invite stress and anxiety. Sailors that are able to navigate the waters and thrive in such an environment can do so because a *fearless environment* has been created onboard the ship, and they have done the work so they can show up intentional rather than reactive. If they don't tend to what they need to show up as their full, authentic selves, and if the environment feels too risky, it's nearly impossible for them to collaborate and effectively navigate the ship. The same holds true for workplaces. There's an old saying that people need to leave their car windows cracked during the day when they're at work so their real selves can breathe. It's exhausting (and not sustainable) to wear masks and armor, trying to be one person at work and another in our personal lives; we are *one* being.

Just as the mind, body, and spirit are interwoven parts of the greater whole of our individual humanity, the well-being of organizations and their people are inextricably interconnected; we call this *The Fusion*. In fact, we sometimes refer to *The Fusion* as mind, body, and spirit for organizations. When organizations are thriving, their people can weather the VUCA storms and flourish; however, it's nearly impossible for people to thrive when the organization is sick. We need to foster environments where people can be both engaged and thrive in their well-being; the future depends on it.

Now that the context has been set for why we need to rehumanize the workplace, we can begin to look at how to move from a good idea to reality. We can help people fuse their personal and professional lives by applying the five key rehumanizing principles we mentioned at the beginning of the book:

1. *Build a lighthouse.* Having a clear purpose, operationalized core values, and clarity of expectations can help cut through the fog, provide calm in the VUCA storm, and create passion to keep forging ahead.
2. *Create fearless environments.* We must intentionally create psychologically safe teams to support people in taking off their masks and armor so they can show up as their full, authentic selves and be vulnerable to take risks and grow.
3. *Wade in the messy middle.* Change involving humans is complex and evokes discomfort. We need to embrace the discomfort and be in the middle of the mess so that we can make the adaptive leaps the VUCA world demands.
4. *Show up as a leader.* Leadership is a **behavior**, not a title or role. In order to thrive in a VUCA world, we need *everyone* to show up as a leader and make a positive difference—which requires us to *wade in the messy middle* and do the necessary transformative work.
5. *Find your tribe.* This is not a solo journey. Find your tribe by building diverse relationships; and leverage the energy and collective wisdom to remove silos and build community.

It is critical to recognize and honor *The Fusion* and move away from siloed, old-paradigm, whack-a-mole approaches to change. Not only does this mean resisting the temptation to hit fast-forward but also *creating fearless environments* that make it safe enough for people to embrace the discomfort of *wading in the messy middle.* It is the combination of these two principles that help people show up whole and authentically human, embracing our imperfections. In chapters 6 and 9 we will begin to unpack more specifics of how to *create fearless environments*; and in chapter 7 we will detail how we can develop ourselves and others to *wade in the messy middle* and show up without masks and armor.

The very nature of doing this work is asking you to enter into a space of significant adaptive change—and inviting others to join you. While it is necessary for our VUCA world—and rewarding—it will be uncomfortable at times and it won't be perfect. It is important to remember this because our armored instinct can easily move us from a healthy striving for excellence to an unproductive and unattainable search for perfection.

In *The Gifts of Imperfection*, Brené Brown says this about perfection: "Perfectionism is a belief system that if we are perfect we can somehow avoid or minimize painful feelings of shame, judgment and blame. It's a myth and an unattainable goal."[85]

Embracing Our Imperfect Selves

Rachel Druckenmiller is a member of our Paradigm Pioneer community and is an incredible force for possibility and human connection. She describes how she's always been *really good* at appearing like she has it all together and how much it cost her.

> Growing up, I internalized on the stress of my parents' marital dysfunction and became the Golden Child in my family. I learned from a young age that being smart, accomplished, and responsible led to adult approval and acceptance. It gave me a sense that I mattered.
>
> In my head, I told myself I had to do well in school, follow the rules, be the best, avoid disappointing people, be nice to people, look the part of the health coach that I was, and never outwardly show anger or emotional pain. When my parents went through a rough patch in their marriage and briefly separated when I was six, I held it together. When my mom had a miscarriage and sobbed at the kitchen table, while I sat by her side as a seven-year-old, I held it together. When I wasn't invited to a classmate's birthday party that everyone else was invited to and felt the deep pain of social rejection, I held it together. I didn't let anyone but the pages of my journals, and occasionally my dad, into the middle of my messiness.
>
> I carried the weight of that pressure with me into adulthood and continued to be who everyone expected me to be—impressive and accomplished. I received the ultimate recognition in my field nearly a decade into my wellness career when I was named the number 1 Health Promotion Professional in the United States. I had made it.

> But now the pressure to have it together was even stronger. If the industry said that I was "the best," then I told myself I had to have all the answers and the best ideas and not appear incompetent in any way. I was a one-woman department with inconsistent support. I needed help. I needed insights and guidance and a listening ear from other people, but I was too proud to ask for any of that. I started missing deadlines, not responding to people in a timely manner, being unapproachable, and having a bit of an attitude.

It was all a facade for the chaos and overwhelm Rachel was feeling inside. She was afraid to let anyone into the mess she was feeling. She started having dreams of drowning and noticed she was having trouble with her memory. She was irritable and defensive. On the surface, she appeared to be this impressive, have-it-together professional who was winning awards and posting inspirational quotes on social media. But deep inside, she was struggling.

Eventually, she burned out. Rachel was diagnosed with Epstein-Barr virus, an acute form of mono that can take months, if not years, of rest and recovery to feel somewhat normal again. For a period of time, she lost her voice, which is a major issue, considering she makes her living as a speaker. Her coworkers at the time had no idea what she was going through because she didn't tell any of them; and they grew more frustrated with her for her brevity and lack of responsiveness. Hiding was hard. She cried a lot and felt hopeless, especially in the first few months of recovery. During the first few months of her diagnosis, she needed over ten hours of sleep a night to feel rested. As much as she resisted it, she started saying "no" to people, late night socializing, and exciting "opportunities," so she could take care of herself.

> I emailed my boss and our CEO, letting them know the seriousness of the virus and asking for support in terms of recovery time and staffing. It was the first time I'd been honest about needing help and acknowledging that I couldn't do it all myself anymore. Within the year, we hired a part-time assistant to work with and support me. I cut down my speaking commitments to two gigs per week instead of the four I averaged prior to getting sick. I couldn't be everything to everyone and had to care just as much about disappointing *myself* as I cared about disappointing *other* people.

As I recovered, I had difficult and uncomfortable conversations with colleagues, as I apologized for not showing up for them fully. I explained how my own pride and fear of disappointment and failure caused me to armor up and push people out when I needed them the most. As someone who finds it easy to be alone and crawl into a hole when I'm feeling inadequate and overwhelmed, I started reaching out to people and bringing them into the muck with me. They didn't reject me or shame me. They surrounded me. They checked in on me. They hugged and held me as I cried snotty cries all over their shoulders. They hung out with my husband when I had no energy to do anything. They prayed for me. I now have stronger friendships and a more supportive and loyal community than I ever have. I no longer believe I'm alone, and I no longer believe that I have to do it all and have it all together. A significant part of my message as a speaker and writer now comes through my courage in sharing the messy parts of my journey. It's what people relate to because they see themselves and their humanness in it, too.

If you're going through a difficult illness or feeling overwhelmed and burned out, you are not alone. It might feel incredibly uncomfortable—even impossible—at first, but find the courage within you to say, "I'm struggling"; "I need to talk. Are you free?" or "I need help." Be willing to invite people into the messy middle *with* you. Let them see you unmasked and with your armor off. No one expects you to be as together as you expect yourself to be.

Trying to be perfect and running on self-limiting stories of the Reactive Mind caused Rachel to burn out. Yet, it was also a gift. She took the wake-up call as an opportunity to *wade in the messy middle* and do the work to shift her inner narrative and start advocating for herself. As she took off her masks and armor and showed up as her beautifully flawed, authentic self, it didn't push people away; it invited *more* connection with others. And as she has become more intentional about tending to her personal well-being, her work life has also flourished.

Our self-limiting dialogue can not only lead to our well-being eroding, but it can keep us safe and small and prevent us from being able to lead and influence change. We need to realize that **everyone** has the opportunity to *show up as a leader*. In her book *The New Alpha*, Danielle Harlan has a definition of leadership that we really like and leverage: "Leadership is about becoming the best version of yourself in order to maximize your positive impact on the world. It's about developing into someone whom people genuinely respect and admire and want to work with—and using that power and influence to be a force for good in the world."[86]

In her book *Dare to Lead*, Brené Brown defines a leader as "Anyone who takes responsibility for finding the potential in people and processes, and who has the courage to develop that potential."[87]

And Simon Sinek defines leadership as "The awesome responsibility for those around us—to see those around us rise."[88]

With each of these definitions as inspiration, we define leadership as

> **Maximizing our positive impact on the world by becoming our best, fully authentic selves and supporting those around us to break past barriers and step into their greatness.**

At its core, leadership is a mindset and a behavior, not a role or title. Every single one of us has the potential and opportunity to choose to *show up as a leader*—to do the courageous, difficult work required to show up authentically human, become a better version of ourselves, and create a space for others to do the same. And when we do, amazing change can happen.

Carley Kammerer (founder of Wildflyer Coffee) put it well when she described what it means to *show up as a leader*: "Just taking action makes you a leader because most people don't take action. A lot of us are like, 'That problem needs to be fixed.' But then we don't do anything about it. I think a lot of us sit there thinking, 'Yeah, there are a lot of problems in the world but someone else should do it.' So, I think if you're someone who is willing to say, 'Okay, I'll fix it or I'll try to fix it the best I can,' that does make you a leader."

As we go through each component of the Thriving Organization Pyramid, please beware of any self-limiting dialogue that emerges for you. **You** have the ability to *show up as a leader*. **You** have the ability to influence and lead positive change. It's about accepting the open invitation to step into your greatness and show a path to a better, more human future—one person, one group at a time.

What's Possible When You *Show Up as a Leader*

Michelle Spehr is another phenomenal leader in our Paradigm Pioneer community. On more than one occasion over the past few years (including while taking our Thriving Workplace Culture Certificate training program), she would say something like "I get all of this and believe in it; but what can I possibly do? I don't have the credentials you do. I'm just a wellness person." Over time, between being engaged with her fellow Paradigm Pioneers and doing her own transformative work to change her inner narrative, Michelle slowly but surely started to set aside her self-limiting dialogue and step into her greatness.

In April 2017, the Benefit Services Group, Inc. (BSG®), the organization Michelle worked for, had merged with Hausmann-Johnson Insurance (HJI). BSG was founded in 1987 and is a privately held company that specializes in health and welfare benefits consulting services, wellness consulting, and health care data analytics. BSG provides services for mid- to large-sized employers, health care systems, and carriers. BSG is in Pewaukee, WI, and has forty-five employees. HJI is an insurance agency with expertise in designing and implementing risk management and employee benefits strategies for clients across the country. Based in Madison, WI, this privately held agency traces its roots back to 1946 and has ninety employees. After a few years of sharing a mutually beneficial working relationship, BSG and HJI merged. The BSG|HJI organizational structure includes a board of directors, executive management team (EMT), and twenty-six shareholders.

In the weeks that followed the merger announcement, Michelle had informal conversations with several members of the leadership team to let them know she was interested in being on the integration work group responsible for bringing these two employers together. It made perfect sense to her that a well-being practitioner should be at the table, and this merger would likely threaten employee well-being and engagement. She was thrilled when she received an invitation from the president to discuss her ideas for how to add value to the vision/values process.

In early November of 2017, she stepped out of her well-being comfort zone and began working on the "*Start with WHY*" project plan. The plan outlined the specific steps for leveraging the **WHY** discovery process and collaborative sensemaking techniques to create a unified sense of purpose and to define what the combined organization culture is like when it's operating at its best. By early December, she made the case to the EMT that they should move forward with this plan and that she would be the best person to lead the effort. In this meeting, Michelle reviewed the key components of Simon Sinek's Golden Circle framework and discussed how important it was at this point in the integration process to identify and align the clarity of "**WHY**" (why they do what we do), the discipline of "**HOW**" (their values, guiding principles, strengths, and beliefs), and the consistency of "**WHAT**" (aligning everything they say and do with what they believe).

They also discussed how this process would create alignment between how they think, act, and communicate as one organization. The meeting ended with agreement to launch a four-phase process starting in January 2018:

- **Phase 1: WHY Discovery Workshop.** The purpose of the **WHY** discovery workshop was to find and articulate the combined BSG|HJI "**WHY**" in simple language that would create a unified sense of purpose.

- **Phase 2: Defining Core Values.** The purpose of these workshops was to bring the organization's core values to life by leveraging the contribution action phrases that were identified in the **WHY** discovery workshop and translating them into simple, everyday actions they display when they're at our best. A core values subgroup was assembled, and they grouped all the contribution action phrases into three general themes: *how we work together*, *how we approach our work*, and *how we show up for others*.

- **Phase 3: WHY Town Hall Meetings.** The purpose of the **WHY** Town Hall meetings was to create an opportunity for associates not involved in the **WHY** discovery workshop to hear about and feel inspired by the **WHY**, so they would be able to take ownership and put it into practice.

- **Phase 4: Live the WHY.** The focus now is to keep the **WHY** alive over time by keeping it front and center, communicating it, and committing to living it with purpose, on purpose, every day. They are currently working on a proposal to name their president as the "Chief **WHY** Officer" and possibly evolve Michelle's role so that she can serve as a **WHY** "technical lead."

Michelle has absolutely come alive over the past year and is making such a positive difference in her organization. And it's all because she reframed her self-limiting dialogue, *waded in the messy middle*, and chose to *show up as a leader*. So think again if you're doubting your ability to impact positive change beyond whatever your role is at your organization!

The Fusion in Action

Amazing things can also happen when you *build a lighthouse* (which we'll be detailing more in chapter 8) and *find your tribe*. In the fall of 2016, we gathered a multidisciplinary team and began planning a new conference; two years later (November 2018) we launched the inaugural Fusion 2.0 Conference. As we continued to see the benefit of breaking down silos and leveraging *The Fusion* of organizational and employee well-being, we became increasingly frustrated with the lack of integration at professional conferences. HR professionals go to HR conferences; wellness and well-being professionals go to their industry conferences; safety and risk management professionals go to their industry conferences; and the pattern of siloed learning continues. We also noticed how many conferences seemed to have the same old sessions and short-lived impact; people would go home inspired for a few days but then not be able to actually influence or lead any meaningful change (and many times forget what they learned within a few short weeks).

Our vision was to further build community by bringing together people working in disciplines that are normally siloed (HR, wellness, organizational effectiveness/organizational development, safety/risk management, training and development, and leadership), so they could stop undermining each other and work to create one thriving human experience at work. We wanted it to feel different—be inclusive, accessible, and create a safe space for people to be real and authentic. We wanted it to be energizing and transformative. And we wanted it to be **actionable**—helping these amazing change-makers process what they've learned and equip them to be able to take action and lead positive change when they went home.

Building the Fusion 2.0 lighthouse required us to be intentional to operate from clarity of our purpose and core values. Our company values kicked into high gear, starting with *choosing courage over comfort*. We put great intention behind the design and content of the event. This started with working to ensure our speakers were not only credible and amazing presenters, but also diverse in as many ways as possible. Living our value of *honoring sound science* meant being careful and selective to ensure that any company involved as a sponsor or exhibitor supported humanity at work and that their products and services were credible. Consequently, even though we needed the funding, we had to make decisions to turn down potential revenue.

Our value *we are stronger together* was also a major focus of Fusion 2.0. From conversation starters at tables to purposeful networking opportunities to a Listening Wall, we wanted to create a safe space where people could genuinely and authentically connect as humans and build relationships that would hopefully last beyond the conference. In order to *pave a path so others can thrive*, we knew we needed to emphasize sustainability. We gave everyone a learning journal and guided them through a synthesized learning session at the end of each day to help them process what they learned; provided a conference learning summary; and had thirty-, sixty-, ninety-, and one-hundred-and-twenty-day post conference reinforcement emails, webinars, and tips to keep the momentum going.

We knew we were taking a **huge** risk with Fusion 2.0. Nothing like it had ever been done. Staying true to our core values was challenging at times yet provided the guidance and clarity we needed to cut through the fog in this unknown territory. Initially, we had a hard time finding our voice and figuring out how to help people see what Fusion 2.0 was, how it would be different, and why it is needed. Yet it was **so** aligned with our purpose and had so much energy surrounding it that we knew we had to forge ahead. Being intentional paid off. The event itself was amazing and surpassed all expectations. People came out of the woodwork to be involved and were still talking about it months later. We received hand-written and emailed "love letters" thanking us for this event, saying how needed it is, and asking to be involved in the next one. In addition to the actionable content, people said they felt welcome and human, made real connections with people, and felt *loved*. People removed industry, geographic, and other silos to make diverse connections; they *found their tribe.*

We also learned that being on the leading edge comes with financial pain; we ended up taking a massive financial hit in getting Fusion 2.0 going that nearly bankrupted our business. In spite of that, we knew we had to rally and find the partners and resources to not only have another event but to make it a regular gathering so that change-makers can come together and learn from and support each other in putting people back at the forefront of business. When you *build a lighthouse* and *find your tribe*, people will *show up as leaders* and rally to make some pretty amazing things happen.

We're so excited about growing this tribe and seeing more people step up and advocate for rehumanized workplaces!

Speaking of *finding your tribe*, it's also critically important to remember that culture is not a C-suite thing, an HR thing, or a leadership thing; it's an **everybody** thing. So, as we go through each section of the Thriving Organization Pyramid, think about who your partners are; grow and diversify your tribe and leverage it to create energy to put humanity back at the forefront of our workplaces.

Chapter 5

TWENTY-FIRST-CENTURY ORGANIZATION DESIGN

Our organizations don't need to be reinvented. All of the basic parts are present, it's just a case of unlocking the structure to allow people to be their best. —ANDY SWANN, *The Human Workplace*[89]

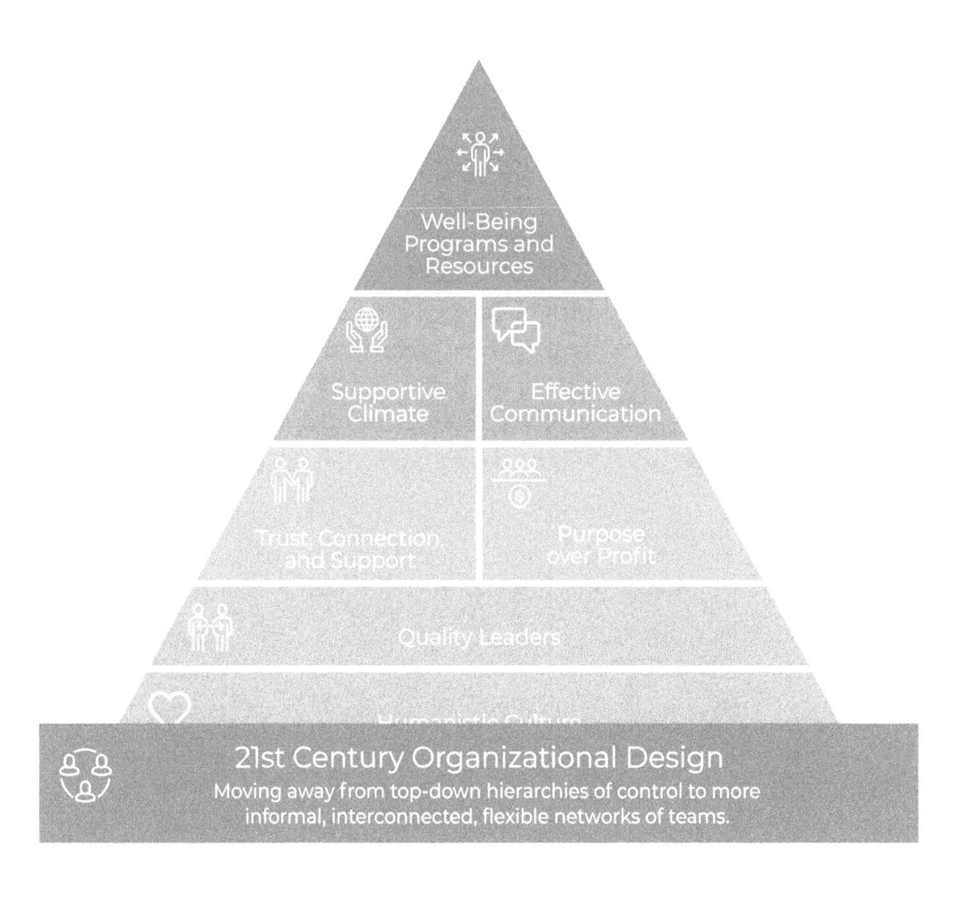

Imagine if all the shipwrecked sailors decided to cling tightly to their familiar structure of command-and-control they had aboard the ship. Instead of people tapping into their resourcefulness, organizing into tasks to learn their new surroundings, and finding a way to thrive, they would have likely been stuck. The sailors would have been waiting for the formal leaders to figure out a plan, meanwhile wasting precious time critical for their survival. Anxiety and stress would have grown amongst the crew as they waited for some guidance and reassurance. Consequently, their ability to make the adaptive leaps necessary to thrive in this new environment would have been greatly diminished.

Instead, the new-paradigm sailors adopted a new structure where they removed the hierarchy, formed functional teams, and created the opportunity for everyone to *show up as a leader*. This is what effective, forward-thinking, future-ready, and human organizations are doing; they are relationship-oriented and change-agile. This is why the anchor of everything related to rehumanizing the workplace is rethinking organizational design.

Most traditional organizational structures neglect to support the biological imperatives of living systems—of being human. Instead of supporting people as self-authoring, relationship-oriented beings, organizations inhibit this with rigid hierarchies. In his book *The Human Workplace*, Andy Swann suggests that the problem with hierarchy isn't with the structure itself but with how the structure is used to repress information; it impedes people's ability to contribute fully to realizing the purpose and goals of the business.[90]

Take a look at an example of a traditional organizational chart. It shows rows of rectangular boxes neatly stacked on top of each other.

Sample Organizational Chart

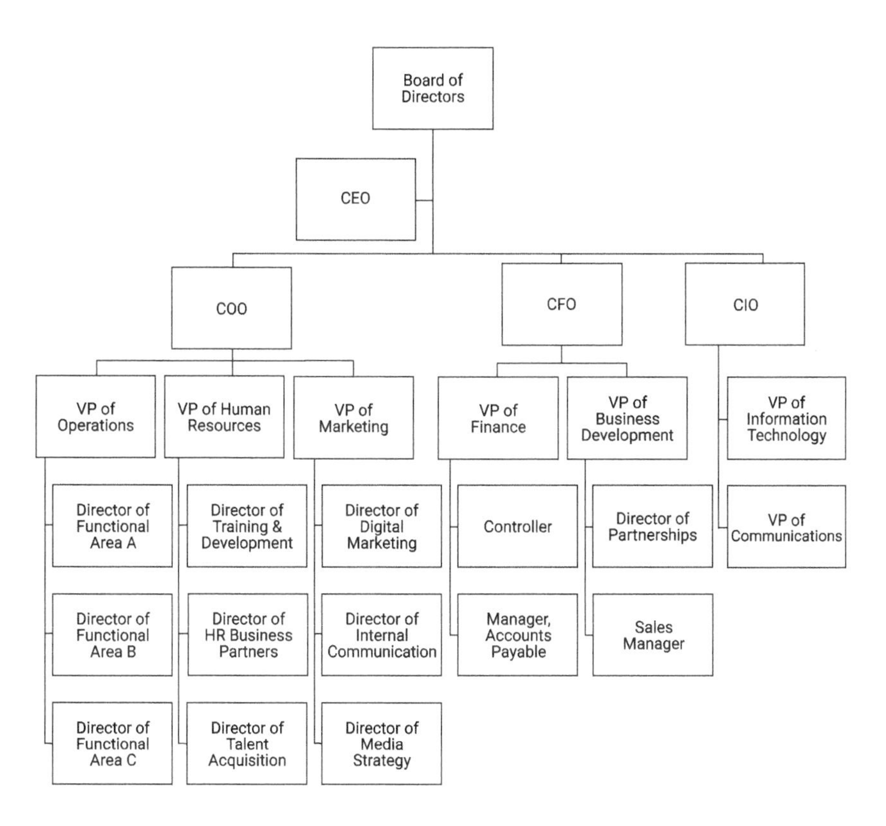

When organizations have rigid structures that require information to go through several layers of approval, it sends a message that they don't trust their people. And the more structure that is applied, the more rigid the organization becomes. This is counterproductive to being able to adapt in our rapidly changing VUCA world. In their *Global Human Capital Trends 2016* survey, Deloitte called out the need to redesign organizational structures to better represent the new business realities. They suggested that instead of rows of neatly stacked boxes, the new focus needs to be on creating flexible networks of teams.[91] And Swann echoes this, suggesting that the organization has a responsibility to get out of the way and reduce complexity and unnecessary distraction by removing obstacles and encouraging people to take action. The key is to provide just enough structure to thrive and allow great work to happen; he calls it "freedom with parameters."[92]

Future-Ready Organizational Structures

What does "freedom with parameters" look like? Well, take a look at an example of an organizational chart that reflects this—and how humans actually work:

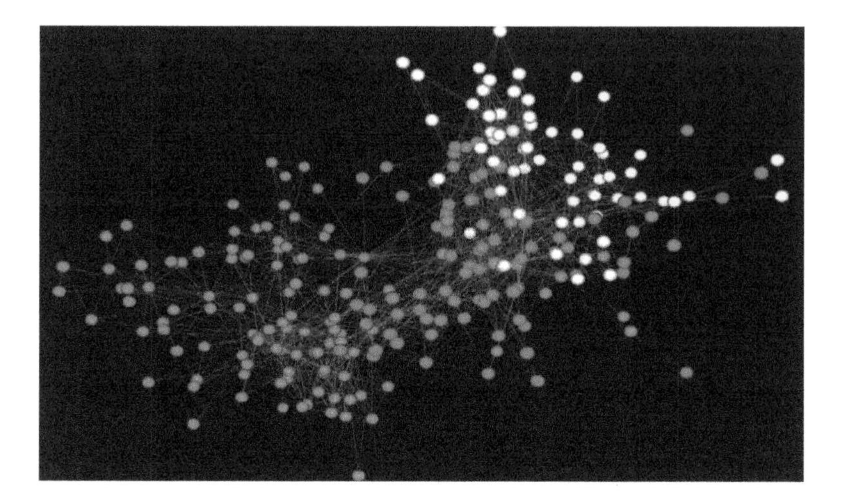

© Morning Star Company. Used with permission.

This is the partial "organizational chart" of the Morning Star Company. You've probably consumed their products if you've ever put ketchup on a burger, eaten pizza, or poured sauce on pasta. Chris Rufer founded it in 1970 as a one-truck owner-operator, hauling tomatoes to other canneries. Today, Morning Star is the largest tomato-processing company in the world, accounting for over 25 percent of the California tomato production, supplying 40 percent of the US ingredient tomato paste and diced tomato markets, with industrial sales of approximately $500 million.[93]

What makes Morning Star unique is that they are completely self-managed; they coordinate their own activities and communications without taking direction from others. You read that correctly—no managers or bosses (more on them in a little bit). With that as background, Morning Star's organizational chart makes sense (and is quite a contrast from rigid, hierarchical structures). In fact, they actually refer to it as their "web of commitments" rather than an organizational chart; it shows a more realistic visual of the networks of relationships and how communication actually occurs between real, live human beings.

The Power of Understanding and Mapping Human Networks

Morning Star is not alone in going "beyond the boxes" to map their organizational structure. Vikas Narula founded a company called Keyhubs in 2009 as an answer to what he calls "the Dilbert problem," which he describes as the dysfunction inherent in hierarchical organizational structures. Vikas realized that the real work within organizations happens through the web of human connection; after all, we are social beings.

Keyhubs began by helping organizations and leaders see and leverage the hidden web of connections underneath their formal hierarchical structure through what they call "human networks mapping." By 2012 they started using the network data to help leaders see and understand their influence (or lack thereof) and uncover the tapestry of workplace relationships that largely dictate how work gets done. As a software and services company, they combine unique survey methodologies with state-of-the-art mapping and application software to provide insight around internal talent and team dynamics that surprise, enlighten, and transform. Here is an example.

A Fortune 500 financial services company wanted to improve their sales performance through strategic mentorship, onboarding, and their existing relationship capital. While this organization had a good handle on their top performers based on sales numbers, they had a desire to understand the existing "culture of selling" and determine if and how it may be impacting sales performance in various regions. They wanted to foster and strengthen a culture of collaborative solutioning and selling by way of key informal influencers.

Like many multidivisional sales organizations, the leaders struggled with identifying the "secret sauce" of success. Why is this division outperforming the other? What separates a top performing culture from a low one? Do we have the right sales leaders providing mentorship to the right group of entry-level salespeople? Why does our retention vary so greatly from division to division? Traditional engagement surveys and Net Promoter Scores were not giving this organization's leaders the data they needed—relational dynamics. So, with a desire to put their finger on these pressing issues, Keyhubs set out to uncover the unseeable—to unpack the cultural fabric of the sales organization and to use this data to help them make better people and team decisions that would result in increased sales.

They designed, developed, and deployed a sales organization–wide relational survey, which was sent to approximately three thousand team members with over 80 percent participation. In a matter of weeks, Keyhubs very succinctly and elegantly uncovered the "secret sauce" of sales success and the common patterns that were keeping divisions from outstanding results. They use their proprietary methodology to map social networks. Each circle (node) represents an employee, and the arrows represent the answer to the survey question. The first question asked was

"Who is a sales role model and inspires you to be the same?"

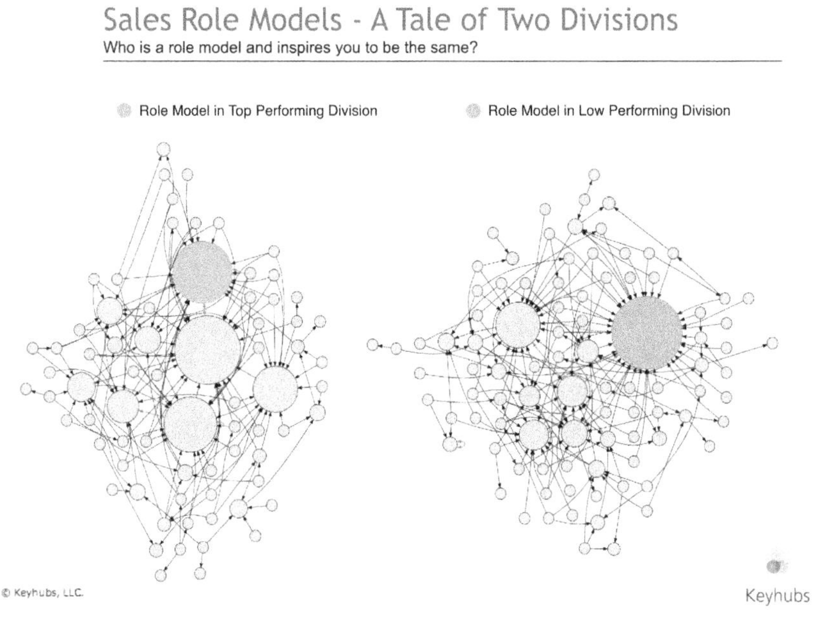

© *Keyhubs. Used with permission.*

As you can see, the larger nodes have more arrows pointing to them. These "hubs" represent the people whose names were given in answer to the survey question. These are key individuals who have more followship and positive influence within the organization.

The second question they asked was

"Who do you most frequently collaborate with in the sales process?"

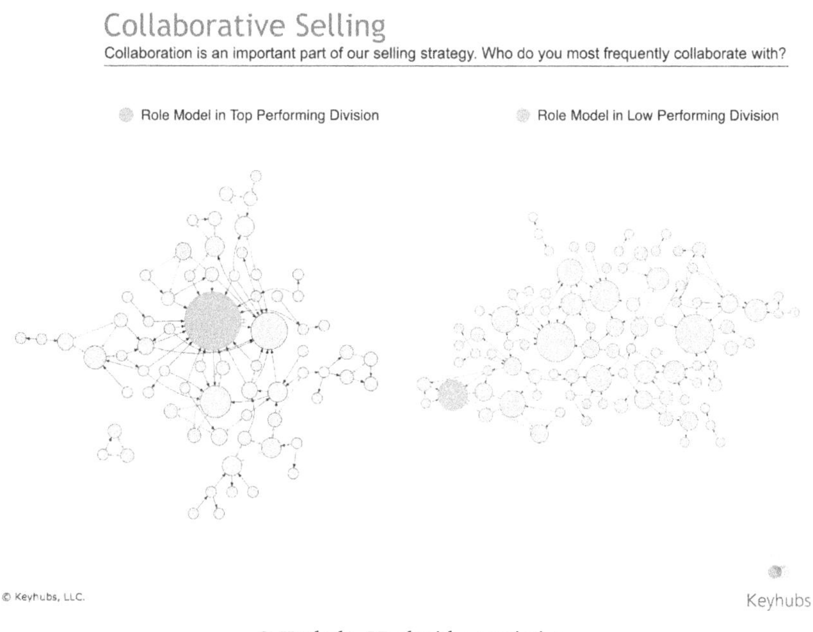

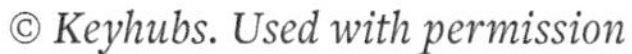

© Keyhubs. Used with permission

These Keyhubs maps show how differently two influential sales role models from two different divisions (one high performing, the other low performing) show up in the collaborative sales network. In the high performing division, the sales role model is central to collaborative selling efforts, while in the low performing division, the sales role model is on the periphery of the collaboration network. These differences in relational dynamics impact overall sales.

Keyhubs was able to identify a few key patterns that were contributing to sales success. The top performing sales divisions had:

- Stronger, tighter alignment between key influencers
- A higher number of salespeople connected to sales role models
- Influential sales leaders in formal mentorship roles

They also learned that those sales divisions with two or more of these traits significantly outperformed the average sales organization. With this data, the organization was able to design and direct new strategies of engagement with their sales leadership and key influencers across their sales organization. This included heightening awareness of key leaders regarding the influence patterns in their division, coaching key influencers and leaders for more intentional alignment and collaboration, and putting key influencers in positions of formal influence through collaborative mentoring. As a result, over the next twelve months, the organization experienced double-digit sales growth.

The Keyhubs methodology has not only been used to help improve culture and leadership through networks at many large organizations (Accenture, Medtronic, Thrivent Financial, the YMCA, and Bremer Bank, to name a few), their work has been used to foster significant revenue growth through the understanding of human connection, relationships, and networks. They also have found some recurring patterns that show up in organizations (regardless of industry or size) and that these patterns show up in our professional networks and communities:

- Talented, influential, highly collaborative individuals are often hidden in lower levels of the organization.
- Birds of a feather flock together, forming cliques and even polarized cultures.

In his 2017 TEDx Talk,[94] Vikas references recent research that suggests the biggest predictors of career success are having diverse networks (where you are connected to different networks and can help serve as a translator of different perspectives and points of view to bridge the gap between those networks) and open networks rather than closed networks.[95] In other words, we need to expand beyond people who are just like us to *build a tribe* of diverse people to bridge the gap, break down silos, and foster greater human connection. Understanding this provides an important framework for how self-managed organizations, like Morning Star, work—and why they are so successful.

Self-Managing and Self-Organizing in Action

In order to be relevant, effective, and future-ready, we must stop approaching organizations and people as if they were machines. We already stated that biologists consider the two fundamental prerequisites of life as being able to create themselves (*autopoiesis*) and striving for and needing to be in relationship. With that, human beings (like all living systems) are capable of and seek to be self-organizing and self-managing. Top down, authoritarian, scientific management flies directly in the face of these innate tendencies.

Think about birds flying in their typical V formation, especially when they are traveling long distances. While it may look like there is only one leader, all of the birds actually take their turns being in the front of the V. Similar to how bicycle racers draft off each other, the birds rotate their positions, leading until they are tired and then dropping back into the formation to let others take their place. What's even more fascinating is that they actually teach themselves how to do this; it is not something they are born knowing how to do.[96] In order to be effective, and safely get to where they need to go, every one of the birds needs to *show up as a leader.*

Or think about the human brain, consisting of one hundred billion neurons processing four hundred billion pieces of information every second. There are structures and coordinating mechanisms, but no boss or CEO directing traffic.[97] Even just a single human cell has thousands of chemical processes happening concurrently and in a coordinated fashion. Again, no boss in charge.[98]

Consider the last time you traveled somewhere via an airplane. You likely had to decide which airline and flight to take, what hotel to stay at, and then make your reservations. As the trip drew closer, you decided what to pack and how to get to the airport. When you arrive in your destination city, you decide how to get from the airport to your hotel, figure out your meals while there, and so on. No one was managing you or telling you what to do; you were in charge—as were the hundreds of other travelers you encountered.

Yet this process is not anarchy. There are guidelines and rules you need to follow. You have to have a ticket and abide by regulations at the airport and during the flight; and you can't just take your neighbor's car to the airport (unless you had permission and prearranged it). These parameters help provide clarity of expectations and avoid anarchy; yet there is incredible freedom regarding how you operate within such guidelines.

Being in charge of our own journey (self-determination) with respect to work is often referred to as autonomy, a concept we will come back to over and over again; it is not only at the core of being human, but it is critical for both organizational and employee well-being. Organizations that honor what it means to be human create structures that leverage human networks and foster our innate need for self-determination. As a result, they have demonstrated the ability to greatly outperform those who ignore this and operate from mechanistic, hierarchical structures.

Self-Management Success at the Morning Star Company

Even though Chris Rufer had a traditional MBA education (favoring rigid hierarchies and control), he aspired more to honoring the innate needs of human beings when building his company. Self-management started somewhat naturally at Morning Star because it started with truck drivers. Chris said, "How the heck do you manage truck drivers? They're in a truck. What are you going to do . . . have a supervisor for every driver? Of course not; that makes no sense. Besides most of them were students. They weren't looking to get a day off or hurt themselves so they could get Workers' Comp for the winter. They wanted to earn money to advance their education. They required very little management, so it became natural."

After all, we self-manage every day in our personal lives. The key for Morning Star is structuring everything around a clear purpose and mission. Chris describes it well:

> Whether you realize it or not, you're adhering to a very consistent mission in your personal life; and everything you do is structured to help you achieve that mission. What kind of glasses and clothes you wear, who you associate with, what you eat, where you go to school, etc.—everything is structured around that mission. You're weighing the options and all of these considerations through some sort of formula in your mind—an algorithm for what will bring you the most happiness over time.
>
> Let's say you're at college. One night you decide to go study when all of your friends are going to do something else that would have been fun in the short term. But you're sitting there weighing your options against your vision of where you want to be in the long term. So you take the long-term consequences into consideration as well. It's a discounted cash flow of your happiness.

Self-management works at Morning Star because they have very clear parameters to guide decisions and operations. As an example, they have a formal, written process for gaining agreements. If you have a difference with someone and are unable to come to an agreement, the process is to bring in a third person who is preferably familiar with the situation or has the capabilities to help facilitate the decision. Usually the next step is to bring the situation to your group or team to see if you can obtain an agreement there. If there's still not agreement, then it can go to an enterprise team. Finally, it goes to Chris, the president, or someone they appoint; but then there's a final decision where all of the other parties are involved.

All of these steps occur with everybody present who is involved. This is important because many times what gets in the way of agreement are a lot of misunderstandings or not enough information being applied to the decision. Other times what gets in the way is people not wanting to risk someone not liking them if they push things further; so they'll drop something and won't take it far enough. By intentionally putting disagreements out into the open and having this process, it helps Morning Star advance toward *creating a fearless environment.*

Chris is also the first to admit that self-management isn't perfect. He believes that any system that's going to be viable long term needs to work for most people, not all. The most difficult issues he experiences are consistent with the developmental gap we described in chapter 2; self-management really demands people can show up with greater mental complexity (i.e., at least self-authoring). Chris describes his frustration in terms of what he sees as a lack of emotional intelligence and people not having a "satisfied ego" and being driven by what they lack (i.e., our *not enough* narrative).

> I believe the concept of self-managing is quite good. But now you're injecting human beings. We may be able to manage ourselves; however, I see people struggle making the tough decisions and the tough actions that have to be taken. Frankly, there are very few who can do that. A long time ago I read a book, *Ants at Work*. Even though they have a Queen, ants really have no hierarchy. They have their own system of following based on certain built-in genetic pathways or reactions. They have a very clear system and routine that allows them to be resilient, move, and get their tasks done every time. But ants also don't think.

We've got a system that is formally set that is really good. We have a clear mission and methods in place to gain agreement when we have differences.

But now you put human beings into that system. Well, it doesn't work as well as the ants. So, the system is fine. I'm still not convinced that it's really the right system for today's culture; I'm talking about the psychological makeup of the vast majority of human beings.

So many people don't want to use their social capital to deal with a person who's not doing the right thing—even though it will hurt our total performance as a company and their capability of earning money. They can't internalize it. They can't see far enough down the road to see the true ramifications of their hesitancy to risk their social capital. Then there are some who don't have ego satisfaction, so they drive for power. And whenever there's a little opening that they have to acquire power over other people, they take it.

Then there are other people who, frankly, don't want to take the initiative. They want to come to work, do their deal, and go home, take care of the kids, watch a baseball game, go fishing, do something, right? And they're great folks. But they don't want to do anything more. And they are very happy to be sitting there and do a good job like this, and allow somebody else to, quote, "be their boss." So, they don't take advantage of the system.

I am absolutely convinced that adequate emotional intelligence is essential. Frankly, there have been three or four people terminated in the last month or so at Morning Star. Every one of these individuals is amazing—very high performers, sharp and really good. However, their emotional intelligence was getting in the way for too long where they just couldn't work well with other people. And they disrupted the organization more. So we put a lot of energy around helping people build emotional intelligence so they can effectively work with others.

And, as people become more self-aware and emotionally intelligent, and they are charged up about their mission and their job, they do much better, and they love it. So self-management works really well for them. It gives them more freedom to actually pursue things. Producing tomato products and satisfying our customers the best we can, in the most cost-effective, environmentally responsible manner, is our operating mission. Self-management is our prime mission, our larger purpose. It's really trying to develop a workplace environment that is enthusing and engaging.

Chris believes that developing people so they can operate from more of an internal locus of control (i.e., self-authoring) is essential for self-management to work well and reach its potential. It requires people who have a strong sense of self, can bring forward ideas and take initiative. In other words, self-management not only requires *building a lighthouse* and *creating a fearless environment*, but it requires intentionality so people can *wade in the messy middle* to develop themselves so they can show up in a way that fosters success.

More Self-Managed Companies Reinventing "Business as Usual"

Morning Star is just one of many companies who have done away with their control hierarchies and instead leverage "freedom with parameters." Buurtzorg, a home nursing health care organization in the Netherlands, is another shining example of a self-managed company. Some ten thousand nurses operate with no bosses, no middle management, no human resources department, and minimal staff. Almost all decisions (budgets, hiring and firing, and even day-to-day questions about care) are made by teams of ten to twelve nurses. Disputes are overseen by regional coaches who guide discussions but have no decision-making power.

One of the most fascinatingly unique components of Buurtzorg and other self-managed companies relates to how decisions are made. Here is how the process works. In principle, any person in the organization can make a decision, even one involving, for example, buying an expensive piece of equipment. It is the decision-makers job to consult with anyone in the organization who will be impacted by the decision, as well as anyone who has expertise in the space. The advice of all these parties must be seriously considered (this is called *the advice process*), but the decision-maker is under no obligation to incorporate their suggestions.

We typically think of decisions in an organization being arrived upon by two methods. Either the leaders at the top make decisions and pass them down, or people get together, discuss, and compromise to come to a consensus. In the first case, these approaches often end with people being frustrated because they have not been a part of the process. In self-managed companies—since, for all practical purposes, there are no bosses—it is generally concluded that consensus must be the chosen decision-making process.

However, the problem with consensus is that the decisions are often ineffective, watered-down compromises that satisfy nobody. Furthermore, almost anyone in a position of power can veto the decision. In addition, often no one really takes ownership of the decision; therefore, whether it succeeds or not, it is not clear who should take responsibility. In self-managed companies, these problems are alleviated by the use of *the advice process.*

So, back to the case of Buurtzorg. How successful is the company, compared to other home nursing care organizations that are not self-managed?

- Patients require 40 percent fewer hours of care.
- One-third of hospital admissions are avoided.
- Absenteeism is reduced by 60 percent.
- Turnover is reduced by 30 percent.

Scaled to the United States, this would save almost fifty billion dollars a year for home health care alone![99]

You might be saying to yourself, "Well, maybe self-management can work in home health care, but what about a blue-collar shop? Can the workers on the floor similarly be the ones in charge of making these types of critical day-to-day decisions?"

FAVI is a celebrated brass foundry in France. They develop and supply complete sub-assemblies and technical parts for industry in brass, copper, and aluminum die casting. Like Buurtzorg, they are run by teams of workers (mini-factories) that make all decisions regarding rules and regulations, hiring, firing, purchasing, planning, and scheduling. Unlike Buurtzorg, however, they were originally run like any other factory—from the top down. In the book *Reinventing Organizations*, CEO Jean-Francois Zobrist chronicles the dehumanizing reality of those days:

> The analysis of our organization chart in the early 1980s reveals without a doubt that men and women were considered to be:
>
> - **Thieves** because everything was locked up in storage rooms.
> - **Lazy**, as their working time was controlled and every late showing was punished by somebody . . . who didn't even care . . . about the reasons . . .

- Not dependable because . . . production was controlled by somebody else . . .
- Not intelligent, as a "manufacturing engineering" department did the thinking for them.[100]

Basically, employees were not to be trusted, were not capable of thinking for themselves, and needed to be controlled! Good for machines, but not so good for humans! Zobrist and his colleagues defined three new assumptions that over time have become mantras inside the factory:

- People are systematically considered to be good. (Reliable, self-motivated, trustworthy, intelligent)
- There is no performance without happiness. (To be happy, we need to be motivated. To be motivated, we need to be responsible. To be responsible, we must understand why and for whom we work, and be free to decide how.)
- Value is created on the shop floor. (Shop floor operators craft the products; the CEO and staff at best serve to support them, at worst are costly distractions.)[101]

FAVI is famous for impeccable customer service. As an example, one of the mini-factories was concerned that they might be a few hours late with a client delivery. Without checking with anyone, they ordered a helicopter to deliver the goods. The puzzled client contacted FAVI about the helicopter that had just landed on their premises, saying it really had not been necessary because they still had some of the items in stock. Zobrist responded proudly by saying it demonstrated the commitment and pride the employees had for their work. Not surprisingly, the company has not had a single late order in thirty years![102]

Another self-managed company finding great success is Sun Hydraulics. They are a global designer and producer of high-performance screw-in hydraulic cartridge valves and manifolds for worldwide industrial and mobile markets. In 2018, I (Jon) visited their headquarters in Tampa, Florida. When I met with the director of human resources, I noticed that his name tag did not include his job title. He told me that the founder of the company insisted that all employees display their names but not their roles so that everyone would hopefully be treated equally and humanely. According to company lore, the only exception was the woman who came through the buildings and watered the many plants that adorned the ceilings and walls. On her lapel was her name followed by the title "plant manager."

The desire of the company to attract autonomous, self-managing employees is quite clear from this message on their website: "If you're looking to be told what to do, Sun Hydraulics is not the place for you. There is no organizational chart. There are no formal job descriptions here. No reserved parking spaces or executive offices."[103]

Amazingly, just like the self-managed nature of the human brain and our cells, this process works for Sun Hydraulics. At any given time, there are hundreds of engineering projects going on at the same time. Yet there is no boss approving all of the projects and project plans; and timelines, budgets, reports on progress and the like are rarely written down. They spend their time on the work that matters, trust one another, and fully embrace autonomy. When asked why they don't spend the time documenting things like what is traditionally done with projects, one of the company's leaders put it simply: "We don't waste time being busy."

These companies are just a few examples of many (from a wide variety of industries) who are thriving by humanizing their workplaces and honoring our innate need to self-manage. In his book *Reinventing Organizations*, Frederic Laloux explains the seeming paradox: "These companies are highly profitable, despite the fact that they seem to be, compared to traditional corporations, quite careless about profits. They don't make detailed budgets, they don't compare budgets to actuals at the end of the month, they don't set sales targets, and colleagues are free to spend any money they deem necessary without approval from above (as there is no one above to approve the spending).They focus on what needs to be done, not on profitability and perhaps precisely for that reason, their efforts are rewarded with stellar profits."[104]

You may be thinking, *That sounds great but will* NEVER *work at my company.* So we want to pause here before continuing, to be clear about our purpose for including these stories about self-management. As exciting and groundbreaking as they are, we are certainly not suggesting that self-management is right for every organization or, for that matter, every employee. However, there is much we can learn from them. Led by enlightened servant leaders, these companies have carefully and systematically taken autonomy and self-determination to their extreme logical conclusions; and they've been incredibly successful.

Though not for everybody, what we have seen is that movement in this direction of greater autonomy and flexible networks of teams (versus rigid hierarchies) is becoming more and more important for businesses to be able to thrive, and even survive, in the rapidly evolving VUCA world. We believe that every organization who brings more humanity into play will greatly increase their likelihood of sustainability and financial success.

And even if you're working in a hierarchical organization, you can still take lessons from these organizations, *show up as a leader*, and make a difference. Start small and experiment with your own team on some simple tasks and projects; see how it goes and build from there. Or experiment outside of work and see how the principles of self-management can make a difference in the lives of those around you. One individual did just that; and we think his lessons have the potential to transform youth sports.

Can Self-Management Transform Youth Sports?

Scott Life is a phenomenal, humanistic leader. We met him in the fall of 2016 when he completed our Thriving Workplace Culture Certificate (TWCC) training program. During one of the sessions, we discuss the concept of self-managed companies. Being a person who likes to practice what he preaches, Scott wanted to experience the concept of self-management for himself. He was in a career transition; he had just spent the last thirteen years of his career as president of an industrial safety products manufacturer and was now transitioning to independent consulting.

Scott thought, "Where could I experience self-management in an organization that had only known traditional management principles? My son's 13U travel baseball team?" After seven years of coaching recreational and competitive (a.k.a. "travel") baseball for his son's teams, he had seen the good, the bad, and the ugly of modern youth sports. He thought he had experienced it all . . . or had he?

Here is Scott's experience, in his own words:

> In the increasingly micromanaged and hypercompetitive world of youth sports, what would happen if we turned the model upside down, got rid of the coaches, and let the players have full autonomy?
>
> Our season was drawing to a close, and we had one remaining league game to play. We were playing the first-place team in our division. We were in third place—too far behind to jump up in the standings—but we knew our result would determine if our opponent would win the division outright or if they would be co-champions

with the team currently in second place. And when you add in the fact that our players went to the same middle school as several players on the other team, I knew it would be a competitive game.

At our final practice, I announced to our players that we were going to try something different for the last game of the season. They hung on my every word as I described what must have sounded like Utopia to these teenagers: there would be no coaches involved in any aspect of the game and they would have complete autonomy to decide their batting order, defensive assignments, pitching rotation, etc. They were energized. It was a great practice.

I thought of the words that Rosie and Jon repeated throughout our TWCC course: "People will support what they help to create." And the three principles applied by FAVI were still ringing in my head. They resonated for me because they were easily adaptable to the context of a baseball team, particularly the third assumption: **Value is created on the baseball field. Players craft the plays; the coach and coaching staff at best serve to support them, at worst are costly distractions.**

And now it was game day. Our players filed into the dugout thirty minutes before our game, just like normal. There was considerable chatter amongst the players, as I assume they were discussing batting order and defensive/pitching assignments. There were nine players playing that day, so they did not have the difficulty of deciding who would sit out on defense. I know they had a whiteboard and marker in the dugout, but I'm not sure if they used it like I always used it. The players then began their stretching routine, just like normal. They then progressed into warming up their arms with a throwing progression, just like normal. Several players then proceeded into hitting stations, just like normal. I looked down at my watch . . . they were right on schedule. Could this really be happening with an unsupervised team of thirteen-year-olds?

I had alerted the umpire and opposing coach about our plans ahead of time. I'll never forget the look on their faces when two of our players, Dylan and Calvin, walked up to home plate for pregame instructions as our "coaches." The umpire's smile seemed to indicate shock: "Wow, they are actually going to go through with this?" Meanwhile, the opposing coach's smile seemed to indicate overconfidence. "Yes! They are actually going to go through with this!" And when Dylan and Calvin shook hands with the umpire and opposing coaches, there was no turning back. It was time to play ball.

Our team took the field, and it was fun to see what positions they were playing. A few players were in unfamiliar spots, and I could hear some of the parents in the bleachers making comments along those lines. Speaking of parents, there were more parents in the bleachers than usual. This was a function of it being our last game and the fact that the players were talking about it so much at home. Plus, there were three coaches now sitting in "unfamiliar spots"—the bleachers!

Despite giving up a single and a walk, our players held the other team scoreless in the top of the first inning with some great pitching and solid defense. It was now our turn to bat, and with that, a few more surprises surfaced. The "normal" batting order was thrown out the window. But I have to be honest—I really liked the batting order they came up with that day.

Our leadoff hitter singled to right field. And to our players' credit, they were organized and had our eighth and ninth hitters in the lineup at first base and third base, respectively, as base "coaches." The "coach" at third base was giving signs to our runner at first base. After the first pitch, he gave our runner at first base their "steal" sign. But, in a departure from the norm, our third base "coach" did not give our batter their "take" sign ("take" = don't swing). Our batter popped out to the second baseman, and the runner on first base was not able to get back in time—it was a double play. I thought it had to be an oversight by our third base "coach" and that he forgot to give the "take" sign to our batter. But based on the reaction of our players, it was exactly what they had wanted to try. It was aggressive to call the hit-and-run, and they were willing to take the risk. Our players were very positive, and they were quick to console our batter who felt bad for hitting into the double play.

Our next batter was hit by a pitch. So, with another runner at first base, would our third base "coach" stay aggressive? After taking ball one, our third base "coach" gave our runner at first base the "steal" sign and, again, did not give our batter the "take" sign. Oh, no . . . another hit-and-run?!? But this time, our batter lined a double to left-center field. Our runner, already running on the pitch, was able to score from first base. Our players did not let the failed hit-and-run shake their confidence. They had the early lead. They were playing to win.

	1	2	3	4	5	6	7	R	H	E
Traditionally Managed	0							**0**	1	0
Self-Managed	1							**1**	2	0

There was a noticeable buzz from our side of the field. Parents in our bleachers were talking amongst themselves, and our players were high-fiving as they transitioned out to play defense. The opposing coach had a few choice words for his team as they entered their dugout, and he ended his rant with something to the effect that they were now losing to a team without any coaches! But he was wrong. We had a team with nine "coaches."

The other team put together a few nice hits and scored three runs in the top of the second inning. After that big swing in momentum, our players showed great discipline at the plate (two walks) and hit the ball hard, but the other team played great defense to strand our two base runners:

	1	2	3	4	5	6	7	R	H	E
Traditionally Managed	0	3						**3**	4	0
Self-Managed	1	0						**1**	2	1

The top of the third inning was another big inning for the other team. Their hits and our errors were piling up quickly. Maybe this experiment wasn't such a good idea?

	1	2	3	4	5	6	7	R	H	E
Traditionally Managed	0	3	4					**7**	6	0
Self-Managed	1	0						**1**	2	2

There was a noticeable buzz in our bleachers . . . this time, not in a good way! I was getting anxious looks from parents. I could sense the assistant coaches were getting uncomfortable. But I stayed committed. I trusted our players. And our players responded beautifully in the bottom of the third inning. For our team, this was exciting.

Our players were having fun. For their team, this was nerve-racking. Were their players playing to win—or not to lose?

	1	2	3	4	5	6	7	R	H	E
Traditionally Managed	0	3	4					**7**	6	2
Self-Managed	1	0	5					**6**	4	2

The momentum swung back and forth over the next few innings. Our players were playing great baseball, while their players seemed to be hanging on for dear life. Going into the final inning, we were still trailing by a run. In the top of the seventh, the other team was able to increase their lead to three runs. Unfortunately, there would be no Hollywood ending . . . there would be no walk-off grand slam in the bottom of the seventh inning.

	1	2	3	4	5	6	7	R	H	E
Traditionally Managed	0	3	4	0	2	0	2	**11**	9	6
Self-Managed	1	0	5	1	0	1	0	**8**	7	3

After the game, our players huddled in right field, just like normal. While I don't know exactly what was said in that player-only huddle, there was positive body language and a healthy amount of laughter. Despite what the scoreboard said that day, I was proud of our players for finishing the season on a high note.

Scott realized that one baseball game wasn't enough to prove whether or not self-management could work in youth sports. But this single game allowed him to experience how certain behaviors emerged when a group of players were given autonomy:

- They were fully invested, and they were having fun.
- They were able to "take off their armor" and focus all of their attention and energy on making plays.
- They were willing to take risks without fear of criticism from a coach.

Scott thought, "What if I, as 'CEO' of this baseball team, would have been willing to put my trust in the players and, in return, they brought the best versions of themselves to the baseball field each and every day for an entire season?" As he watched the players walk off the field with big smiles that day, he was beginning to imagine the possibilities for youth sports and the development of youth athletes if self-management principles were universally applied. Scott has since then experimented with leveraging self-management principles in coaching other teams and says, "The question isn't 'Can self-management work?' The question is 'Are you ready to take the leap?'"

Again, we want to be clear. Self-management may not be the goal for your organization; and that's okay. But it is important to see how this understanding of innate human needs is being leveraged within organizations—and that they are also successful and profitable. Rehumanizing the workplace demands that we relook at traditional organizational structures that go against the grain of being human and result in being rigid, slow, and unresponsive. We need to move toward more "freedom with parameters" in order to thrive in a VUCA world.

How to *Show Up as a Leader* and Influence Change at This Part of the Pyramid

The more structure we put in place, the more we go against the grain of being human. Yet we need *some* structure. Additionally, the incredible work of Keyhubs and the lessons from these self-managed companies show how important relationships are. We need to honor the self-managing nature that is in our DNA and support freedom within clear parameters. Here are some ways you can *show up as a leader*, support humanity, and influence change for relevant, future-ready organizations:

- **Diversify your tribe.** As we learned from Vikas Narula and his work with Keyhubs, we need to think less about formal hierarchical structures and more about leveraging, growing, and diversifying our networks. So even if you work in a hierarchical organization, you can help build and grow networks. Expand your influence by seeking out people who are different than you; work to understand their perspectives and strengthen relationships. Then you can *show up as a leader* and work to help bridge the gap between your networks by encouraging additional connections with people and including more people in the process.

- **Start engaging in conversations with the people doing the work.** Organizations with a flatter structure leverage the expertise of the people doing the work and support them in *showing up as leaders*. You can be an advocate for others. Find the informal leaders within your organization who have profound influence; start engaging them in conversations and idea generation for what can help nurture autonomy and support growth. And when you're in meetings with others, be a voice for those who are doing the work or who will be impacted by decisions; ask the group, "Have we included or discussed this [process, change, etc.] with those who do or will be impacted by this?"

- **Pilot autonomy-boosting structures.** Find a department that might be open to trying out some new processes and structures that support autonomy and give people the opportunity to self-manage. "Pilots" tend to feel less risky because they are set up as an experiment. Take a clue from our friend Scott, and see where else in your life you might try trusting our desire and ability to self-organize and self-manage. It's about starting small and experimenting; he started with one game. You'd be surprised how quickly momentum can build.

- **Seek and create clarity.** "Freedom within parameters" works when the parameters are clear. Don't sit back and wait for someone else to clarify expectations or the vision. Start *building a lighthouse* by asking for the clarity you need. Better yet, invite others into conversations to collectively begin the work to create clarity regarding where the organization is headed and how you can support the purpose being realized.

Chapter 6

HUMANISTIC CULTURE

A people-first workplace regards all people as of equal importance and the relationship must be two-way—adult.

—ANDY SWANN, *The Human Workplace*[105]

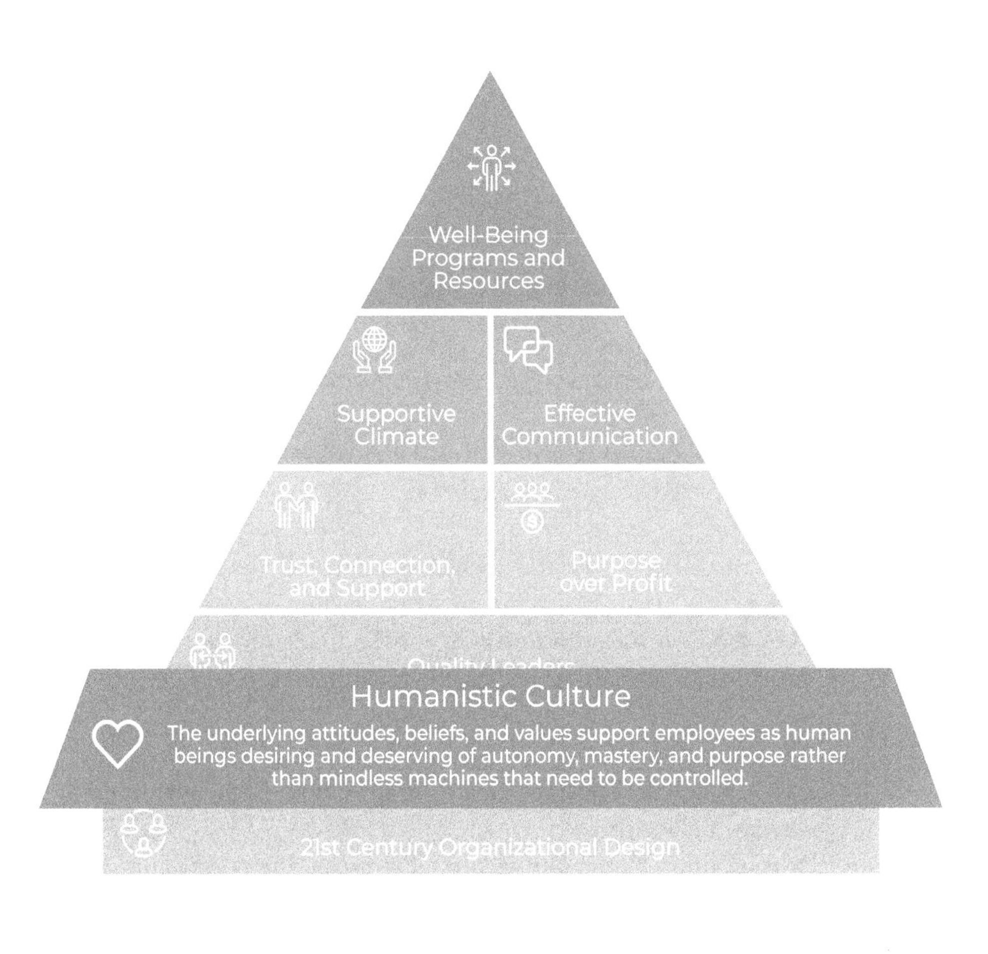

We know that life on a stranded island is nothing like life onboard a highly structured ship at sea. A rigid, hierarchical, command-and-control structure aboard the ship leaves very little autonomy for the crew. It might even send a signal to the crew that they are not valued and become disempowering. However, in our opening story, we quickly saw the new-paradigm sailors rise to the occasion. They had a clear purpose—to collectively work together to survive and thrive. They leveraged each other's strengths and supported autonomy as they all *showed up as leaders* to do their part and contribute to their shared purpose.

As we saw in the previous chapter, twenty-first-century organizational design favors nimbler networks of teams than rigid, hierarchical structures. This helps provide the flexibility needed to adapt to the disruption our VUCA world brings. However, simply redesigning organizational structure is not enough by itself. If we are going to rehumanize workplaces, we must also have a foundation where our innate human needs can be better met—where we all can be treated as self-authoring adults. **We must nurture a humanistic culture where the underlying attitudes and beliefs are that people are valued as *human beings*, not as predictable, controllable machines.**

Before we begin looking at specific aspects of a humanistic culture, we need to level set on what culture is and is not. Culture is **not**:

- On-site fitness classes, social events, ping-pong tables, nap rooms, or other perks
- What's in the physical environment (i.e., workspace design features)
- "The way we do things around here"

These are all examples of *climate*, which is ultimately the manifestation of culture. Edgar Schein, PhD, is the guru and leading researcher on organizational culture. He describes culture as "the hidden force that drives most of our behavior both inside and outside organizations."[106] Schein says of culture:

- It includes the unconscious, taken-for-granted beliefs, perceptions, thoughts, and feelings.
- It goes beyond "it's the way we do things around here," the company climate, basic values, etc. These are all *manifestations* of the culture.
- The culture of an organization plays a significant role in shaping employee behavior and fostering organizational change.[107]

In his book *The Culture Blueprint*, Robert Richman echoes Schein when he describes culture as the "mindset and habits that drive behavior."[108] Therefore, changing culture first and foremost requires changing our *thinking*, which requires *wading in the messy middle* to upgrade our Inner Operating System. In other words, in order to have a conscious, humanistic culture, we have to start seeing people as **humans**, not as predictable or controllable machines. We need to honor the biological imperatives of self-determination and self-organizing and *create fearless environments* where everyone can show up as authentically human—feeling *enough* just as they are at the same time they continue to grow and seek excellence.

Rehumanizing workplaces starts at the local level; culture is ultimately built team-by-team. Humanistic businesses understand this and put great intention in building human-focused cultures at the team level as well as creating deliberate practices at the broader organizational level. A key aspect of this is providing a framework for people to intentionally shift their mindset.

Valuing People as **Humans**: Moving from an Inward to an Outward Mindset

In order for us to truly see and value others as human beings, we need to recognize our triggers to dehumanize and then apply strategies that rehumanize. You may be thinking, "Of course I recognize people are humans." However, as we've seen, when we're triggered and operating from our Reactive Mind, it's a different story. We end up operating from an inward mindset.

Research from the Arbinger Institute has found that when we become inward focused, we start to see people as objects:

- as **vehicles** to help us accomplish our goals and objectives;
- as **obstacles** preventing us from accomplishing something; or
- as **irrelevant** to us and what we're wanting to accomplish.[109]

When we operate from this inward mindset, we don't acknowledge or care that other people have their own needs, objectives, and challenges; our focus is on ourselves, our department and work, our company, our location, our teams, etc. Consequently, we become primarily concerned with others' impact on us, resulting in a lack of collaboration, turf protection, and entire workplaces focused on **me** rather than **we** . . . entire workplaces where people don't feel that they matter. And when people are feeling stressed or threatened in some way, this inward focus only increases. Arbinger describes the heart of the inward mindset issue: "At its heart, the problem is pretty simple; incentive structures, company metrics, career goals, and personal egos all conspire to keep people focused on themselves and their own perceived needs and challenges, usually to the detriment of the team and the enterprise. In short, organizations and their people get inwardly focused, and as a result, they get stuck."[110]

Quite simply, an inward mindset makes things harder. We become attached to our own stories and *rightness* and end up with significant blind spots, silos, blame, *stuckness*, and low morale.

One of our clients is a large engineering and architectural firm. They were going through incredible changes, from acquisitions to leadership changes and more. Not surprisingly (given what typically happens in the face of adaptive change), people's self-protective triggers were going off all over the place; and they didn't even realize it. Every time we spoke with an individual or team, we heard things like "Ugh, they just don't get it! This isn't going to work for our team/location. Why are we the ones having to make all of the sacrifices?" They were completely **me**-focused and operating from an inward mindset. Consequently, they ended up in an unproductive loop of blame and being problem-focused because they were all too busy justifying their "rightness" and clinging tightly to what was familiar to them.

At one of their offices, the principals (main leaders of that location) were so stuck in their own inward mindsets that there were massive culture issues; as a result, they were losing key talent—particularly younger employees. Senior leadership and human resources leadership expressed concerns, but these principals couldn't see it and brushed it off. As we met with each of them, they expressed frustration about "those damn entitled millennial employees."

One of the principals, Brad (not his real name), was particularly rigid and stubborn in this thinking. He ended up viewing most of the millennials as obstacles; they were annoying and got in his way of getting his own work done because they are "too needy" and expect too much. He also expressed great frustration with human resources. He vented: "Why are we expected to bend over backwards and completely change how we do things just to meet the demands of these folks? They [millennials] should have to make changes too."

Brad "grew up" in the industry in an era of sink-or-swim and expects his employees to do the same. He said, "Why should I have to show them how to do their job? They should figure it out; that's what we hired them to do. I don't have time for this!" Ouch! Brad was so focused on himself and being "right" that he had lost the capacity to effectively lead. And as he lost the capacity to lead, his workload increased—as did his stress. He started dropping the ball on projects and having colleagues lose confidence in him—all because he couldn't move beyond his own inward mindset. It wasn't until after a lot of hard work of *wading in the messy middle* that Brad could see where his inward mindset was getting in his way of having the impact he wanted.

Unfortunately, workplaces are full of people operating with an inward mindset, largely as a result of our Reactive Mind hijacking us. The good news is that we can learn how to leverage an outward mindset, which also helps us better leverage our Creative Mind.

An *outward mindset* is a way for individuals, teams, and organizations to be more effective by transforming from being inwardly focused to focusing on the needs and impact of all stakeholders. It is a framework that helps clarify and align people around a common, collective vision, and result rather than operating out of a scarcity mindset and self-protection.[111]

When we embrace an outward mindset, we are able to see each person as a **human**. We focus on our impact on others and then look for ways to adjust our efforts to be more helpful by leveraging the SAM model:

- See others as PEOPLE. Acknowledge (and care about) the needs, objectives, and challenges of others.
- Adjust our efforts to be more helpful. Think about what we can do that might help others get their needs met, achieve their objectives, or address a challenge they're facing. Find a win-win.
- Measure our impact. Hold ourselves accountable for the impact (positive or negative) we're having on others. Are we on track, or do we need to course-correct? Then work to maximize our positive impact on every stakeholder.[112]

Every person contributes to the current state of the workplace culture. If we want to have a collective mindset shift at the organizational level from one of employee-as-machine to honoring what it means to be human, we have to go beyond ourselves. A 2014 McKinsey & Company study found that "failure to recognize and shift mindsets can stall the change efforts of an entire organization."[113] And another McKinsey & Company study found that organizations who identify and address pervasive mindsets at the outset are four times more likely to succeed in organizational change efforts than companies that overlook this stage.[114]

So if we can equip people to *show up as leaders* and leverage an outward mindset, it makes things easier; it leads to a broader visual range, collaboration, accountability, innovation, and engagement. It makes us smarter, open, curious, and aware. In other words, we have to *build a lighthouse* to see what's possible when we move from a guarded, self-protective inward mindset to a curious, open, collaborative outward mindset. Then we need to *create a fearless environment* and invite people to *wade in the messy middle* to look at their own inner narrative and do the work to shift their thinking and upgrade their IOS.

Putting an Outward Mindset in Action

We were working with a leadership team in the grocery industry. During a period of growth, they decided to expand some of their existing stores while they were also building new locations. The leadership team squabbled about which factors were most important for the remodels and store expansions—each focused on their own area and teams rather than the whole and the big picture. None of them wanted to have to sacrifice anything or deal with the anticipated drama with their teams due to the disruption and inconvenience that would inherently emerge. They were stuck and unable to effectively lead their teams because they were approaching the situation from an inward mindset perspective.

We walked them through some self-reflection exercises to help them realize the triggers that were leading them to show up in a reactionary, self-protective way. Then we introduced the concept of an outward mindset by engaging them in a silly, yet powerful exercise adopted from improv comedy—the colonial person/flight discussion.

We ask people to find a partner. One person plays the role of a person from historic, colonial times and needs to be rigid about staying in that role. The other person's role is to take a couple of minutes and try to describe to their colonial friend about airplanes and how they fly. There's usually a healthy dose of laughter as the colonial person asks questions and expresses confusion over concepts they don't understand, such as electricity, engines, and more, while their friend struggles to find ways to explain flight in terms that might resonate.

When we debrief and ask the people describing flight what they noticed and tried that was helpful, many describe trying to figure out what their colonial friend might understand. People commonly try to use comparisons to a horse and buggy, oil and fuel from lanterns, or birds in flight. The point is that they had to put themselves in their partner's shoes, think about their partner's frame of reference, and then adjust their efforts to try to be helpful—so their friend could understand. They essentially needed to embrace and leverage an outward mindset.

After debriefing the exercise with our grocery leadership team, we invited them to identify their major stakeholders: employees, customers, local community, and vendors/suppliers. Then we broke them up into four groups and asked each group to take on one of the stakeholders; we asked them to embrace an outward mindset (much like the colonial/flight exercise) and spend time listing what they thought the needs were for their respective stakeholder as it relates to the store remodels and expansions. After they listed the needs, we asked them to identify what they thought the objectives and challenges were that their stakeholders were facing.

One by one, a spokesperson from each group took turns presenting the needs, objectives, and challenges of their stakeholder group. We captured the collective responses on flip charts. As we did, the leadership team began to see shared needs and objectives between the stakeholders and common challenges they were facing. As they were challenged to move beyond a **me**, inward mindset to a **we**, outward mindset, they started to see the broader system; they started to see the situation with greater clarity and complexity.

With that newfound awareness, we asked them, "If you weren't triggered and focused on self-protection and being right, what's one thing you would do to be more helpful to ______ stakeholder? What's one thing you could do now that would add value to that stakeholder?"

This simple, yet powerful exercise can be done with individuals and groups. By asking people to look beyond themselves and see people as humans, we start to build a foundation for better listening, empathy, and connection. In fact, an outward mindset is also one of the keys to Morning Star's success with self-management. Within their "freedom with parameters" structure, they have two clear parameters regarding decision-making:

1. When making decisions at Morning Star, people are expected to focus on who is impacted. If someone will be materially impacted, employees are expected to discuss it with that person.
2. If there are other people (either inside or outside of the company) who could bring meaningful additional information or knowledge to the decision, employees are expected to consult with those people.

An outward mindset is critical to creating a humanistic culture so we can truly see one another as *people* rather than as objects. This is also imperative in order to foster not only diverse but fully inclusive workplaces.

The Importance of Diversity and Inclusion in Building a Humanistic Culture

We can't have a human workplace without being intentional about nurturing diversity and fostering true inclusion. We have to admit, our eyes have been opened to broaden our perspective of what it means to have a truly inclusive workplace. Most people typically think about gender, age, race, culture, and mobility when considering diversity and inclusion; however, it goes far beyond those factors.

In the spring of 2019, we invited an amazing woman, Ragen Chastain, to enlighten our Thriving Workplace Culture Certificate Annual Licensing community. She is an internationally recognized thought leader, writer, and speaker in the fields of body image, Health at Every Size®, Athletes at Every Size, size acceptance, and corporate wellness, and she has worked with many companies including Google, Apple, Sony, Panasonic, Intel, Warner Bros., Paramount, Fox, and Microsoft, as well as many universities. Ragen challenged us to think about our workplaces and whether we are welcoming diverse bodies in our spaces by considering the following three questions:

1. **Who can access this space?** While the Americans with Disabilities Act (ADA) regulations have been an improvement for people with mobility issues, ADA compliance is a bare minimum and excludes many groups. For example, people using mobility devices (i.e., electric scooters) may not have access to all spaces or room to maneuver or park their device. Or people with limited mobility may be excluded if your facilities require long distances of walking without adequate seating along the way for taking breaks. I (Jon) experienced this

firsthand during our Fusion 2.0 Conference when I realized how much walking was required during the event and how challenged I really am with so much walking due to my multiple sclerosis.

Mobility is only one consideration when thinking about accessibility. Are your locations in areas where people of color will feel comfortable and not seen as "suspicious"? Then there are considerations regarding size diversity. Let's face it: we're a fat-phobic nation and tend to forget about some basics regarding being inclusive of all body sizes. For example, does your seating restrict the ability for people with larger bodies to sit (i.e., chairs with arms)? Do your uniform, safety, or medical equipment vendors accommodate larger sizes? And are you welcoming of all genders, including people identifying as transgender and nonbinary, by having gender-neutral options for restrooms and changing areas?

2. **Who does not see themselves represented positively in this space?** The bottom line is that everyone who enters your space should see themselves represented positively. Consider your marketing; do the images and messages avoid stereotyping? Are there options available for people with hearing impairments? Or how about any artwork you may have on display? Do you purchase from diverse artists and foster appreciation rather than appropriation (i.e., ignoring or belittling certain aspects of culture and their original significance)? If you have waiting areas, consider the messages any magazines you have might send in terms of exclusion or devaluing groups of people; do they show diverse bodies (might be a good idea to avoid fashion and fitness magazines all together)? Do you have any braille options for those with vision impairments?

3. **Who might not feel welcome in this space?** People with disabilities end up being excluded and minimized by many of the common programs and initiatives workplaces promote. "Take the stairs" campaigns frequently have a shaming tone for people who need to take the elevator for a variety of reasons. Inflated claims that "sitting is the new smoking" (even the American Council on Exercise criticized such claims in 2019) also tend to shame people for whom standing for any length of time is painful, problematic, or impossible. Or having a company-sponsored 5K run or a bike-to-work program without any

viable option for those who can't participate also minimizes people.

Then there's the language factor. Our words matter and frequently minimize, exclude, and even dehumanize people (we'll expand on this a little later in this chapter). For example, using ableist language (i.e., any word or phrase that turns a disability into a negative thing) can minimize and elicit shame; some examples are *crazy*, *insane*, *lame*, or *mental*. Then there's language and practices that dismiss people of color and foster more racism. And we also need to be mindful of bigotry and heteronormativity regarding gender orientation and sexual preference. For instance, do your forms only have binary choices of male or female? We also can't forget about language, practices, and programs that promote sizeism, such as off-hand jokes, Biggest Loser, and weight-loss competitions; having events at non-accommodating spaces; or not having t-shirts in large enough sizes at special events.

Adam Grant put it well during his keynote speech at the 2017 Workhuman Conference when he said, "If we want to build a truly human workplace, figure out whose voices are not being heard and then invite them into the conversation."[115] *Finding your tribe* requires leveraging an outward mindset and intentionally seeking out others who are different from us to broaden our relationships and network. **If we don't *create a fearless environment*, invite everyone into the conversation, and work to align (rather than compete) with each other, it's nearly impossible to have a truly human experience at work.**

Showing Compassion for People, Regardless of Their Background

We also can't talk about a humanistic, inclusive culture without talking about people who are commonly ignored—people who are denied opportunity for growth and personal success because they are defined for the rest of their lives by the worst mistake they made. Yes, we are talking about incarcerated men and women in the United States. True, some are violent criminals; however, many people in our prisons are not. Their lapse in judgment came with a different consequence than us.

Why should we care? Because we are at a time in our history where as many as one in three American adults have a criminal record. And each year seven hundred thousand men and women are released from prison and reenter society, where many want to find jobs. Yet, despite the growing need for workers, formerly incarcerated applicants face a huge obstacle in achieving gainful employment: criminal background checks.[116]

It has been over twenty years since "ban the box" laws came into existence, yet in recent years there has been a renewed focus on fair-chance hiring policies. These laws require employers to remove criminal-history questions from employment applications; the intent is to protect applicants and candidates convicted of a crime from automatically being disqualified during the selection process so that employers are only considering criminal history until either after an interview or when a job offer has been made. To date, "ban the box" laws have been enacted in thirty-three states and more than one hundred and fifty cities and counties.[117] Although they primarily cover the public sector, many also apply to private-sector employers; and efforts are being made to broaden this at the Federal level.

Johnny C. Taylor is the president and CEO of SHRM (Society for Human Resource Management), the world's largest HR professional society. In 2018, he stated that second-chance employment (i.e., hiring employees with a conviction history) is a SHRM priority and initiative, noting that "willingness to hire in theory doesn't necessarily mean willingness to hire in practice."[118] He is a passionate advocate, evangelizing the need and opportunity to let go of some of our judgments and give people second chances.

Televerde is one such company that believes in second chances. They provide sales and marketing alignment, strategy, and services. More importantly, they have a socially responsible business model that helps disempowered people find their voice and reach their human potential. Televerde works to reduce recidivism by partnering with the Departments of Corrections in Arizona and Indiana to invest in training and employing incarcerated women in their call centers for their customers that range from technology companies to manufacturers and health care. This is how they describe their model:

> The inmates at Perryville and Rockville who make up our Televerde family aren't any different from you and me. They are women—daughters, sisters, wives, mothers, aunts, grandmothers. They seek personal and professional fulfillment. They want their children and families to be proud of them. They, like all of us, are working to better themselves in every area of their lives.

> By investing in people through education, job training and opportunity, we help those who are disempowered successfully re-enter their communities, reunite with their families, and build meaningful and rewarding careers.[119]

The women of Televerde are paid a fair market hourly wage. They have immediate access to a portion of their wages for discretionary spending, and the remaining portion is set aside in savings for when they are released; this allows these women to have financial resources to assist them as they reintegrate into society. They also earn college credits for completing company-sponsored training programs and can take online college classes at their facilities. Additionally, they have the opportunity to work for Televerde post-release. In fact, Televerde employs more than one hundred ex-offenders at their corporate office in Phoenix; and hundreds more are able to gain successful employment leveraging the skills they developed while working with Televerde. They are creating opportunities for these women to *show up as leaders.*

Televerde also works in partnership with a nonprofit, Arouet Foundation, to help women learn how to transition back into society, address everyday challenges, form meaningful relationships, discover their hidden talents, continue on to higher education, and strengthen confidence in themselves to reach their goals. They are going far beyond "ban the box" to treat these women as people, reduce stigma, foster inclusivity, and create meaningful opportunities while growing their business and addressing a large social issue.

Another organization going above and beyond to foster inclusivity and lift up humanity is Twin Cities R!SE, a nonprofit organization with locations in Minneapolis and St. Paul, MN. They assist individuals with social and economic challenges on the path to long-term and stable employment. In 1993, Steve Rothschild was motivated to find a solution to the poverty experienced by many people of color in the Twin Cities, so he founded Twin Cities R!SE. They provide free comprehensive career skills training to ex-inmates, underemployed, and unemployed individuals that reached far beyond technical training. Their eight-week career training programs also focus on building emotional intelligence, personal empowerment, and interpersonal skills. Then they partner with organizations to place these individuals in internships, at temp agencies, or in full-time jobs.

We have to admit that we never even had this group of people on our radar when thinking about diversity and inclusion until recently. And it blew us away to learn of organizations like Televerde and Twin Cities R!SE and SHRM's renewed interest in bringing this issue back to the forefront. As the job markets get tighter, organizations like Televerde and Twin Cities R!SE are *building a lighthouse* to broaden people's perspectives of what's possible and how to leverage a still widely untapped group of talented people who want a second chance. It gives us even more hope for rehumanizing workplaces! And to take it a step further, one organization is working to help people much earlier in their lives.

From Hopeless to Hopeful: The Power of Investing in the "Usually Forgotten"

The purpose of Wildflyer Coffee is to help youth experiencing homelessness. Carley Kammerer (Wildflyer's founder) has seen it all. She is such a great example of what is possible when we don't assume or marginalize people who happen to be disadvantaged and give them some love, support, and opportunities.

Carley told us the story of one of their youth, whom we'll call Alex. Alex started with Wildflyer the summer of 2018. His first several months on the job were an incredibly challenging transition. He was late all the time, would walk off during his shift and just take an hour-long break, and more; Alex didn't think this was a problem. Carley and Ben wondered if they should let Alex go. Then Carley said, "Well, our program exists for this purpose, so I don't want to let him go." She had numerous conversations with Alex about needing to be on time, calling (not texting) if he was going to be late, needing to be better, and more. Over time, something finally started to sink in, and he started to *show up as a leader.*

Alex slowly shifted from being late with no notice to being late with a text, to being late with a call, and finally being on time. Then he would actually show up twenty minutes early—before the coffee cart arrived at a farmer's market; he would call Carley saying, "I'm here. Where are you guys?" Alex started taking ownership and went from not caring to being really involved and taking pride in his work. During his shifts, he would constantly talk to customers about Wildflyer's mission and what they're trying to do. He would call Carley to make sure she was on time (talk about a shift!). In fact, Carley included Alex during a really big weekend market. Before the weekend, she called him and said, "I really need you to be on your A game because it's just going to be me and you, and it's going to be a really busy weekend." Alex responded, "I'm always on my A game. We got this. I'll be there. I'll be there half an hour early, and I'll make sure to help out with the new employee." He's grown from someone Carley couldn't rely on to calling Alex if she needs a reliable employee for something.

Carley described the value of seeing beyond labels and limitations to seeing the humanity in people and then investing in them:

> I think Alex is one of many great examples that youth really do want to work. A lot of people will say things like "They're just lazy and don't want to get a job or work hard." But Alex was working and stayed with us. I think he just didn't know how to show up or be successful in a working environment. He was struggling because I don't think he really cared about anything for a long time. But having those continued coaching moments really helped him learn how to handle situations. And it showed him that someone **does** care. Once people have pride for what they're doing, they're committed to it and care a lot more.
>
> We try really hard to cultivate a work culture of "dignified employment." We also work really hard to make sure our product is really good and competitive, and I think that starts to reflect in our youth. They see the community wanting to come to our cart because they know our coffee is good, and that gets them excited. They feel like they're part of something that the community cares about, so now they care about it too.

Carley could have easily operated from an inward mindset, only being concerned with how Alex was impacting her and the business. Instead, she embraced an outward mindset and saw Alex as a person with his own needs, objectives, and challenges. She let Wildflyer's purpose further guide her and adjusted her efforts to be more helpful—to Alex and to furthering the mission of her company. She created a safe space—a *fearless environment*—for Alex to mess up and learn so that, ultimately, he was able to see his own value, *show up as a leader*, and maximize his positive impact on those around him.

Humanistic Cultures Require *Creating a Fearless Environment*

If we are going to have human, diverse, and inclusive workplaces, we need **everyone** within the organization to be able to see people as humans rather than objects; and we need people to be able to set down their armor and move from self-protection to curiosity and collaboration. This can only happen by starting at the local level. We must be intentional to *create fearless environments* within every team. Then we can invite people to *wade in the messy middle* and embrace the work so they can be more self-aware—of their inner narrative, their triggers, and when they're operating from an inward mindset. And then we need to develop and equip them with the tools and skills to be able to pause, move from operating from a Reactive Mind to a Creative Mind, and embrace an outward mindset.

As we mentioned in the introduction, Amy Edmondson (one of the leading researchers on psychological safety) defines psychological safety as "the belief that the work environment is safe for interpersonal risk taking . . . Psychological safety is present when colleagues trust and respect each other and feel able—even obligated—to be candid."[120] And it resides at the local team level. We will be looking more closely at psychological safety in chapter 9 and considerations for enhancing it. For now, it's critical to understand the importance of it and how interrelated it is with our inner narrative and our subsequent behaviors.

In her book *Dare to Lead*, Brené Brown states that what frequently gets in the way of psychological safety in teams includes judgment, interrupting, unsolicited advice, and sharing outside the team.[121] If you think about it, these are behaviors that usually stem from people operating from their Reactive Mind, where they're triggered and in self-protective mode. Yet the behaviors we need from our fellow team members include listening, staying curious, being honest, and maintaining confidence.[122]

Building a solid foundation for your organization to have a mindset where people see and value one another as human beings demands that we *create fearless environments* and help people upgrade their IOS and build the skills to talk **to** people rather than about them (we'll be expanding on this in chapter 10). It also demands that we become more thoughtful about the words we use.

Words Matter! Being Mindful of Our Language

Nurturing a humanistic culture requires us to be mindful of our language. We already mentioned earlier in the chapter how important it is to be aware of and intentional about the words we use. And this goes far beyond diversity and inclusion efforts (though that's an important aspect for consideration).

The great English writer and storyteller Rudyard Kipling said this about the power of language: "Words are the most powerful drugs used by mankind. Not only do words infect, egotize, narcotize and paralyze, but they enter into and colour the minutest cells of the brain."[123]

Our words convey a message to people about whether or not they are valued and how they are regarded. In order to create and support more humanistic, inclusive cultures, it is essential for us to work to replace words that dehumanize with words that humanize. We do this by shifting from using language rooted in the old paradigm of mechanism, reductionism, dualism, and patriarchy to using language supporting the complexities of what it means to be human.

Even though we may not realize it, so much of our traditional language of business is rooted in military terms—further supporting this notion of needing to "armor up" and be ready for battle. And when we're not using words reflective of battle, we're using words more appropriate for predictable, controllable machines or rodents than self-authoring human beings. This is certainly not a comprehensive list, but we suggest in the table below some key shifts that can start to set the tone for a more humanistic culture.

Considerations for moving from language that dehumanizes to language that humanizes our workplaces:

Old, Mechanistic Language	Humanistic Language
Drive, motivate, get people to . . .	Foster, elicit, nurture, create the conditions for . . .
Human resources, human capital, assets, staff	Humans (period), people, partners, team members
Supervisor, manager	Leader, mentor, coach, advisor
People who report to you, people on your team, direct reports	People within your span of care
Work–life balance	Work–life integration, work–life harmony, fusing work and personal lives

When we start to leverage an outward mindset to see people as human beings and upgrade our language to be more humanistic, we can begin to transform our workplaces to be thriving and successful.

What's Possible When You *Wade in the Messy Middle* and Leverage an Outward Mindset: Bringing Humanity Back to the Technology Business

Envision IT has put great intention behind the language it uses, including titles. As you will learn, they are very much a conscious business and anchor their entire company on the pillars of Conscious Capitalism. So it makes sense that their president is called *chief evangelist of stakeholder value*. Their business development team members are called *stakeholder value seekers* because what they're trying to do is not transact a product or service but identify where Envision can deliver value. Their marketing person is called the *cultivator of connection*, and their employees are called Envisioners. They also don't use "manager" or "supervisor" titles because they feel people don't want to be "managed."

Before we get to their story and how these titles came to be, and in order to understand how phenomenal Envision IT is as a company, it's important to have some background and perspective about the technology industry. We learned in the beginning of the book about the benefits and challenges technological advances bring to workplaces; but what about the businesses that make up the technology industry? Well, the industry is known for being pretty challenging; it is notoriously hypermasculine—aggressive and very "dog-eat-dog," where success is defined by how much money you make and how fast you make it.

Today, there are a lot of venture capital and private equity firms that typically invest in technology companies expecting to receive a return on their investment quickly—and multiple, multiple times over. So expectations are really high for entrepreneurs, and the shareholder-only mentality quickly sets in. Many who start a technology company are looking at how quickly they can inflate it and then exit; unfortunately, when they exit, the people that are left behind suffer as they are the ones having to meet the often-unreasonable expectations of the new ownership.

Enter Nancy Pautsch, a phenomenal, humanistic leader with miles of energy, courage, and compassion oozing out of her four-foot-ten frame. She is a stellar example of someone who *waded in the messy middle, shows up as a leader*, and is *building a lighthouse* to shift a dehumanized industry; she is bringing humanity back to the technology business. Nancy "grew up" in the technology industry as it was going through explosive growth, and tells of her experiences that shaped—and shifted—her approach to business.

> I half joke that I'm a "recovering" perfectionist, Type A3, and a people pleaser. So, entering the industry, I was naïve, intense, and eager to please. In the wrong hands, easily exploited. And sometimes that happened . . . however, I also thrived with the pace and "success." I was the oddball as a four-foot-ten woman among (mostly) tall skinny white guys, and sometimes had to achieve more to get the same recognition. And I did it—hook, line, and sinker. It was competitive and hard hitting. As sales folks, we made a lot of money for the organization and for ourselves—and the more money we made, the more we were pushed. Commissions defined us—and our egos were in high gear.
>
> My workstyle and personality traits helped me earn promotions into leadership. At one company I met my "brother from another mother," Bill Crahen. As I built a rock star sales team, he built a stellar technical team of engineers, project managers, etc. Together, our respective teams were "killing it." We earned a track record as a great leadership team. We worked together many years at that company, which was a "value-added reseller" or VAR. VARs typically focus on the infrastructure of technology, which is a tough sector in the industry.
>
> Unfortunately, the company was sold to private equity (PE). The original owners were good people; they just followed the well-trodden path of building up a company and selling it. It's the norm and now the expectation. After the sale to PE, we experienced the suffering firsthand of the "profit maximization fallacy" and shareholder-only focus. It was like watching our baby being ripped apart at the limbs—heartbreaking.
>
> About a year after the acquisition, I was struggling with a decision. I was discussing it with a friend but of course wasn't asking for help since my ego-driven workstyle was still in play. Anyway, as we were talking, my friend offered, "Nancy, just listen to your gut." That made me curious . . . what is my gut? I immediately thought . . . I need to learn about this "gut" thing and then maybe I'll know better what to do. So I went on a search for my gut, which launched a

spiritual and personal growth journey. It became my side hustle and started with trying to understand my purpose. Why am I here? What matters? I was learning about love, connection, compassion, empathy, intuition, the growth mindset, etc., and these were so against my grain and trained behavior! It was all so new, yet resonated, and so I studied and studied and studied. I reflect now, perplexed yet grateful that something sparked my curiosity to learn about my "gut."

About a year or two into my journey, something shifted, and my fierce determination to do things differently commenced. The catalyst was Bill's affliction with Bell's palsy. You see, in our business partnership and friendship, Bill was the rock: he was always even-keeled, grounded, kind, and stoic. He'd seemingly move mountains without a sweat. Turns out, that's not healthy. In the post-sale toxic culture, there was a lot of pressure to reach unreasonable objectives, and a lot was piled on Bill's plate. Bill took it on. Until one day, it took its toll. Bill came into work with a droopy face and visibly in pain; he developed Bell's palsy. It was a textbook case, and all we could do was wait.

As a routine, a group of us used to meet up later in the afternoon at a bar near the office for "stress relieving" beverages. We were there one afternoon during Bill's experience with Bell's palsy, and I noticed Bill was standing there with no beer in hand. I asked him, "Why aren't you drinking? If you ever needed one, certainly now is the time." He softly explained to me that he physically couldn't drink out of a glass. My eyes filled with tears, and my heart sank like I'd never experienced before. Here was my rock suffering and physically weakened by the craziness of our workplace. With that, I grabbed a straw for my glass of wine and ordered him a beer with a straw. Sadly, we had a couple that night.

That was the definitive turning point for me. I swore to myself and to God that I would never contribute to a destructive organization's success. I was at a crossroads and at a loss. One night, I said to my husband, "Honey, I can't do this anymore. I think I've got to hunker down in a cave in Nepal or something and just meditate." And, God bless him, he said, "You can't do that. What are you talking about?" Oh yeah—reality check. At that time, we were a single-income household.

So I felt trapped. And I thought, "God; what am I doing?" With all my studying and self-work, I was becoming a more caring and

> nurturing leader to my team, but I couldn't change the company directives, which fed the toxic culture. I saw my team working harder and harder—suffering on the proverbial gerbil wheel. Then I came across the book *Firms of Endearment*; and it opened me up so much and offered hope of a new way that I thought, "Maybe I don't have to go to a cave in Nepal after all! Maybe I can use my twenty-plus years of experience in this industry and lead a company that is doing good in the world. Maybe all companies in this terrible industry don't have to be like this."

Nancy shared *Firms of Endearment* with Bill, and he also thought it was amazing that businesses could be successful and conscious—centered around purpose, conscious leadership, and benefiting all stakeholders, not just the shareholders. It didn't have to be a zero-sum game.

At this point, people were leaving the company left and right. As one of Nancy's team members was leaving, he asked her to do him a favor and meet with his neighbor's friend. She agreed and met Beau Smithback, the young thirty-year-old founder of Envision. Beau started the company part-time in 2001, while he was still in high school, and continued it as a side hustle through college. Upon college graduation, Envision had several happy clients, and Beau realized it could be a real business.

After their initial introduction, Nancy wanted to learn more about Envision, and Beau wanted to learn more about her as a leader. Then she gave him *Firms of Endearment* to read and said, "This is what I want to build." After Beau read the book, he responded, "That's what I want Envision to be. Why don't you come and help build it? Let's do this!"

So toward the end of 2013, Nancy and Bill joined Beau to become the executive leadership team (ELT) at Envision. Nancy heads up the business, Bill leads the technical teams, and Beau (who is one of the best enterprise architects in the nation) spends most of his time consulting with clients. Envision was still young enough that they could really shape its future; and they declared that they were going to operate as a Firm of Endearment (FoE).

At the outset, Nancy and Bill met every employee just to understand what they were about and to share the intentions of being a FoE. After about three months, they leveraged their history and knowledge in the industry to design a plan for success. This included defining a differentiated business strategy, which would also lay the foundation for building a conscious culture. As Nancy puts it, "You can be as conscious as you want, but if you don't have a sound business strategy that you can execute, then the company won't thrive. You need to be profitable in order to deliver on your purpose." They knew they had a young and nimble enough company that they didn't have to undo much; they could start out with good engineers providing quality professional services. So that's what they did.

During this transition, most of the former employees left (either on their own accord or they were assisted in their departures due to not being a good fit). Many people didn't want to change or be part of a conscious culture; it was too uncomfortable. They didn't want to have to *wade in the messy middle* and grow; they wanted to just keep their heads down and work. Sometimes being intentional about your culture has growing pains, but the temporary pause to slow down is what helps us speed up.

So who is Envision IT today? They are a group of curious and compassionate people growing a soulful company. Envision exists to improve the lives of their stakeholders. An anomaly in the tech industry, they don't plan to exit—ever. They intend to be an inspiring employer, caring partner (to their clients and business partners that serve them), and contributing member of their communities for a very long time. Envision is based out of Madison, WI, with people and business in Minnesota, Iowa, and Illinois.

They have flipped what it means to be a technology partner. Nancy and Bill saw how the traditional world of VARs (value-added resellers) fueled poor behavior and said, "Why does it have to be this way?" Some companies will still try to put Envision in the "VAR box" because they don't know what to do with them since Envision is so different.

A typical VAR has twenty or more technology manufacturers (e.g., Cisco, Palo Alto, IBM, Hewlett-Packard, Dell, etc.) they partner with to resell their products and implement them.

The typical structure of a VAR business is a mix of selling product (mostly hardware and software) and professional services. The revenues for traditional VARs are mostly comprised of product resale with very slim margins—some as low as 0.05 percent. Significantly less revenue is earned from professional services; however, margins are better at more than 40 percent. Oftentimes a VAR can earn greater margin with a manufacturer if they sell more product, and individual sales are incentivized with SPIFs; this is when VAR motivations can get clouded and motivate bad behavior.

Maximizing profits with inauthenticity doesn't sit right with Nancy: "A VAR that represents multiple competing manufacturers can offer a technology assessment for a customer's environment. Ideally, they're objective and prioritize the customer's needs. However, all too often we've seen a sales rep have a predetermined bill of materials in his back pocket to recommend to the customer. And that bill of materials includes the products that offer the highest SPIF that month or where the rep or organization is short on their manufacturer's sales quota."

As they reflect on their years in the industry, Nancy and Bill share observations from their firsthand experience as well as the general VAR swim lane of the industry:

> Looking inward, the historical VAR model can incite unhealthy behavior—and this is exacerbated with the "profit maximization at all costs" mentality. Typically, professional services accompany a product sale for implementation of the product. And engineers are specialized in a specific product line or technology and are billable consultants. And their performance is "measured" by utilization. With professional services being the highest margin line of business, engineers are typically driven hard—the more billable hours, the higher profitability.
>
> To incentivize consultants to bill as much as possible, VARs will often offer bonuses tied to utilization. So, for example, if an engineer hits 90 percent utilization, that person gets a bonus. And if that same person crosses the 100 percent threshold, there's an even bigger bonus. And sometimes there are "team" bonuses on top of individual incentives. But at what costs to the person, the corporate culture, the customers, and the business?
>
> Here are some of the problems we've observed . . . starting with the person. Most engineers enter the industry because they love technology. If they are billing near 100 percent of the time, they don't have time to learn new technologies. Most of these folks like to build labs and test new capabilities, but they simply don't get the time to play and learn. So their passion dulls. They also don't have time to spend with their families or outside hobbies. And in fact, many of them feel torn to work more in order to get the bonus for their families that they rarely see, or get the bonus for vacations that they can't take. It's sad.
>
> The corporate culture also suffers. An engineer relies on sales for billable work. So if a salesperson isn't selling enough products and accompanying services, then the engineer may not get billable work

to get the bonus and blames the sales person. One tricky thing here is that VARs often add new manufacturers to their line card. This gives more products to sell, but also more technologies for engineers to learn for implementation—but the engineers have little or no time to learn.

The suffering continues as engineers stretch for billable hours. They may take a project with technologies they aren't trained on and then ultimately deliver poor service. In this case, the negative results are multifaceted . . . the customer is disgruntled with poor quality, reputations suffer (the VAR, the engineer, and the salesperson), and infighting ensues as the salesperson and managers blame the engineer. And in the case that the engineer turned down that billable work? Then not only would salespeople and management be upset, but also peer engineers who may lose out on their "team" utilization bonus. People feel like a failure, infighting perpetuates, customers are unhappy—everyone is stressed. Rinse and repeat.

And then when employees finally get fed up and want to leave, it can be difficult for them to find jobs because their personal brand is scarred.

Nancy and Bill thought, "What if we actually didn't do the hardware game?" They believe in the Age of Transcendence where ultimately experience is more important than the stuff. They said, "What if we really just went in and focused on optimization and focused on the end users?" So they started with the end user—the people. They recognize how much technology impacts people's lives and how frustrated people get when it doesn't work; and that impacts the technology and even the culture of a company. They talked to many chief information officers and other leaders in organizations and asked them, "What do you feel is missing from your technology partners today?" The answers were consistent and clear: "Could they please just do what they say they're going to do? Could they just follow through? And could they actually be good at doing what they say they're good at?"

Envision basically decided to start with a blank slate and to define their passion, their engineering strengths and interests, and what matters. They realized that people just want to be seen, heard, and know that they matter. And that's true in work life too. People want to meaningfully contribute and be acknowledged for it; and technology is a growing part of being able to contribute at work. We rely on technology in order to do our jobs in many cases. If that doesn't work, how can we contribute?

Starting with the end user means leveraging an outward mindset, and looking at how people want to work and how technology can enable them to do their jobs and also enable employee engagement and business success (rather technology being an obstacle). Envision has seen how technology can enable people to have a really good day at work; or it's a nonfactor because it's so easy or helps them get out of the way so they can focus on their talent. And when people have a great day at work and can contribute and be acknowledged for it, they likely go home and have a pretty good night with their family. Or they go out into the community and are great at the PTA meeting. Or they get to enjoy a hobby. Enabling them means they can do something that helps them thrive.

So Envision works to really understand an organization's strategic and tactical objectives and then considers how they can actually help them achieve those objectives through what they do. If Envision can't, they try to see if they know anybody else that can. Or they may simply try to help bring them clarity (that's not manipulated to make it fit in their box of services). They want to enable everyone's whole life. And they also want to turn technology into an enabler with authenticity rather than try to sell a bunch of products to people. They said, "How about if we go in and just make it all work. If they do need something, certainly we can recommend something; but we will do so with absolutely no skin in the game." So Envision is quite different than most stereotypical technologists. They do partner with two technology companies from a resale perspective—Citrix and Microsoft. They partner with them intentionally because both operate with conscious leadership, and the quality of their products supports Envision's mission.

This intentional disruption of "technology business as usual" and the focus on the pillars of Conscious Capitalism have brought Envision great success. They have focused on mindful and healthy growth rather than stereotypical technology company growth. Because they are owner-operated and not taking any outside investments, all of their growth has to come from what they generate. Rather than being given a territory and trying to work with everyone, they try to find good companies. So their stakeholder value seekers (a.k.a. business development team) are well trained at qualifying potential clients. They specifically seek out companies who actually care about their employees (as they likely also care about their end-user experience) and who value and understand that technology is important to the success of their company. Then they have to understand the stakeholder perspective from a partnering perspective so that it's a mutual benefit. This is critical because people join Envision because of their culture; they're not going to bait and switch by putting them into a toxic customer environment. They will only work with good companies who care.

With thirty Envisioners currently working for Envision, they are small but mighty—and growing. They have found great success so far as a conscious company:

- In the past five years, they have grown their top line eightfold.
- They've won awards locally for their contributions to the economy and community.
- In the technology industry, Envision has been globally recognized as the "best of the best" for engineering excellence, project delivery, and customer satisfaction.
- In 2017 they were one of three finalists (among thousands of entries) for the Innovation Award for work they did with their client Exact Sciences, which is working to eradicate colon cancer. The award recognizes companies that find innovative solutions to IT's most complex challenges, fuel business growth, and forge strong connections with clients.

They are also earning fiercely loyal clients. Interestingly, their "Endearment Team" (a.k.a. help desk people that work directly with end users) have been compared to nurses or caregivers; not only do they have deep technological knowledge, but they genuinely care about helping people—which comes through. Envision also has a very healthy hiring pipeline because the people who work there love how it's part of living a whole life; and many new hires and candidates are referrals from current Envisioners.

Should I Stay or Should I Go?

Just like Envision experienced, when organizations decide to become conscious and intentional about their culture, there will be casualties along the way; and that's okay. It takes courage and discipline to stand firm in our purpose and values to craft a truly human, inclusive, and equitable workplace. And it takes time for people and workplaces to transform. So how do you know when it's time to leave an organization and when it's time to dig in, *wade in the messy middle*, and work through the transformation?

Well, we're dealing with human beings, not machines; so there is no clear-cut answer. That said, we have seen that as long as there's some momentum and some willingness among people within the organization to recognize the need to evolve and work toward a more intentional, human, and thriving future, it can be worth the effort. Yes, it will be uncomfortable. Yes, there will be setbacks. Yes, it will be *messy*. But there are no shortcuts to anywhere worth going. It requires leveraging the energy of the small successes along the way to help you through the challenging times.

On the other hand, if you find yourself unable to *show up as a leader*, if you find your own well-being eroding no matter how hard you try, and if the toxicity is greater than any energy for transformation, you may be better served putting your energy toward a different organization. There is no magic "breaking point," as everyone is different. But, from what we've experienced, most people know when it's time to part ways with an organization or when they're simply avoiding *wading in the messy middle*. And if you are in a situation where it's time to go, the good news is that the rehumanizing workplaces revolution continues to grow.

How to *Show Up as a Leader* and Influence Change at This Part of the Pyramid

Culture is **everyone**'s responsibility, not just the HR department. Here are some ways you can show up as a leader and bring a humanistic culture to life:

- **Start doing the work to challenge your own assumptions and embrace an outward mindset** with others within your organization. If you lead or attend meetings, speak up and show up as a leader; challenge people to consider the needs, objectives, and challenges of other people. Walk them through an exercise like we outlined with our grocery store leaders.

- **Be mindful of your language.** Abandon language that marginalizes or dehumanizes individuals or groups. Be curious and ask questions that invite others to be thoughtful and intentional about their language.

- **Honor the absent (a.k.a. avoid gossip).** One way we build psychological safety is by talking **to** people, not about them. When we gossip about others, we ignore that there's more than what's merely apparent going on and let our judgment take over. If others try to gossip to you, say something like "I don't know because I wasn't there," or "That hasn't been my experience," or something even bolder like "I make it a practice to not talk about someone who isn't here." Lead by example and invite others to do the same.

- **Expand your inclusion efforts.** Most discomfort we feel around any aspect of diversity and inclusion stems from not recognizing our own privilege. Embrace an outward mindset and think about inclusion more broadly. Start paying attention to your physical environment and language used within your organization. If you're not familiar with it, ask questions to understand your hiring practices. Start building relationships, asking questions, and engaging others in conversations to broaden your perspective on diversity and inclusion.

Chapter 7

QUALITY LEADERSHIP

The process of developing extraordinary leadership is the same process as becoming an extraordinary person. —W. A. (BILL) ADAMS[124]

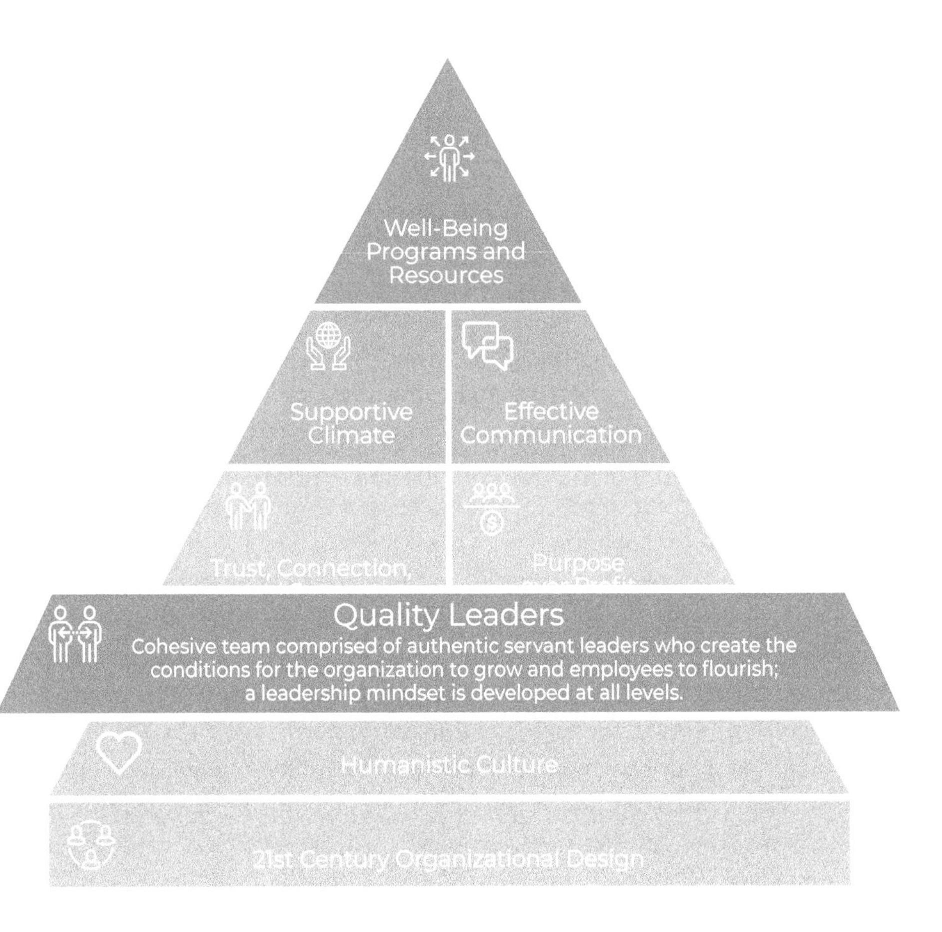

The new-paradigm group of shipwrecked sailors didn't sit back and wait for inspiration or direction; they all *showed up as leaders*. In the midst of stressful and uncertain circumstances, they were able to find their inner strength, challenge their own assumptions, and support one another. They even embraced an outward mindset and let go of their righteousness toward the old-paradigm sailors so they could collaborate and collectively realize their common vision of surviving—and even thriving. Without everyone *showing up as a leader*, the outcome could have been very different. They embodied our definition of leadership: **"Leadership is maximizing our positive impact on the world by becoming our best, fully authentic selves and supporting those around us to break past barriers and step into their greatness."**

We have already seen countless examples of what's possible when people move beyond viewing leadership as a role, title, or position of authority or power to viewing it as a **behavior**. This broadened view of leadership is becoming increasingly needed, given our rapidly changing, VUCA world. It requires embracing the principles of Conscious Leadership, one of the four pillars of Conscious Capitalism. As we mentioned in the introduction, conscious leaders operate from a place of purpose and service to others rather than power and self-interest. They are self-aware and intentional so they can effectively mentor, develop, and inspire people; consequently, they are able to call others to greatness and foster high levels of engagement, creativity, alignment with the higher purpose, and performance.

We need to develop **everyone** to make the adaptive leaps necessary in our VUCA world; we need everyone to be able to leverage a higher level of mental complexity, operate from a Creative Mind, and *show up as a leader*. In fact, a study looking at longitudinal organizational development efforts found that organizations cannot progress beyond the consciousness or development level of their leaders; the researchers found a direct correlation between cognitive developmental stage and whether or not CEOs were able to successfully lead organizational transformations.[125] And since "business as usual" does not support what we know is required for people and organizations to thrive today and in the future, we must focus on expediting our development in a meaningful, sustainable way; and it starts with shifting our mindset.

In an interview with *Inc.* magazine, Simon Sinek pointed out the issues we face with leadership when he said,

> Leadership is a practicable skill; and it's rarely taught, unfortunately. When it is taught, it's not taught well. Most of the MBA programs don't really teach leadership; they call it "leadership," but they teach management. **Leadership is this really sophisticated change in mindset** . . . [W]e have to go through this transition where we are no longer responsible for the results; **we now become responsible for the PEOPLE who are responsible for the results**. We are no longer responsible for taking care of the customer; we're now responsible for the **people** who are taking care of the customer. **This** is what leadership is.[126]

Bob Chapman, CEO of Barry-Wehmiller, also describes a key distinction between management and leadership:

- Management is the manipulation of others for your gain.
- Leadership is a stewardship of the people whose lives are entrusted to you every day.[127]

A 2019 article published in *Harvard Business Review* examined the future of leadership development—where it needs to be and what the current gaps are. The authors declare that the leadership skills that helped people succeed in the past are not what are essential in today's VUCA world. Leadership development can no longer be reserved for the few who are in or close to the C-suite. In fact, more than 50 percent of senior leaders believe their talent development efforts are not adequately building skills or organizational capabilities because they focus on traditional skills like strategy development and financial analysis; however, they fail to focus on the *interpersonal skills* essential to thriving in today's networked and increasingly collaborative environments.[128]

In order to equip people to thrive in this disruptive, relationship-focused environment, organizations need to undo much of what their leaders learned. Javier Pladevall, the CEO of Audi Volkswagen, Spain, put it well when he said, "Leadership today is about unlearning management and relearning being human."[129]

The reason why most development efforts produce short-lived (if any) results is that they are teaching knowledge and skills that are not supported by the underlying IOS. It's like trying to install complex graphics software on a DOS operating system or trying to install a gaming app on a flip phone;

it won't work properly because the operating system can't support it. As we've stated earlier, there are no shortcuts to development. We must *wade in the messy middle* and do the adaptive change work to upgrade our IOS; only then can we effectively apply the knowledge, skills, tools, and techniques that help us *show up as leaders*. And our well-being depends on it!

Why We Should Care: The Leadership–Well-Being Connection

Let's be honest, there are tons of movies and TV shows that leverage the negative impact poor leadership has on individuals and the organization; it makes for good entertainment. But when you live it, it's not so funny.

When I (Rosie) led the well-being/culture consulting practice for an organization, I experienced both the upside of great leadership and the downside of crappy leadership. In the early years, I had full support of my leader and the senior leaders for challenging the status quo and trying out new approaches with our clients. I had fulfilling work, great colleagues, happy clients, and led my team to grow in revenue—all while also becoming a new mom.

Then life threw me a major curveball, and I found out just how awesomely human my organization was. Our son, Peyton, was nine months old and had been sick and crying nonstop for two days with a high fever. I stayed home with him and was tired and sleep-deprived. My husband, Dave, told me to go upstairs and get some rest. I wasn't even asleep twenty minutes when I was awakened to Dave yelling at me. "Rosie, get up! Look at Peyton—call 911!" There he stood holding our limp, almost lifeless-looking baby. The next few minutes were a blur, and it seemed to take an eternity for the paramedics to arrive. I called my sister who lived two miles away and could barely get a word out between the hysterical crying. I rode in the ambulance with Peyton for the long trip to the hospital, praying he wouldn't die en route. The doctors said they think he had an atypical form of a febrile seizure.

Fast-forward thirty days . . . Peyton had another fever lasting four to five days, averaging a temperature of 103 with fever-reducing medicines and sometimes spiking to 105 and above. He was sitting in his highchair while Dave was getting him breakfast, and I was upstairs preparing for an interview with Public Radio that was to start in ten minutes. Once again Dave starts yelling, "Rosie, it's happening again; get down here!" Peyton starts turning pale and bluish and slumps over in his highchair. Another 911 call and paramedic visit to the Ward house. And this started to become the norm for us; nearly every thirty days he would have a week-long fever and one of these lifeless collapsing episodes. Dave and I would take turns not sleeping at night and place Peyton in the bed between us so we could watch him breathe and maybe somehow catch it if something changed; we were terrified he would die in the middle of the night. We were in and out of every specialist you could think of, trying to get answers for what was going on with our son. Every month we'd scramble to figure out who could stay home with Peyton; and we were both negative in our paid time-off balances at work. On more than one occasion we would look at each other and say, "This is how people lose their jobs."

During this time, my leader and organization wrapped their arms around me, loved me, and supported me in being able to take care of myself and Peyton. Every month when I'd call or text my leader with the "it's happening again" message, he would tell me not to worry about anything and take care of Peyton. He'd check in on me to see how we were doing and if we needed anything. And in between these episodes, I still managed to effectively lead my team, serve my clients, and grow our area in revenue. I was engaged and supported in tending to my personal and family well-being; and that was worth more than anything! But it didn't stay that way . . .

My company joined part of a larger, national organization. Initially it seemed to be positive, with lots of growth opportunities. I had practice leaders from other locations throughout the country calling me and asking for mentoring support to do things differently in their consulting work. I felt like I could make a bigger difference by developing others to do what I was doing. Up until this point, my company valued challenging the status quo—even prided themselves on it. Now that was becoming a liability; people who spoke up, questioned things, or challenged the "establishment" were slowly managed out the door; and I was no exception. (True confession: In *How to Build a Thriving Culture at Work*, this story was featured with much less detail as a case study of "Jones Corp," with "Robin" really being me. We did that because I was still riding out a noncompete agreement at the time and didn't want to rock the boat. So now I'm sharing the full, human story.)

To this day, I have no idea why, but I suddenly went from being my boss's "golden child" to metaphorically being shit on the bottom of his shoe. Every time I turned around, I was getting my hand slapped for something that didn't make sense, being told my work didn't matter, and that I should stop talking about culture and leadership and go back to coordinating wellness programs. I then got put on a written performance improvement plan (PIP) because I was bringing in too much "Rosie-related" consulting revenue rather than revenue attached to the core business (insurance). Yeah, figure that one out! I managed to meet the requirements of that PIP only to receive another one; this one had nothing that was being objectively measured. When I questioned it, my boss literally said, "Well, you figured out how to meet the other one, and we're still not getting what we need from you." *What the hell?!* This PIP literally said that I was not showing up as a leader because I wasn't participating in the daily stretching program (even though we were measured based on billable hours). I swear you can't make this shit up! Then he had the nerve to say to me, "Rosie, I want to support you in being successful." To which I replied, "Oh really. It's pretty evident I'm being shoved out the door"—which, of course, he denied. My only response was "Well, I guess we'll see come December 21st, won't we?" That was the deadline date on the new PIP.

I kept trying to figure out what happened; the only explanation I could come up with is that I continued to speak up and advocate for a new-paradigm approach like I always did; but now that had become a liability with this old-paradigm national company. I also advocated for my colleagues in other states who were asking for help; and I think they took offense to that or something. I presume that me speaking up against the mighty and powerful and pushing boundaries became too much of a liability. I don't know if my boss really believed that I was as bad as he accused me of or was just a mouthpiece for the "establishment" and protecting himself and his job. It doesn't matter; it sucked!

Regardless, there was no longer a *fearless environment*, and I shut down and went into survival mode. I felt a pit in my stomach every day driving into work. I ended up making a *Rosie's Survival Playlist* on my iPhone and played "Roar" by Katy Perry on repeat just to get my mindset in a spot where I could take on whatever they threw at me. I went from being open, creative, and productive to armored and ready for battle. It was like a bad game of chicken—wondering each day if I was going to be fired before I could find another job and quit. We had also just bought a new house and were still dealing with Peyton's health issues. I was a walking ball of anxiety and would come home and cry and fall apart at the dinner table; this started to take its toll. Peyton was now three years old. Where he was normally a loving, chill toddler, I was starting to get calls that he was biting another friend at preschool. I can only imagine he was acting out the stress he was witnessing at home.

The cherry on top of this dehumanized work environment came when my mom's only brother, my dear Uncle Buford, passed away from an aggressive form of brain cancer. I never so much as received a token "sorry for your loss" from my boss that most people would say to a complete stranger. Instead, hours before I was leaving to catch a plane for Buford's funeral, I was called into the COO's office to meet with her and my boss. She was scolding me for no longer being an energetic, engaged, outgoing employee (*seriously?!*). I'm pretty sure I was going to be fired in that moment; this is one time when my Reactive Mind self actually saved me. I didn't mince words with the COO when I said to her, "What the hell do you expect from me when every time I turn around, he's [pointing to my boss] telling me how much I suck?" He tried to deny it; but I quickly fired back, "Are you seriously going to sit here and lie? All you do is point out everything I'm doing wrong and how much I suck!" Then I turned to the COO and said, "And excuse me for not being happy-go-lucky, but my uncle just died and I'm trying to arrange my work life so I can hop on a plane in a few hours for his funeral." She looked stunned, looked at my boss with an *oh crap* look, and then he slid a paper he had partially out back under his folder. I went home and told Dave, "I'm pretty sure I was about to be fired today," and then had a red-wine-and-dark-chocolate dinner.

Human workplaces require intentionality. When organizations do not tend to their culture, and don't *create fearless environments* for people to *show up as leaders*, they can quickly become dehumanized; and it takes its toll—on the employees and their loved ones. In these dehumanized environments, people are merely trying to survive. Perhaps my boss actually thought he was acting reasonably and trying to help me. Perhaps he thought it was all bullshit and was just protecting himself, knowing enough to not rock the boat himself since senior leadership had already made up their mind that I was a liability. It doesn't matter; it was time for me to go.

Thankfully, I was able to quit about a month after my near-firing incident and purged nearly everyone from that organization from my LinkedIn and Twitter accounts. As I found myself in my next organization (while I rode out my noncompete agreement), I realized how much damage this dehumanized workplace had done to me. My new leader was amazing; yet I was constantly waiting for the other shoe to drop.

I will never know what caused the Dr. Jekyll and Mr. Hyde transformation with my former boss; and many times, others don't know either when they experience something similar. What matters is that we can recognize the toxicity, find ways to survive, and find a path forward to a better future. And, in time, we can find and appreciate the gifts that such experiences give us. I sometimes think that if I was to ever run into my old boss again, I would thank him for being such an asshole to me; while it sucked at the time, it lit a fire under me to do what we're doing now, prove them wrong, and become an even fiercer advocate for rehumanizing workplaces. Without him pushing me out the door, I might still be there playing it safe and small; who knows.

The good news is that eventually I healed from this ordeal, but it took its toll. And the even better news is that, just before Peyton turned five years old, we finally found an amazing specialist who gave us answers for his health condition; thankfully, a simple surgery cured him, and Peyton is a happy, loving, awesome nine-year-old who keeps me on my toes and challenges me to grow each and every day.

My experience of horrible leadership and a dehumanized organization is one thing, but what do we know from the research about the consequences of poor leadership? Well, for starters, we know from several different studies that transactional and more top-down, control-oriented management is associated with eroding emotional and physical well-being:[130]

- Bad bosses are associated with an increased risk of heart attacks.[131]
- Chronic stress from dealing with bad bosses on a daily basis has been linked to high blood pressure, sleep problems, and anxiety; it's also associated with smoking, excessive alcohol use, and overeating.[132]
- A meta-analysis of 228 studies conducted by Harvard and Stanford researchers found that workplace stress and bad bosses have negative health effects as bad as what are seen in people exposed to significant amounts of second-hand smoke.[133]
- However, we know that transformational and servant leadership is associated with actually boosting emotional and physical well-being.[134]

So if you're trying to implement programs to support employee well-being and safety, how effective do you think you're going to be if your organization is full of "bad bosses"? Who really cares if your managers participate in and promote wellness programs if they're treating people like crap?

Who cares if your managers promote working safely if they then turn around and push results that put your people at risk for not going home in one piece?

Additionally, leadership effectiveness is highly correlated to business performance. Being a more effective leader starts with people being more self-aware, building the skills to reduce autopilot reactivity, and thereby, being more intentional about the action they take. So it makes sense that, as people evolve into later stages of adult development and mental/emotional complexity (i.e., move from a Reactionary to a Creative Inner Operating System), so does their leadership effectiveness. In their book *Mastering Leadership*, Robert Anderson and William Adams describe two games of leadership that we'll paraphrase here:

- *The Inner Game* (a.k.a. our Inner Operating System). This game consists of what drives us; our internal beliefs and assumptions that make up our identity and guide our actions; our meaning-making system that we use to make sense of the world; how we analyze and make decisions; and our level of self-awareness and emotional intelligence.

- *The Outer Game* (a.k.a. Leadership Practices). This consists of our domain knowledge, experience, managerial capability, leadership competencies, and behavior.[135]

Anderson and Adams point out that, although the *outer game* is where most of us spend most of our time (and it is important), the *inner game* runs the *outer game*. "Mastery in anything is a well-honed outer game arising on a highly mature inner game." They go on to show how evolving both games results in greater leadership effectiveness in VUCA environments. Their highly validated Leadership Circle Profile (LCP) 360 assessment measures eighteen key Creative Competencies that make leaders effective. It also measures the kinds of Reactive behavior that reduces their effectiveness. Additionally, the LCP includes a measure of leadership effectiveness consisting of the following items:

- I am satisfied with the quality of leadership that this person provides.
- This person is the kind of leader that others should aspire to be.
- This person is an example of an ideal leader.
- This person's leadership helps this organization to thrive.
- Overall, this person provides very effective leadership.

Anderson and Adams show a very strong correlation between Creative leadership and effectiveness. They also show that Reactive leadership is strongly associated with ineffectiveness. The really good news is that we can develop people so they can "upgrade" their operating system, leverage greater mental and emotional complexity, and become more effective in VUCA environments. As they do so, they also evolve into more of the fullness of their humanity.

Relearning What It Means to Be Human

Part of the human condition is being triggered to operate from a place of self-protection. As we saw in the examples in chapter 2, our childhood experiences shape our internal stories and assumptions; and the stories we hold shape our behaviors. The key is to recognize our stories and then *wade in the messy middle*. We must embrace the discomfort and do the work to change our stories that are not serving us or are coming at too great of a cost. As we do, we are able to progress in our developmental stage and move from a Reactionary Mind (i.e., *not enough*) to a Creative Mind, where we can recognize we are *enough* just as we are **and** continue to work to grow and improve and step into our full, authentic selves. But it's still a lifelong journey.

Growing up as the youngest of five girls in an overachieving family shaped my (Rosie's) stories and assumptions. For a variety of reasons, I created a huge internal narrative of not being *enough*—in most areas of my life. My meaning-making system interpreted pretty much everything as another "validation" that I wasn't *enough* or that I needed to prove to myself and others that I was *enough*. So I thought if I became the best I could at everything, somehow it would fill this void and prove to myself and others that I was lovable. In seventh grade I played first chair flute in the ninth-grade band (even though I hated it—but if I had to do it, I was going to be the best). Then I was terrified of being labeled a "geek," so I became a cheerleader in eighth and ninth grade to be "cool." I was captain of the danceline team in high school, competed in performing lines for a dance studio, was on the A honor roll and taking advanced classes, and the list goes on and on. I assumed that my value didn't come from who I was but from what I accomplished.

At the same time, I so desperately wanted to feel like I belonged. But even when I was invited to "cool kid" parties or hung out with people, I always had this underlying fear that they didn't really want me there and that I was an imposter. In looking back at my school years, I was always waiting for the other shoe to drop; so I pushed myself to achieve even more. And this reactive pattern didn't stop when I went to college. On the surface I had a lot of friends, but I didn't let people in much to the real me out of fear of being rejected, being found out, etc. This even bled into my dating life; any time I started to really care about a guy, I would break up with him to somehow preempt getting hurt (I know, it makes no sense!).

Fast-forward to being a working adult, and this pattern only got worse. I taught group fitness classes and wanted to have the highest attendance and best time slots, so I poured myself into creating choreography and playlists. I became a national trainer teaching continuing education classes, and pushed myself to create the best workshops and have stellar evaluations. I was constantly overachieving to have my leaders like me and praise me. I was trying to do it all to receive accolades and feel *enough*. My friends even had this ongoing "joke" about me being Wonder Woman. The truth is, for years I prided myself in the amazement people expressed about how I managed to somehow do it all. But it had its cost. At one point it nearly eroded my marriage. And more times than I can count, my body has finally had to step in to stop me with illness or injury before I'd slow down long enough to listen, reflect, and reprioritize my life.

On the outside I was highly successful; on the inside I was exhausted! After years of this Reactive Mind cycle repeating itself, I finally hit the pause button and started *wading in the messy middle* to do the transformative developmental work necessary to upgrade my operating system and began to change my meaning-making system. I tiptoed into this work by completing therapy and then the *Curriculum for Living* with Landmark Education. Then I was introduced to the world of coaching in 2004 and began my training and development in Intrinsic Coaching®. These all helped me build the skills to pause and start to think about what I really wanted for myself—to hear my own voice versus what I assumed others and the world expected of me. I journaled, read countless books, and completed all sorts of exercises to further help me be self-aware and operate from a place of intention. I was definitely shifting my IOS.

But life isn't clean and easy. The toxic work experience I previously shared completely threw me back into a reactive mode where I was armoring up to prove how *enough* I was. Thankfully, shortly after I left that organization, I was introduced to Immunity to Change (ITC) work from

Bob Kegan and Lisa Lahey.[136] My new organization was having all of us on the leadership team complete several months of ITC coaching to help foster our development and become more effective at having courageous conversations.

The process started with our coach, Barbara Sanderson, walking us each through creating our four-column ITC map. This is a process where you set an adaptive change goal—some behavior you want to get better at (column 1). Then you start telling on yourself by listing all the things you are doing or aren't doing that undermine your column 1 goal (column 2). Next comes the time to embrace the discomfort and *wade in the messy middle*; column 3 is where you list all your worries and fears—what's at risk for you if you imagine actually doing the opposite of your column 2 behaviors. Then you translate those fears into "competing commitments"; what you begin to see is that our brain is unconsciously spending an enormous amount of energy to keep us "safe" and ensure our column 3 fears never see the light of day. So the harder we push ourselves on our column 1 goal, the harder our brain simultaneously pushes back to keep us safe. It's like having one foot on the gas and one foot on the break at the same time; this is our psychological immune system. Finally, in column 4 you create your Big Assumptions (BA). These are our underlying meaning-making systems. Our Big Assumptions create rules for us about how we show up and operate to stay safe; they anchor our IOS and psychological immune system. Here is my initial map:

Column 1: Improvement Goal	Column 2: Doing/Not Doing	Column 3: Competing Commitments	Column 4: Big Assumption(s)
To be better at speaking up directly and timely—at work and at home	Ignore frustrations at home and don't say anything Make excuses for any poor performance for my team and jump into hyper-support mode (i.e., "train them to success") Procrastinate having corrective conversations Get sucked in during corrective conversations; apologize, fumble over my words, get derailed, etc. Ruminate for days before and days afterwards when I've spoken up; then go into hyper-doing mode to try to "make up" for having the conversation	**Worries/Fears:** I won't be perfect. People won't like me = I won't be loved. I'll be rejected. I'll appear selfish. **I'm committed to:** being perfect having people like me . . . at all costs never risking being rejected never appearing selfish	If I speak up, I might be subjected to explosive anger; people won't like me; I will be rejected and will end up alone. My sole value comes from what I accomplish and from being perfect. People can't disagree with me or be upset with me and still love me; they can't coexist.

When I look back at my original map, I just think how exhausting this was! While I had one foot in the self-authoring developmental stage, I had another anchored in the socialized mind that was keeping me stuck as I desperately tried to feel *enough*—in this case, to feel lovable. And, as you can see, all the books and training in the world applied on this IOS wouldn't work as long as my meaning-making system (i.e., my Big Assumption) was at play. The only way to upgrade my IOS was to *wade in the messy middle* and do the work; you can't fast-forward this development!

Barbara *created a fearless environment* and graciously held the space for myself and my colleagues to *wade in the messy middle* for several months while we began the upgrade process, moving through the ITC coaching arc. This included reflecting on childhood moments that formed our Big Assumptions and starting to see how we created our meaning-making system on a brain that's at a lower level of development.

Many times when I was a young child I was yelled at when I messed up; enter the script of needing to be perfect (to be loved, so I won't get yelled at, etc.). I also had moments where I felt like I only received love or validation when I did something extraordinary and "performed"; enter the story underlining my hyper-doing, overachieving tendencies. Most of the time I felt like I was being compared to my older sisters. I was expected to attend their band and orchestra concerts throughout the year, but no one ever came to my dance competitions and bitched the one time per year when they had to attend my dance recital; then I'd get crap for being upset by their lack of support (enter more stories about not being lovable or enough and not being selfish).

Once we became more aware of where our Big Assumptions (BAs) came from, the process began to start observing our BAs; this allowed us to become keenly aware of the costs when our BA hijacks us—and also when it doesn't, and what casts doubt on its validity. Then eventually we moved into testing mode; we started designing and running experiments that, one by one, started to cast doubt on our BA. It helped us start to form a new story and new meaning-making system that would serve us better than the one we've been carrying since we were young children.

What I realized through this process, and in my work since then in becoming a certified Immunity to Change coach and supporting countless people through this process, is that we are all so similar; we all have our own ways of putting on our armor that keep us "safe" but keeps us from being fully alive and from being effective. I armor up with data and research and get into full-blown, pain-in-the-ass, hyper-driven, get-shit-done mode. And while I'm productive, there are great costs—including becoming more disconnected from others. Thankfully, I know it and can frequently catch myself. But not always; I'm a work in progress too.

As an example, I know that people connect more with stories than data. And I know that, in the past, when I've shared my stories, people have appreciated it, thanked me, said how helpful it was, and it fostered some amazing connections and friendships I have to this day—all because I shared a little more of myself. When we share ourselves, we give others permission to do the same. But somewhere along the line in working hard to have our company be successful, I got triggered and didn't even realize it. I stopped sharing our story and focused on sharing other people's stories. *Who cares about our stories? We're nobody*, I thought. In my mind, our value was bringing other people's stories to light and giving them a platform. Even as we were first proposing this book, the publisher graciously came back and said we need to tell more of our story; and my reply was something like "Really?!

We are this small firm and don't really have a story to tell." Wake-up call! I realized there was an underlying narrative I was holding to do whatever it took so I didn't appear as an egomaniac. The irony is that the more I armor up with data and the less I share of myself, the more arrogant I probably appear—like a know-it-all. Oy!

But when I just show up as me, it's enough. And when we listen to the gifts the universe has to offer, we can see how our former stories were just that—a made-up story and interpretation. Last year a dear childhood friend, Emily, passed away after a long battle with cancer. Going to the funeral was a bit like a mini junior high and high school reunion. We're all much older and were just being humans connecting—not teenagers trying to hide our inadequacies. The genuine love and connection present with everyone was amazing! As we reminisced about this time in our lives, I realized that the stories I was telling myself back then were absolute bullshit. If only we had a time machine to go back and have a do-over!

How we armor up may be different, but at the core, we're all walking around with some version of our own *not enough* script. And when we let it hijack us, there are great costs. Consider that nearly 75 percent of people are operating on a Reactive Mind, with their meaning-making system rooted in the socialized mind and worried about being *enough*. Put us all together within organizations and add in all kinds of stress and triggers that the VUCA world inherently brings, and we have these dysfunctional, dehumanized workplaces. Yet, when we *create a fearless environment* and equip people to recognize when their own *not enough* stories are triggered so they can pause and choose a different story, they get out of their own way and step into their greatness; they are able to *show up as leaders*, and it's profoundly inspiring. We regularly tell Bob and Lisa that their ITC work is such a gift to the world!

We also must remember that development is a lifelong journey. Just because we may do the work to overturn our psychological immunity and upgrade our IOS doesn't mean we're done. We are humans; we will still get triggered and default to a reactionary mode. But the more self-aware we are, and the more skilled we are at knowing how to pull ourselves out of reactionary mode, the more we are able to *show up as leaders* in an authentic, effective way.

It's also important to note that it's not just stressful or negative things that can trigger our reactive tendencies; sometimes we can be triggered by so much joy, love, compassion, etc., that we don't know what to do with it or how to accept it. How many times have you witnessed someone who can't accept a compliment or gratitude? Or how about times when people short-circuit heartfelt moments with humor or other strategies to lighten the space? Sometimes it can be hard to hold these incredible gifts of love, joy, and compassion.

When we launched the inaugural Fusion 2.0 Conference, it surpassed our vision and expectations. From the start of the conference, we had people saying it felt different. They said every little touch was noticeable and that they felt loved and that they could show up authentically human. People were inspired and hopeful and appreciative for no longer being on an island and for *finding a tribe* of people who are fierce advocates for humanity at the workplace. They were creating action plans to be able to go home and actually apply what they learned. And, more importantly, they were creating meaningful connections and building a community that would last beyond the conference. It was so big and radiated so much love that I (Rosie) didn't know what to do with it.

I was so focused on the *doing* parts of the conference and making sure it was a transformative experience that I was only partially present and couldn't fully take in the gratitude and love. I had people coming up to me saying they were "geeking out" to meet me and thanking me for the conference. Instead of just saying "thank you," I'd reply with some self-deprecating comment like "Well, once you know me, you'll know there's nothing to geek out about." And even though I know how much work and effort I personally put in to make Fusion 2.0 a reality, I immediately deflected and gave credit to the village that made it possible. Now, it's true there were many people that helped make it a reality; and it's great to share credit. But this was me not accepting or embracing my part or the gratitude they were gifting me, because my reactive story kicked in—that is, making sure the rest of the event stayed perfect and not wanting to appear like an egomaniac.

Countless people during the event stopped me, grabbed both of my shoulders, stood six inches from my face, looked at me with tears in their eyes, and said, "Thank you for this event. Thank you for your work. This is amazing. This is life-changing. This is the best conference I've ever been to. This is **so** needed. You **have** to do this again and keep this going!" I also had countless people advise me to just take it in. Jon gave an amazing heartfelt public speech of gratitude acknowledging me and the work—which ended with a room of two hundred people giving me a standing ovation. *What if the remaining days bomb? How are we going to pay for this and do this again?*

How can I live up to this? That's what was going through my head rather than being fully present and accepting these amazing gifts. It was too big—too much for me to hold in those moments. I received hand-written cards, emails, and calls from people afterwards also expressing how much Fusion 2.0 meant to them; yet I still couldn't process it. I was in hyper-doing mode trying to figure out how to cover the large debt we incurred to get it going and how we could make another one happen. It wasn't until several weeks afterwards that I was able to actually give myself permission to take it in; and when I did, I cried buckets of gratitude and gave myself the gift of self-compassion for being human.

As much as we need to *create fearless environments* and develop people to adopt more effective stories when they're negatively triggered to operate from their Reactionary Mind, we also need to create the conditions that nurture and foster being able to give and accept gratitude, love, and joy.

Sustainability Is Developing a Leadership Mindset in Everyone

We share all of this as context for why it is so important to develop **everyone**; so that we all have the opportunity to upgrade our IOS and *show up as leaders*. Think about the birds flying in a V formation, which we mentioned in chapter 5; if every bird does not *show up as a leader*, they will never be able to make it when traveling long distances. The same is true for organizations.

We need to all be able to show up as *enough* at the same time we work to become better versions of ourselves so that we can handle the adaptive challenges that the VUCA world presents us. The only way to do this is to approach development from the inside out; we can't fast-forward it. This is why this component of rehumanizing the workplace rests on a foundation of a humanistic culture; we have to *create fearless environments* where it is safe enough for people to reflect, *wade in the messy middle*, and try on new, more effective stories.

We need to stretch ourselves, embrace adaptive change work, and be able to transform ourselves and our organizations in order to thrive in this VUCA world. Grace Lee Boggs, a lifelong activist and philosopher for social justice, describes key leadership behaviors essential for transforming organizations:

- **Develop every member as a leader.** Organizations cannot depend on just a few charismatic leaders.
- **Leaders of a revolution must become more human.** In order to transform the world, we must transform ourselves.
- **Leaders must learn to think dialectically.** In other words, we need to leverage greater mental complexity because our reality is constantly changing.[137]

So if you want to join the revolution already underway to rehumanize workplaces, it's imperative to develop everyone to embrace discomfort, become more human, and upgrade their IOS. Research on more than thirty thousand leaders from thousands of companies in more than one hundred countries further supports this.[138] Being an effective, conscious leader starts with being self-aware and able to manage our own thoughts, behaviors, and actions. This requires being aware of when our ego or Big Assumption is in the driver's seat (triggering us to show up in self-protection, reactionary mode) and preventing us from learning from our mistakes. We also need to embrace our imperfections and start being curious so we can see others as *people*. When we do the developmental work to operate from the late self-authoring developmental stages and beyond, we are much more likely to be effective navigating the VUCA world.

A Four-Step Framework for Developing **Everyone** as a Leader

Keeping in mind the research on what it takes to have meaningful change, high-performing, human organizations, and thriving individuals, we follow a four-step framework for leadership (a.k.a. **people**) development that takes an inside-out approach and focuses on upgrading our IOS. There's a lot that goes into each step, so we are intentionally providing you with a few key concepts and exercises we use at each step with individuals and teams that help them *show up as leaders* in all areas of their lives. Our hope is that you can use these to grow yourself and share with others so our collective leadership capacity grows.

Step 1: Enhancing Self-Awareness

Margaret Wheatley said, "We can't trust ourselves to be perfect or to never cause harm and hurt. But we can get curious about who we are and how our mind works. We can learn to know our triggers, habitual reactions and our strengths and weaknesses. The more we know ourselves and our filters, the more we can see beyond them—and the more trustworthy we can become. A natural consequence of getting to know ourselves is humility."[139]

Too often people want to skip past this step. However, self-awareness is a cornerstone of developing emotional intelligence and resiliency. It is essential to being able to do the transformative work required to work on the *inner game* and upgrade our IOS. You can't expect people to behave differently while using an outdated operating system. The late leadership guru Peter Drucker said, "You cannot manage other people unless you manage yourself first." Most leadership training and education is backwards; it starts with strategy, finance, operations, and people management. According to Drucker, this approach is like building a house starting with the roof; it starts at the end and misses the beginning.[140]

This step is all about us getting to know ourselves at a deeper level—when we have gifts and strengths to leverage, when our triggers self-protect, and where we need to pause and self-manage more in order to maximize our positive impact on those around us. We could spend an entire book just on this step, as it is that important and transformative. It's amazing how lacking we collectively are in self-awareness—and what's possible when we start paying attention and owning our own stuff.

This step is where leveraging various assessments can be useful to foster greater self-awareness. Whether or not you have access or training to use assessments, the value of spending time doing work on self-awareness helps people pay attention to their inner narrative and see the impact they're having, illuminates what happens when their reactive selves take over, and provides groups a common language to use to foster greater understanding. For more than a decade, we consistently start all people development work with describing the concept of The Frame[141]—the lens through which we view the world that influences the choices we make and actions we take.

The Frame

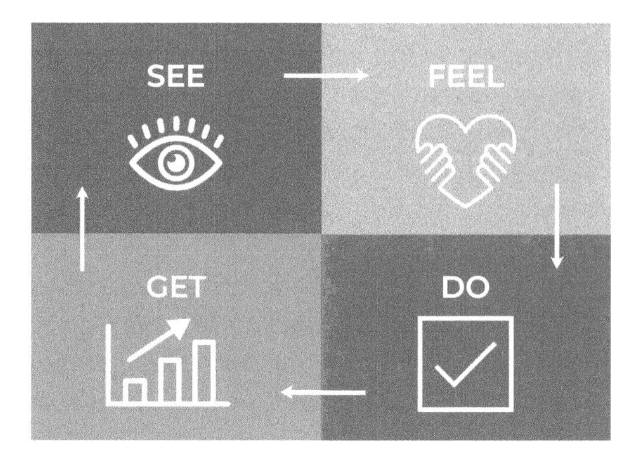

How we choose to **see** a person, ourselves, or a situation (i.e., our inner narrative) influences how we feel about it and ultimately what we **do**. What we **do** gets us some kind of result that we usually use to reinforce how we **see** it. Here's the example we always use: Let's say you're going for a walk, you look over in some nearby woods, and you **see** an angry-looking tiger. How are you likely going to feel? If you're like most people who we asked this question to, you probably instinctively said "scared." And if you're scared, what are you likely going to do? Again, if you're like most people, you probably instinctively said "run." That will get you a pretty predictable, physiological fight-or-flight response that will reinforce your **see** of averting a near-death experience. And now you'll probably have a nice, dramatic story to tell at social gatherings for months, or even years, to come.

Now, let's say you're going for a walk, you look over at the same nearby woods, but you don't actually see a tiger; you see a cardboard cutout of Tony the Tiger, the Frosted Flakes mascot. Now, how are you likely going to feel? Like most people, you probably didn't have a quick answer. Perhaps you said "amused" or "confused" or "hungry" or "grrrrreat!" And with those guiding your **do**, you probably didn't say you'd run. Perhaps you'd keep walking. Or perhaps you'd go up and take a selfie with it. Regardless, you're not going to have that same fight-or-flight response and have a much less dramatic and significant result that you may not ever even mention it to anyone.

The point of these examples is that, in either case, your actions make complete sense based on how you saw the situation. If you honestly thought your life was in danger, of course you're going to run; if you don't think your life was in danger, it would be a little odd to run. If we honestly perceive a threat, of course we're going to self-protect. Our behaviors are the outward manifestation of our thinking, our IOS, or how we **see** things. So if we want to behave differently and have lasting change, we need to *wade in the messy middle* to rewrite our inner narrative and how we **see** things. This is why learning to pause is so critical—so we're not instinctively reacting as if there's a tiger ready to eat us when there's nothing more than a cardboard cutout.

After we introduce The Frame to people, we spend time anchoring all other work in step 1 on the **see** box. This is about helping people start to challenge their inner narrative and see how different their experiences are based on the stories they tell themselves. One of the staple exercises we use is based on *The 15 Commitments of Conscious Leadership*[142] and what we refer to as The Choice Line. How we **see** things is fundamentally different depending on whether we are "above the line" or "below the line." When we are above the line, we tend to be more open, curious, collaborative, empathetic, resilient, and energetic; as a result, we tend to be more committed to learning. When we're below the line, we tend to be judgmental, defensive, closed off, guarded, pessimistic, and sometimes apathetic; as a result, we tend to be committed to being right. And, as we learned in chapter 2, when we're committed to being right, we cannot show up authentically.

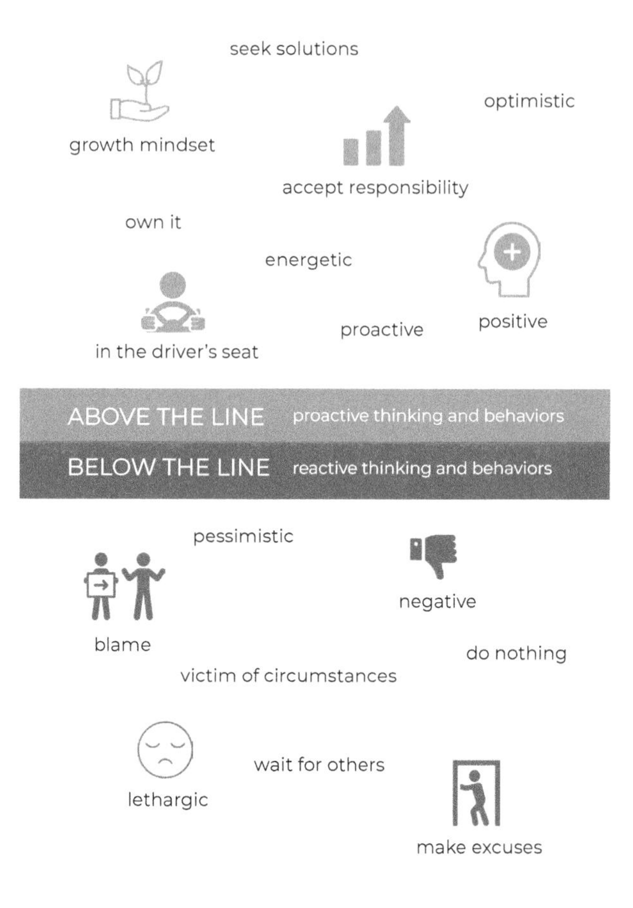

We walk people through self-reflection questions to help them identify how they show up and know they are above the line and below the line. We also ask people to identify how they **see** others (i.e., their inner narrative) when they are above vs. below the line. For example, if we're above the line, we're likely to see our colleagues and loved ones as caring, hardworking, well intended, smart, and creative. However, when we're below the line, we're likely to see them as annoying, lazy, disrespectful, incompetent, and uncaring. Then we ask people to identify their triggers that tend to easily pull them below the line. If we can be aware of our inner narrative and know our triggers, then we can hopefully break the Reactive Mind cycle. So we ask people to identify their "trampolines" that can help them spring back above the line when they realize they've dropped below the line or are likely to encounter a trigger. Some common trampolines are going for a short walk, listening to a favorite or motivational song, watching a funny video clip, reading an inspirational quote, looking at pictures of loved ones, getting out in nature, or simply taking a few deep breaths and repeating personal mantras.

When we recognize that we're below the line, or know we're likely to encounter a trigger that will bring us below the line, we can surround ourselves with trampolines that can prevent us from being hijacked by our reactive, self-protective selves. And when we can't find a trampoline large enough to spring us back above the line, the best thing we can do is honor our humanity and then go below the line in a protective bubble. This means avoiding making any major life decisions or having important conversations. It also means letting people around us know we're not in a good spot so they can hopefully support us and not resort to creating unnecessary stories about why we're showing up a certain way.

From a team perspective, this simple exercise starts to give people a common language. We encourage them to check in at the start of their day, meetings, or huddles with a quick pulse of where everyone is in relation to The Choice Line. Some teams even use quick hand signals; thumbs-up for above the line, thumbs-down for below the line, or flat hand for hovering at the line. We encourage people to communicate when they're below the line. This doesn't give them a free pass to be a jerk to others; however, it does let others know this may be a day to give that person more space or not go to that person with something requiring his or her best thinking. It gives them a nonthreatening way to check in with each other and start to be more intentional about owning their inner narrative.

Ingredients to Be My Best

We have numerous other exercises we use to help foster greater self-awareness that build on The Frame and The Choice Line. For the purposes of this book, our intention is to give you the "golden ticket" ones that you can use immediately—with yourself and others. Since the core of *showing up as a leader* is becoming the best version of yourself, one of the exercises we like to use is called "Ingredients to Be My Best." Think about who you are when you're at your best and what the surrounding conditions around you are that allow you to show up as your best self. We literally give people a paper with several of the following statements and ask them to fill in the blanks:

I'm at my best when ______ .

As an example, Roger was doing this exercise and started filling in the blanks of when he's at his best. His answers included the following: *when I've had a good night's sleep; when I start my day with quiet time with the newspaper and a cup of coffee; when I've had time to be fully present with my kids; when I can get out in nature; when I have down time at the end of the day.*

Next, think about what the recipe is that allows the *I'm at my best when* statements to be realized; what are the ingredients that increase the likelihood your *I'm at my best* experience will happen? As Roger thought about his list, he noted the following ingredients:

- Going to bed by ten p.m.
- Setting up the coffee maker the night before and setting my alarm for five a.m.
- Not taking work home
- Putting my phone away when I'm with my family
- Watching the weather forecast the night before
- Planning a walking break during my day; schedule it as a recurring meeting
- Blocking my calendar at the end of the day

It may seem like a no-brainer, but making the list was eye-opening to Roger. He realized there were many simple actions he could take that would support him in showing up as the best version of himself, yet he was mostly leaving it to chance—or ignoring the importance of them. We frequently hear this. We'll ask people, "For how many of you is this the first time ever—or in a long time—that you've actually thought about what you need to be your best self?" Most people's hands will go up. How can we even begin to work toward bringing more of our best selves out into the world if we don't even know what that looks like or what we need for that to happen? And from a team standpoint, we encourage people to share some of their lists so they can support each other in tending to those ingredients; they know that when everyone has the ability to show up as their best selves, the team—and organization—benefits.

When we invite people into self-awareness work, the results are profound. They are able to get off autopilot and start pausing and acting with intention rather than reacting.

We were working with a team to help them communicate more effectively, build resiliency, and improve collaboration. We put them through our Developing a Leadership Mindset program (which we'll detail later in this chapter). This program includes six group sessions with individual practical application work in between each session.

Brad is a member of one of the teams that was participating in Developing a Leadership Mindset. He had a history of being defensive, attached to his "rightness," and blaming others. He was also constantly stressed but wouldn't ask for or accept help. When we introduced The Frame, Brad just sat there with his arms crossed and rolled his eyes. Then we walked the team through The Choice Line exercise. Brad participated and completed the reflections in his workbook, but it was evident he still hadn't bought into the work; from his perspective, everyone else needed this work, not him.

After the first session, everyone completed an assessment—the Judgment Index; this particular assessment measures the thinking behind our choices and the judgments we make—at work and in our personal lives. Everyone received their individual results, and we ran a team composite report. During the second session with this team, we walked through key combinations of scores and how those can contribute to frustrations. Brad had a combination of scores that started to explain how he habitually shows up. He was very perfectionistic and impatient; he also had a strong "I'll do it myself" tendency and was unlikely to ask for help. These tendencies started to create a perfect storm, increasing his stress and leading to neglecting his self-care.

Brad started to see what was contributing to his regular below-the-line thinking and was better understanding his triggers. He also saw how this pattern was preventing him from having the impact he wanted to have—at work and at home. We then walked the team through another exercise where they look at where they've been stuck in an inward mindset with another person. We ask them to write down what the other person does, how they see that person, and how they behave toward that person. Then we ask participants to switch workbooks; they fill in their partner's workbook with how they would see their partner based on what their partner wrote about how they behave toward this other person. Brad got his workbook back from his partner. Under the section for how the other person sees him, his partner wrote, "pain in the ass; uncaring; controlling; jerk." That stung and was a wake-up call for Brad. His knee-jerk reaction to assert his rightness was contributing to his stress and frustration; **he** was part of the problem! By the end of the second session, Brad finally decided to embrace the work. He *waded in the messy middle* to take his newfound self-awareness and begin to do the work to rewrite his inner narrative.

We encourage you to leverage The Frame and The Choice Line and to complete your own Ingredients to Be My Best exercise. These simple exercises can have a profound impact on your ability to be less reactive and help you start to be more intentional. Invite your team members, friends, and family to do these exercises with you; build a common language and equip others so you can all *show up as leaders* and embrace an outward mindset to see others as people.

Step 2: Building Effective Thinking Skills

Once people have greater self-awareness, they can begin the journey to upgrade their IOS and show up in the world in a more intentional way. Viktor Frankl once said, "When we are no longer able to change a situation, we are challenged to change ourselves."[143] We can't control most situations around us; so changing ourselves is all about being able to recognize the stories that aren't serving us well (or are coming at a great cost) and then rewriting those stories to better serve us and others.

We walk individuals and teams through exercises to recognize how powerful their stories are and what happens when they are "married" to their own stories and assume their interpretation is *right*. We can start to rewrite our narratives and stories about people and situations that trigger us by first recognizing that our current reality is based on our own doing. Start using the language, "The story I'm telling myself is ______ ." This helps us realize what we're experiencing is a result of our own inner narrative, and it creates an opportunity to try on a new story. It also forces us to pause and be less reactionary.

Here's an example of how we might begin to rewrite our inner narrative:

Old Narrative/Story	**New Narrative/Story**
My value is equal to how much I accomplish.	I am *enough*, regardless of what I do and don't accomplish.
If I let people see the real me, they'll realize I don't know what I'm doing.	Being myself is not bad; even if it doesn't work out, I won't reject myself.
If I'm not perfect or I mess up, people will think less of me/won't like me.	My authentic voice, no matter how messy, connects me to other humans.
If I have to ask for help, it means I am weak.	People get as much pleasure out of helping me as I get from helping them.

If I want it done right, I must do it myself.	We can create more together than I ever could on my own.
It's all up to me.	When I do it for them, I rob them of their learning and opportunity to grow.
I must do it perfectly right out of the gate.	I am a work in progress.

Rewriting our inner narrative and *believing* it are not necessarily the same thing. However, it helps us start to see that we have the ability to change the stories we tell ourselves. And we can start to create new mantras to help us as we work toward truly believing our new stories.

Another large part of being able to upgrade our IOS and rewrite our inner narrative is embracing our own humanity—our imperfections. We are so hard on ourselves and can set unrealistic expectations. One of the exercises we have people do is a *Self-Gratitude Reflection.* We invite them to spend a few weeks ending their day with two reflection questions:

1. What went well for me today; and what qualities about myself am I grateful for?
2. What did I learn about myself today?

The first question is to help people start to be more self-accepting and to acknowledge their gifts. The irony is that many people struggle with this. The second question is written very intentionally to help people embrace struggle, disappointment, and failure as a valuable gift of learning. If people like to journal, we invite them to actually create a *Self-Gratitude Journal.* Otherwise, we invite them to just mentally reflect. After a few weeks, we consistently hear people say they are starting to be a little kinder and gentler to themselves. We also invite them to use these questions in team meetings to reflect on what's going well collectively and what people are learning. Many people have said they now use these questions at home with their families as well.

Additionally, we also leverage coaching and Immunity to Change work (individually and at a team level) to help people upgrade their IOS. We were working with a leadership team that needed to collaboratively lead one of the organization's locations. We put them through our Building a Cohesive Leadership Team program (which we'll detail later in this chapter). This program includes seven or eight group sessions with individual practical application work in between. Some of that individual work included completing their Immunity to Change (ITC) maps, then going through the follow-up coaching exercises to help them move beyond the grips of their Big Assumptions (BA) and psychological immunity. Prior to doing this work, there were many tensions between the leaders, and trust was pretty low. They were all showing up in self-protective mode; some showed up in a hyper-controlling and judgmental way, while others withdrew and became passive. And they all had unproductive assumptions and narratives about each other.

As the program continued, they each started to see where their Big Assumptions (BAs) stopped them and what it cost them. The controlling leader had a BA that everything was essentially life-or-death and that if she didn't control the outcomes, things would fall apart; then she'd be a failure and alone. She also had a BA that her sole value came from her accomplishments; so if she delegated to others, what value would she have? The passive leader had a BA that if she spoke up, she might look silly and would then be viewed as incompetent, would be rejected, and would further her *not enough* and *unlovable* story. Another leader on this team had a BA that her sole value comes from taking care of things and being helpful; so she was constantly overextending herself with the team she supported and then not doing the work she needed to get done for the leadership team. Each person had a different BA, yet at the core they were all the same . . . behaving in self-protecting ways to overcompensate for or avoid the feelings of not being *enough*.

At one point toward the end of the program, we invited them all to share their BAs with each other (totally optional). As they did, you could see the level of relief and empathy increase in the room; they each began to realize how similar they all were. Once they knew each other's BAs and triggers, they moved from fighting one another to supporting one another and helping to challenge one another's stories when they were triggered. They are a completely different, cohesive team now because they *waded in the messy middle* and dug in to focus on their *inner game*. They take off their armor and start each meeting checking in to see how people are doing and whether they're in a triggered state or not. They embrace an outward mindset and focus on how they can support one another and their respective teams. They have compassion when one of them does get hijacked by their BA and Reactive Mind. As a result of doing the work to improve their thinking, their outer game also improved; their turnover decreased, meetings are more efficient, decision-making improved, and even their customer satisfaction scores for their location improved.

It takes time, intention, and embracing the discomfort of *wading in the messy middle* to build more effective thinking and upgrade our IOS. At the core is rewriting the stories we tell ourselves. It also means we need to embrace our gifts while also giving ourselves and others grace for being imperfectly human.

Step 3: Developing and Fostering Quality Relationships so Others Can Grow

The first two steps in developing people provide such a critical foundation to this step. Most traditional development efforts start here; but it assumes that the skills, techniques, and applications are being installed on an operating system that can support it. Yet nearly 75 percent of us are not operating from a place of awareness, vision, and intentionality. So until we upgrade our IOS, any books, training, or development efforts focused on enhancing leadership practices won't work; the operating system can't support it. If you do nothing more than spend time fostering greater self-awareness and building better thinking skills, you'll be much further along than most people and less likely to be triggered by the disruption of our VUCA world.

Once we've done the work to upgrade our IOS, we can focus on essential aspects of developing and fostering quality relationships. One of the best ways to develop and nurture quality relationships by giving others the gift of our full presence and fully listening to them. Yet we rarely do that in our distracted world; and we are more disconnected than ever. The reality is that most of us don't listen from a place of curiosity with the intent to truly understand another person's experience; we listen with the intent to reply. Consequently, people don't feel heard or seen, and disconnection grows.

Listening well is a skill; and it can't be done if we aren't self-aware and are showing up guarded in self-protective mode. So, once we reach this step of the development framework, we spend time teaching people how to first set a clear intention going into any interaction with an individual or group; take thirty seconds to ask yourself, "What am I wanting for the other person in this conversation? And what am I wanting for myself?" When we set an intention to pause, be curious, and listen to understand, we set a powerful tone for a productive conversation.

Of course we usually have to reset our intentions over and over; when we notice our internal dialogue of judgment, wanting to reply and insert our own ideas, and checking out, we can simply acknowledge it, remind ourselves of our initial intentions, and then choose to turn up the volume of the other person. The next step of listening well is to respond to others with curiosity and open and honest questions; these are questions that help people continue to process their own thinking and gain greater clarity about what is really important in a situation and what matters most. Some examples include:

- Given what you just shared, what are you wanting for yourself in this situation?
- As you hear yourself say all of that, what is standing out that's important to you?
- What else is important here?
- How else are you thinking about this?
- What will tell you that you're headed in the right direction?

These types of questions create a space for other people to expand their thinking. And they also signal that we are truly interested in understanding their experiences (versus inserting ourselves into the mix). We can all practice building our skills to listen better. And it's only when we know how to listen well that we can possible apply any techniques or skills that support others in their growth and development.

With a foundation of self-awareness, an upgraded IOS, and listening well, we are much better equipped to be able to develop others and call them to greatness. So we also leverage and teach people the principles of Kim Scott's *Radical Candor.*[144] One of the benefits of psychologically safe work environments is that they foster candor; if people don't feel they can speak up about something that might be a safety, ethical, or other risk, or withhold new ideas, organizations suffer. Kim Scott defines Radical Candor as the critical intersection of caring personally and challenging directly. In other words, I care about you enough to give you feedback and offer support to help you grow. After all, we all have blind spots. Unless someone cares about us enough to let us know when we're getting in our own way, we have no opportunity to improve.

Keith (not his real name) is a senior leader for a west coast location of one of our clients. He's a people pleaser to a fault. One of his Big Assumptions

(BA) is: *I can't have corrective conversations that might hurt people and have them like and respect me; they can't coexist.* And another BA he has is: *It's my job to shoulder the stress and discomfort and protect people from it. If I ever let people down, I won't be loved.* So it's not surprising that Keith used to avoid any sort of corrective feedback conversation. However, this caused great frustration with the team as they saw him not deal with issues. And when he did, Keith would be stressed for days leading up to the conversation and ruminate for days afterwards. His stress levels were through the roof, and he was struggling.

We started working with Keith on some basic self-awareness with assessments, The Frame, The Choice Line, and other reflective exercises. Then we began the Immunity to Change (ITC) coaching process with him. As he *waded in the messy middle*, we presented the concept of Radical Candor to him. Keith started to reframe his inner narrative from *giving feedback is hard and will have people not like me* to *not giving feedback is selfish and robbing others of the opportunity to grow.* When we reached the point in the ITC process where he was designing and running tests of his Big Assumptions, most of the tests included Radical Candor conversations. Slowly but surely, Keith started to see how he was far more supportive by having these conversations and that people in their office were performing better. His stress also improved. People started to respect Keith more because he cared enough to give them feedback and was no longer shielding them from their own discomfort and growth work.

Fully listening and Radical Candor are essential ingredients to fostering quality relationships and developing others. We find that they come into play with any other technique, framework, or resource that might be used at this step. After all, how can we expect relationships to strengthen or others to grow if we can't be authentic and transparent with them?

Step 4: Growing the Organization

Once people have done their inner work, the outer work can begin. In other words, once they are self-aware, know how to get out of their own way and bring better thinking into their interactions, and can foster quality relationships, they're in a position to help grow the organization. Growing the organization is not just about sales and expansion; it also includes improving efficiencies, processes, and operations that support people in doing their best work and furthering the company's purpose.

Our friends at the Chapman & Co. Leadership Institute have a great process that *builds a lighthouse* to guide organizational improvements and foster alignment with purpose (i.e., **WHY**).

Basically, everything starts with the company's purpose or **WHY** (which we'll be detailing more in the next chapter). We know that we aren't always effective in showing up as our best selves and living our **WHY**; we are human, after all. This simple, yet helpful, process honors that and provides a streamlined way to identify the gaps and root causes for what is getting in our way of being able to live and further the organization's purpose and *show up as a leader.*

With using the company purpose as a foundation, we can work to engage the organization. This is where we put our listening skills into practice and find out where we are effectively living our **WHY** and where there are gaps and barriers getting in our way. Whether it's via formal daily huddles, listening sessions, or informal touch-base conversations, this process anchors on asking people:

- What's getting in the way of you living your **WHY** today? or
- What's getting in the way of you showing up as a leader and being fully effective today?

It's about identifying sources of frustration and improvement opportunities—real time. This allows us to adapt to the ever-changing disruption our VUCA world brings. The key to this being effective, and not just an invitation for unproductive complaining and blaming, is asking a follow-up question:

- And what's the **impact** that has on you?

This second question is important because it weeds out "recreational complaining" or someone who is showing up triggered and committed to being right and blaming others, and helps decipher legitimate frustrations, gaps, and improvement opportunities.

Engaging the organization effectively depends on our quality of listening. As we listen to understand gaps, barriers, and the impact they have on people, we want to listen for key patterns and themes. This is not about jumping to problem-solving at this point; it's about gathering information to fully understand any gaps; it's slowing down so we can effectively propel forward.

Then we can move into the final step of bringing your WHY to life. Essentially, what we do next is to take the common themes regarding any gaps and barriers to living the organization's purpose (WHY), and any suggestions and improvement opportunities, and categorize them into one of three categories: Quick fixes, short-term projects, and long-term change.

Quick Fixes	Short-Term Projects	Long-Term Change
Easy, low-hanging fruit items that can be fixed with minimal cost or effort, yet can make a huge impact in building trust and showing people they are heard *Examples:* Updating an outdated policy Fixing something broken Providing adequate supplies Etc.	Changes that take a little more effort but can likely be accomplished in a fairly short time frame *Examples:* Creating more opportunities for people to get to know their colleagues better Improving timeliness and relevance of communication Etc.	Will take deliberate thought, planning, and resources to support *Examples:* Developing and communicating clear career paths Changing organizational structure to better foster collaboration and reduce silos Etc.

Once we've categorized the gaps and improvement opportunities, we then need to determine if the gaps are due to individual behaviors or ineffective systems. Most of the time, a faulty system is at play (e.g., clunky processes requiring workarounds, outdated procedures, operational hiccups); and a faulty system will circumvent good intentions any day of the week. This is an opportunity to *find your tribe* and engage others in discussions, process-mapping work, and more to create the path moving forward.

We have found this process to be extremely helpful for people. So often people think that this step is reserved for executive leaders or people whose role is business development. However, in a VUCA world demanding that everyone *show up as a leader*, we need everyone to be able to help the organization grow. We need everyone to be able to identify and address gaps and leverage the collective wisdom of those closest to the work. Besides, when people are involved in the process for growth and improvement, they tend to be more engaged and supportive of change efforts.

We do a lot of culture-visioning (a.k.a. *building a lighthouse*) work with our clients. When people are engaged in the process to create a shared vision of what a thriving workplace looks like, and what it will take to make that vision a reality, they *show up as leaders* fueled by energy and passion. The Chapman & Co. Leadership Institute alignment process helps guide people to make productive, solution-oriented contributions.

With one of our clients, we facilitated several Lighthouse Workshops (culture visioning). During each workshop, people were invited to provide their input on what "thriving" looked like for them when they were consistently living their **WHY** and people were able to show up authentically, have fulfilling work, learn and grow, become the best version of themselves, and go home with energy left to show up fully in their personal lives (part 1 of this alignment process). Then we asked people what they collectively need to start, stop, and continue doing in order for that shared vision to be a reality (part 2 of this alignment process).

We summarized the collective feedback and then leveraged their culture ambassadors for step 3 of the process; we asked them to categorize each start and stop suggestion as a behavior or system improvement and whether it was a short, medium, or long-term change. Finally, because we can only do so much at one time, we asked them to determine their priorities for the upcoming year by selecting one long-term change, two to three medium-term changes, and three to four short-term, quick fixes. The culture ambassadors then communicated the improvement plan (and the process for how they landed on their priorities) to their colleagues and engaged them to continue to be part of the process to implement the improvements. By including everyone in the process, there was greater energy to share responsibility for the next steps to grow and improve the organization.

Transforming Workplaces One Team at a Time

We have had profound learning over the past few years that led to us rethink what it actually takes to transform workplaces. As we said at the beginning of this book, while it's true that having senior leadership support is helpful, it's not a deal-breaker. **You don't have to start at the top in order to transform workplaces to become more human. You can start locally—one person, one team at a time.** Much like the spirit of grassroots organizing, momentum can build and spread throughout the organization like a groundswell; it doesn't require a formal strategy being pushed down from the top of a hierarchy.

This realization started with one of our clients desperately seeking help for a team that was struggling with communication, in-fighting, and turnover. We created an early version of our Developing a Leadership Mindset program (DALM) to try to help them. The DALM program followed our four-step leadership development framework to help them be more self-aware, build a common language, take off some of their armor, communicate more effectively, and create a shared vision and guiding principles for how they wanted to show up with each other. Even though none of the people on the team had people leadership responsibilities, we anchored the program on the premise that everyone has the opportunity to show up as a leader and that they each play a role in the current state of the team culture. We also let them know that the content and exercises included in the DALM program were taken from years of life and leadership coaching; if they showed up and did the work, they would likely also experience great personal benefits. It was simply an experiment to see if we could help this team. And it did help: they slowly, but surely, started listening to each other, pausing before they acted, assuming positive intent with each other; and they even reported being less stressed as they were able to also use the principles at home.

The leader of that department was so pleased with the progress and began talking to other leaders. Next thing you know, we had requests to provide DALM for other teams. With each delivery, we refined and enhanced the program. To our delight, we started hearing a common language throughout the halls as teams leveraged the program principles to check in with each other and communicate when they were struggling. We were hearing feedback from leaders on what a positive difference it was making. At the same time, the teams were asking us, "When are the leaders going through this?" Fair question. Here they were experiencing greater self-awareness, being more intentional about how they showed up, and trying to cocreate their desired team culture, but their leaders were still operating on autopilot.

So we tried another experiment and offered Building a Cohesive Leadership Team (BACLT) for a group of leaders that needed to collaborate to lead a department. We used Developing a Leadership Mindset (DALM) as a template and purposely had lots of overlap with content and exercises so they would have a common framework, language, and way of being with each other. However, with BACLT, we focused more intentionally on them becoming a cohesive team and building trust, following some of the principles of building organizational health from Patrick Lencioni. We also included additional content for how they could lead their teams through positive change in a VUCA world, and we added individual coaching and Immunity to Change work.

By the end of the program, the leaders were more cohesive; trusted each other more; were asking for and accepting help, making better decisions, embracing accountability, and experiencing greater harmony between their work and personal lives. Then the same phenomenon happened with Building a Cohesive Leadership Team as we experienced with Developing a Leadership Mindset; the leaders started talking to their colleagues, and the requests came flooding in to help other leadership teams. After eight to ten months, we started to see a profound difference. The work people were engaged in with these two programs was building energy and momentum throughout the organization. And probably because it was organic and at the grassroots level (versus some strategic initiative from the CEO), it became a transformative movement and then started to get the attention of the senior leadership team—enough that they wanted to experience the program themselves.

Think about the strong, courageous students of Marjory Stoneman Douglas High School in Parkland, Florida. Their lives changed forever on February 15, 2018, when they survived one of the deadliest school shootings in US history. Rather than sitting back and waiting for Congress to do something about gun violence, these teenagers stood up and spoke up. They *built a lighthouse* and rallied people across the country, bringing high visibility and eloquent speeches into the mainstream so that their friends' lives were not lost in vain. They got the attention of political leaders, and their incredible display of leadership even made the cover of *Time Magazine*. They started from the ground up and built momentum for positive change.

When people feel connected to a purpose or cause, they *show up as leaders*. So why would we think that things would be any different inside an organization? When people have energy and passion and are engaged in transformative development work that they see is making a difference in their lives, they share. Energy and momentum build and build; and many times much more so than if this started at the top and was positioned as another business initiative to roll out across the organization.

We have since refined both programs and have implemented this grassroots strategy at several organizations—with the same receptive energy. They follow our four-step framework, taking an inside-out approach to development. Building a Cohesive Leadership Team and Developing a Leadership Mindset are designed to have overlap and be run either in parallel or tandem with each other. Both programs include practical application exercises to be done in between each session and are typically offered at three- to four-week intervals to give people time to sit with the previous session's materials and apply the principles. Here is a high-level overview of what we cover in each program:

	Developing a Leadership Mindset (DALM)	Building a Cohesive Leadership Team (BACLT)
	Designed for intact work teams to support them in being more self-aware and showing up as leaders, effectively communicating and navigating change, building psychological safety and resiliency, and aligning with the organization's purpose.	Designed for leadership teams who need to collaborate and support others in aligning with the organization's purpose and achieving business goals. The focus is on parameters necessary to build organizational health and become a cohesive team and move from armored to daring leadership, including: building trust, being more self-aware, effectively communicating a clear vision, navigating and leading change, building psychological safety and resiliency, and aligning teams with the organization's purpose.
Session 1	**Enhancing Self-Awareness** A foundational session focused on self-awareness so people can own who they are during any interaction and be more aware of when their thinking is and isn't serving them well. Participants also complete a psychological safety assessment.	**Building the Foundation for Becoming a Cohesive Team** Review of the importance and framework of organizational health, the Work of Leadership, the realities of VUCA, and upgrading our IOS. The leadership team assesses its current level of effectiveness and trust and then begins self-awareness work central to improving trust and cohesion.
Session 2	**Understanding the Thinking Behind Our Choices** We look at patterns of thinking that guide our choices (leveraging the Judgment Index). The goal is to further self-awareness so individuals and the team can leverage their strengths and manage frustrations.	**Recognizing and Upgrading Our Inner Narrative** We look at what triggers us to self-protect, Inward vs. Outward mindsets, and how to start embracing vulnerability as a path to courageous leadership.

Session 3	**Improving Team Dynamics via Building Effective Thinking** How to leverage greater self-awareness to self-manage and make better choices, communicate more effectively, and increase the likelihood that all team members can bring the best versions of themselves into every interaction.	**Understanding the Thinking Behind Our Choices** We look at patterns of thinking that guide our choices (leveraging the Judgment Index). The goal is to further self-awareness so individuals and the team can leverage their strengths and manage frustrations. Then individual Immunity to Change work starts in between sessions.
Session 3a (optional for BACLT)		**Understanding and Managing Our Reputation to Have Maximum Impact** In this optional session, we leverage the Hogan assessment to help individuals and the team see the impact (or lack thereof) they have depending on whether their Reactive or Creative IOS is in charge.
Session 4	**Reframing Conflict and Leveraging It to Strengthen Relationships** We invite people to reframe conflict as a call to creativity for a win-win by focusing on clarifying needs, letting go of being "right," leveraging Radical Candor, removing drama, and avoiding Unproductive Triangles.	**Improving Team Dynamics via Daring Leadership** The focus is helping leaders start to be more vulnerable with each other, learn how to fully listen to understand, and then leverage an outward mindset to strengthen relationships and grow their Sphere of Influence.

Session 5	**Clarifying Our WHY and Defining Our Desired Workplace Culture** Teams are guided through exercises to help them see how they connect with the organization's purpose (**WHY**) and key behavioral anchors required to live the purpose. Then they engage in a culture-visioning exercise to create their team *Shared Culture and Guiding Principles* that articulates what is needed for them to thrive, live the organization's purpose, and bring their best selves to work; this lays the groundwork for holding one another accountable to be intentional about showing up as a leader and making a positive impact.	**Reframing Conflict and Leveraging It to Strengthen Relationships** We invite people to reframe conflict as a call to creativity for a win-win by focusing on clarifying needs, letting go of being "right," leveraging Radical Candor, removing drama, and avoiding Unproductive Triangles. We then help them leverage peer coaching to support one another and call each other to greatness.
Session 6	**Living Into Our WHY and Desired Workplace Culture** This session focuses on creating a culture of accountability for living the **WHY** and desired culture on a daily basis. People are also taught how to leverage Personal Recognition Messages. We also reassess psychological safety.	**Creating Clarity and Committing to Our Guiding Principles of Leadership** We leverage a framework for how leaders can engage their team to live the organization's **WHY** and thoughtfully identify gaps; clarify non-negotiables and what they need to Start, Stop, and Continue; and commit to what's most important in the next twelve months.
Session 7 (BACLT only)		**Engaging Our Teams to Live our WHY** How to engage teams in a shared purpose, leveraging F.B.I. feedback and recognition, BA sharing, and Team Effectiveness exercise; reassessing trust and team effectiveness; setting intentions; and clarifying next steps.

We've also learned that reinforcing concepts post-program is key to sustainability. So we provide the leader of each team with a program synopsis that includes key actions, conversation starters, and a checklist with actions they can take in team and one-on-one meetings to help keep the content of the program alive. We also send all participants reinforcement and reminder emails at thirty, sixty, ninety, and one hundred and twenty days after the last session. And we started building in a regroup session approximately four months after the last session; the regroup session is customized based on where the group is, and helps continue to support them in keeping the principles alive in their daily work practices.

A little over two years ago, Teresa asked us to facilitate Developing a Leadership Mindset for her clinic team. They were struggling with turnover, engagement issues (her team had one of the lowest scores on the company-wide employee engagement survey), communication challenges, and overall poor morale. Not surprisingly, this was interfering with them being able to effectively collaborate with other teams and ultimately provide exceptional patient care.

Each session, her team showed up fully present and embraced the work. They recognized how much their attachment to being "right" was getting in the way, and started moving from an inward to an outward mindset. By the time they arrived at the last session, it was like being with an entirely new team that acted more like a family than a group of guarded enemies. One of the discussions we have during the last session surrounds keeping this work alive. We ask everyone to set an intention to their teammates for something they want to continue to work on or keep in mind so they can show up as leaders and support living their desired culture they cocreated.

The infusion clinic team was already starting each daily huddle with a quick check-in with each other for where they are in relation to The Choice Line. And they wanted to go further and deepen their commitment to showing up as conscious leaders. They decided they were going to take turns leading a few minutes during their monthly team meeting on some topic from the program. Then they created a book club, reading and discussing books referenced during the program. They are a completely different, and effective, team who are all *showing up as leaders*. Here's how they describe their experience: "Through the Developing a Leadership Mindset program, our struggling team was able to recognize and break down our own behaviors and barriers, resulting in an ability to appreciate and utilize each other's talents and strengths. Our employee engagement survey results even improved from being one of the lowest scoring teams to the second highest scoring team throughout the entire organization."

We share our insights and breakthroughs with our programs to illustrate that this four-step, inside-out approach to development works to nurture leadership at all levels of the organization and enhances individual well-being. Focusing first and foremost on fostering greater self-awareness and then *wading in the messy middle* to upgrade our IOS makes a lasting difference. We invite you to use the resources and exercises we provided to call yourself and others to greatness. It is only when we all work to get off autopilot and be more conscious and less reactive that we can create a critical mass of leaders who can influence positive change.

How to *Show Up as a Leader* and Influence Change at This Part of the Pyramid

If we want people to *show up as leaders*—as the best version of themselves—we have to support their development from the inside out. We have to expand how we define leaders and stop assuming that development is only the job of the leadership development or training departments. Regardless of your role, you have an opportunity to do your own work to *show up as a leader* and also foster and support efforts to create the conditions for everyone around you to *show up as a leader*. Here are some ways you can *show up as a leader* and bring a humanistic culture to life:

- **Start owning and telling your story.** We all have a story to tell. Stories foster meaningful connection with others. At our core, we are all so similar; the more we share and realize our similarities, the easier it becomes to embrace an outward mindset and work together toward a common vision. And when your stories aren't serving you well, start trying on alternative, more productive stories. Challenge others around you to do the same.

- **Be aware of your Frame.** Take a cue from conscious leadership; pay attention to your inner narrative and how it shifts whether you are above the line or below the line. Be aware of your triggers, and leverage your trampolines to move above the line when you've dipped below the line. Consider incorporating these tools in workshops you may lead, or invite your colleagues to do this exercise. There's power in having a common language and framework to support one another.

- Start thinking of yourself as a leader—in all areas of your life. We all have self-limiting stories that stem from our Reactive Mind and can get in our way of true connection and being effective. *Wade in the messy middle*; embrace the discomfort; and do the work to upgrade your IOS and leverage more relevant stories. And embrace the principles of Radical Candor to call others to greatness to do the same.

- Tend to your ingredients to be your best. When you do, you can lead by example. Consider incorporating this exercise in workshops you may lead, or invite your colleagues to spend a few minutes doing this. It's nearly impossible to have collective success if, individually, people are not able to show up as the best version of themselves.

Chapter 8

PURPOSE OVER PROFIT

Creating engagement around a clear, simple set of priorities can function as a lighthouse, orienting behavior and providing a path toward a goal.

—DANIEL COYLE, *The Culture Code*[145]

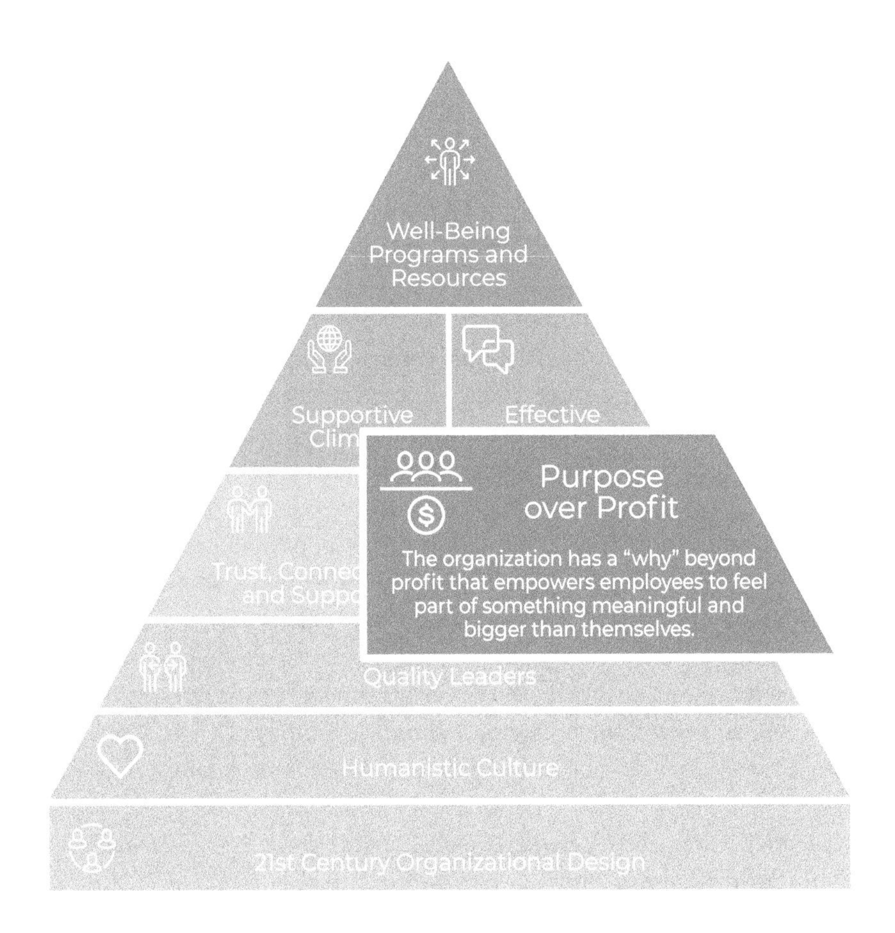

The VUCA seas present many challenges for sailors; some are straightforward, technical challenges, while others are messy, adaptive challenges. When waters become turbulent, it's a natural invitation for anxiety and chaos; how do we know which way to head to find land and safety? We look for the beacon of light cutting through the fog, darkness, and rough waters to help guide the way forward and provide energy to weather the rough patches along the way. In other words, we look for the lighthouse.

In the case of organizations, we must *build a lighthouse* to create that clarity and energy toward a brighter, thriving future. *Building a lighthouse* not only includes having a compelling purpose and vision; it's also setting clear parameters so people know what they need to do in order to *show up as leaders* and help the organization's purpose be realized on a daily basis. **This** is a key differentiator for organizations. Raj Sisodia, cofounder of Conscious Capitalism, articulates this well in discussing why purpose matters so much:

> The ultimate differentiator in the world is the amount of creative human energy that your enterprise is able to elicit and harness and channel. Everything else is a commodity. You can get machines and you can get people to do the physical work; but what you cannot really command is their true passionate commitment and therefore their inspired creativity. That only comes if people are operating out of a sense of purpose, and they're operating with a great deal of autonomy, and when they're operating in an environment of love and not fear. And so creating those conditions is essential.[146]

In his bestselling book *Start with WHY*, Simon Sinek states that great leaders are able to inspire people to act by providing a sense of purpose or belonging; they create a following of people who act for the good of the whole because they *want* to, not because they've been manipulated using fear, peer pressure, or incentives. Great leaders start with **WHY**.[147]

Simon uses the Golden Circle to provide a framework for inspiring action; it starts from the inside out with **WHY** we do what we do:

- WHY is a purpose, cause, or belief that is about our contribution to impact and serve others.

- HOW includes our Core Values (what makes our organization unique and our differentiating value proposition)—and translating those values into clear, actionable behavioral anchors that serve as guiding principles for how we show up each day. It is only through the discipline of **HOW** and being true to our Core Values to guide every decision we make (including holding the organization and every person accountable to these guiding principles) that we can actually realize and live our **WHY**. The **HOW**s allow our **WHY** to be realized; they go hand in hand.

- WHAT is simply what we do: the products and services our organization provides, or—for individuals—our job titles or roles.

Every organization and individual knows **WHAT** they do. Very few know **WHY** they do it—and have the discipline of **HOW** to bring their cause or purpose to life. The **WHY** is a belief; **HOW** are the actions you take to realize that belief. Both should remain constant; what evolves and changes over time is **WHAT** we do to realize our **WHY**. And it *should* evolve, because our VUCA world is constantly changing.

Think about how we typically communicate. We speak about our organizations in terms of **WHAT** we do and even ask people, "What do you do for work?" We speak in terms of function. This is incredibly limiting. For example, Kodak was an industry leader but identified themselves via their **WHAT**; they were a film company. In holding tight to that identity, they eventually put themselves out of business . . . even though they invented the digital photography technology. Imagine if instead they held tight to their **WHY** (which would've probably been something along the lines of *We help people preserve their memories so that they can leave lasting legacies*). Their **WHAT** would have evolved, but their **WHY** would remain constant—and they'd likely still be in existence today.

Of course we need to have good quality products and services and a sound business model, or businesses will cease to exist. Making money is essential for the vitality and sustainability of a business, but it is not the most important reason for existing. Darden School of Business professor Ed Freeman put it well when he wrote, "We need red blood cells to live (the same way a business needs profits to live), but the purpose of life is more than to make red blood cells (the same way the purpose of business is more than simply to generate profits)."[148]

And in an article published in *Entrepreneur*, Simon Sinek echoes this:

> I am inspired by a world where shareholders, corporate boards, analysts, employees and customers demand that organizations exist to advance something bigger than themselves. Who values the long-term growth of their people over the short-term growth of their profits? **Money is important, but money is fuel, not a purpose.** We don't own cars so we can have fuel. We own cars to get places. Fuel powers the car. **Money powers a business, helps it advance its message to bigger and broader audiences. Business can change people's lives and change the world—only when they know why they are in business in the first place.**[149]

We introduced BTM Global in chapter 2. While their **WHAT** is retail systems implementation, their **WHY** is much bigger. Part of BTM Global's culture is giving back and their charity work—especially in Vietnam, where their founder, Andy, was born. They believe it is their responsibility to give back to the communities in which they live and work; and they prioritize efforts that create a brighter future for children.

As their clients and others wanted to contribute, Tom and Andy realized that BTM wasn't really set up as a charity to be able to accept financial donations. So this led to them starting a separate nonprofit nearly three years ago called Kids Promise; its mission is to create lasting solutions to problems confronting kids, giving them a path toward a better future. Kids Promise helps provide safe, adequate homes for rural children living in poverty; scholarships for promising university students in need; and school supplies, clothing, and bicycles for children in need. They support kids in the United States, North America, and Vietnam.

The more BTM grows, and the more money they make, the more they are able to support Kids Promise and their other charitable partners. In other words, as they continue to foster a human workplace and grow their business, they have more fuel to power their business, further their cause, and help kids have a better future.

When people are working hard toward something they believe in and feel a part of, there is energy and passion; otherwise that hard work turns into stress and swirl because there isn't clarity of direction or purpose. And, as we learned earlier in the book, clarity of purpose and passion is what fuels our Creative Mind; without it, our Reactive Mind is more likely to take over and keep us stuck and disconnected. Clarity of purpose *builds a lighthouse* and honors the fact that business is not a machine but rather a complex, living, adaptive system. Andy Swann writes in *The Human Workplace*, "The organizations of the future are no longer machines or systems, they are movements. To make a successful human workplace, you need to start a movement."[150]

Margaret Wheatley defines a movement as "the people willing to stay dedicated to their cause for a long time, those who take risks, work hard, expect defeat, and still keep going."[151] It is in our biological makeup as humans to want to belong and feel part of a community. We are naturally creative when we want to contribute and believe in something. So the key is to have a cause that people want to believe in and create a structure that supports them in congregating around that shared belief.

As Daniel Coyle writes in *The Culture Code*, "Purpose isn't about tapping into some mystical internal drive but rather about creating simple beacons that focus attention and engagement on the shared goal. Successful cultures do this by relentlessly seeking ways to tell and retell their story . . . they build high-purpose environments. High-purpose environments are filled with small, vivid signals designed to create a link between the present moment and a future ideal."[152]

Yet, a shared belief is only one part of the essential ingredients for a thriving, human workplace. We must create the structure and clarity so people can *show up as leaders* and help bring the organization's purpose to life. Then, instead of controlling people's behaviors as if they were machines, we honor their innate biology of being human and need for self-determination and let them take responsibility for their own actions and either align their contribution or leave.

Too often we see organizations that may have done the work to clarify their purpose, but they haven't operationalized their core values into clear behaviors. This is problematic because passion alone isn't enough; it needs structure. Our behaviors serve as a signal for what we believe. Therefore, it is essential to also clarify the **HOW**s to create a structure and serve as guiding principles for our **WHY** to be realized. The **HOW**s become the organization's "playbook" and serve as a filter so people know what is expected, how to show up, and how to approach situations and decisions. They become your deal-breakers. As Cy Wakeman put it, "Buy-in is not an option. Everyone needs a plan either to sign up and support the organization or to sign out of the organization. There is no third option to stay and hate."[153]

In her book *Permission to Screw Up*, Kristen Hadeed describes the process they went through at her company, Student Maid, to identify their deal-breakers. When they finally clarified their core values, they became the filter to "guard their cultural gate"—meaning they would hire by, fire by, and live by:

1. Take your moral fiber. We do what we say we're going to do, and we tell the truth.
2. Roll with the punches. When things don't go according to plan, we adapt.
3. Jump through flaming hoops. We don't just do what's expected; we go above and beyond, not only for our clients but especially for each other.
4. Don't leave us hangin'. We understand how our actions can affect others; we put the interests of the team before our own individual needs.
5. Be classy, not sassy. We show respect to one another, speak with discretion, and maintain a positive and uplifting attitude.
6. Own it. We take responsibility for our work and our decisions, and we care for Student Maid as if it were our own business.
7. Unleash the creative dragon within. We think outside the box to problem-solve and develop new ideas.
8. Pay it forward. We give back to our community, not because we have to but because we genuinely care and want to see the world become a better place.
9. Speak now or forever hold your peace. We maintain open communication with the entire Student Maid team, which means we voice all our concerns, questions, comments, criticisms, and praise.
10. Raise the roof. We work at Student Maid because we love and believe in the company, so we put forth our best effort to help it grow and thrive.[154]

When you do the work to clarify your **HOW**s, your deal-breakers, it creates a playbook that clarifies for everyone what the guardrails are to be effective and successful within your organization. This is what allows self-managed companies (like those we featured in chapter 5) to be successful. They have a clear purpose, clear behavioral anchors to guide decisions, and then treat people like adults who can opt in or opt out. When we (Salveo Partners) did the work to clarify our **WHY** and **HOW**s, it made all the difference in the world. It elevated our passion to bring more of our purpose into the world; and it helped bring clarity to our decisions and the actions we need to take in order to further our purpose.

How Purpose Leads to Greater Humanity, Improved Employee Experience, and Profits

In his powerful 2014 book *The Purpose Economy: How Your Desire for Impact, Personal Growth and Community Is Changing the World*, award-winning entrepreneur (and globally recognized leader in the fields of purpose at work and social innovation) Aaron Hurst lays out the following one-million-year history of human economies.[155]

Economy	Beginning	Worker Proposition
Hunters and Gatherers	(1,000,000 years ago)	Survival
Agrarian Economy	(12,000 years ago)	Survival
Industrial Economy	(1750)	Satisfaction
Information Economy	(1950)	Engagement
Purpose Economy	(present ---->	Fulfillment

Fascinatingly, Hurst's uncle was the individual who coined the term *information economy* and predicted the rise of Silicon Valley, ushering in the new world of the internet and social media that has dominated our economy for almost three decades. Hurst founded Imperative to promote the development of the Purpose Economy. Imperative focuses on research and innovation and provides a talent assessment platform for purpose-driven organizations. They believe that this developing economy is driven by connecting people to their purpose and that value is created by establishing purpose for employees and customers, enabling personal growth and building community.

The first thing that you may notice in the above table is the shrinking time periods between the dramatic changes in economies and how that reflects our VUCA world. And the value proposition for workers has changed dramatically as well. Though employee engagement has been the desired value proposition in the information economy, it is no longer enough in the twenty-first century; people are craving—and demanding—fulfillment.

This is an important distinction with wide-ranging implications.

There are more than fifty identified conceptual definitions of "employee engagement." The Conference Board (a global, independent business membership and research association, working since 1916 to provide organizations with the practical knowledge they need to improve their performance and better serve society) assembled a committee of experts in 2007 that came up with this composite definition: "Employee engagement is a heightened emotional and intellectual connection that an employee has for his/her job, organization, manager, or coworkers that, in turn, influences him/her to apply additional discretionary effort to his/her work."[156]

However, as we learned in chapter 1, engagement rates have not changed in thirty years. We've also learned that since we can be engaged yet stressed and burned out, being engaged plus thriving with our well-being seems to make a profound difference. Enter the new focus to move beyond *employee engagement* to *fulfillment* via nourishing the *employee experience.* In fact, in 2013, The Energy Project surveyed some fourteen thousand global respondents, in more than twenty-four industries, and found that "No single factor in our study comes close to influencing people's job satisfaction and likelihood to stay at an organization as much as the sense that their work gives them a sense of meaning and purpose."[157]

Employee experience goes beyond engagement in describing the relationship between workers and their organizations; it incorporates *fulfillment*, and it is seen as critical to both organizational and employee well-being. While definitions vary, they all have some common threads. McKinsey & Company defines *employee experience* as "Companies and their people working together to create personalized, authentic experiences that ignite passion and tap into purpose to strengthen individual, team, and company performance."[158]

And Glassdoor states that "Employee experience illustrates everything that people encounter, observe, or feel over the course of their time with a company. Employee experience is defined by the sum of its parts—from the daily vibe in the workplace to the employee's purpose and place on their team and how they deliver value for their organization."[159]

Whatever your preferred definition, *employee experience* is being used more and more as a replacement for engagement, with many chief HR and engagement officers retitling their roles as *chief employee experience officers.* David Sturt and Todd Nordstrom, researchers and consultants at the O. C. Tanner Institute, describe this important distinction: "Employee engagement is a top-down philosophy. It's the hope of an organization that employees choose to engage with the company's ideas, culture, work, and results. Employee experience, on the other hand, is a bottom-up concept—where processes, places, and workflow are designed around the preexisting tendencies of the employees. Just like retailers are changing based on customer activity and desire, workplaces are following suit."[160]

We share all of this to help further show how important *The Fusion* is (i.e., how inextricably interconnected organizational and employee well-being are). Many organizations are risking the loss of some of their most engaged and productive and employees due to high stress and burnout. Clearly there is more to the employee experience than just high engagement.

Research from Imperative's "2019 Workforce Purpose Index" gives us some insight into the importance of moving beyond engagement to fulfillment and the employee experience. Imperative defines a "purpose mindset" as "a belief that each of us has the power to make our work meaningful and fulfilling." Their research indicates that people with a purpose mindset are 52 percent more likely to report being fulfilled; and fulfilled employees:

- Serve as your brand ambassadors (with an average Employee Net Promoter Score of 30 compared to −60 for unfulfilled employees)
- Are more likely to be in your top 20 percentile of performance
- Are two times more likely than unfulfilled employees to stay five or more years at your organization
- Are three times more likely than unfulfilled employees to stay ten or more years at your organization[161]

And, as we noted in the beginning of the book, research on conscious businesses (i.e., the Firms of Endearment) who operate from a higher purpose are fourteen times more profitable than the S&P 500. So purpose-focused organizations end up being more profitable and contribute to enhanced fulfillment and well-being; they go beyond engagement.

When a One-Hundred-Year-Old Company Found Its WHY

Harcros Chemicals Inc. is a major distributor and manufacturer of industrial and specialty chemicals. Harcros began business in 1917 as Thompson, Munro and Robins, and changed its name to Thompson-Hayward Chemical

Company (THCC) in 1923. North American Philips acquired THCC in 1961; in 1981 the company again changed hands when Harrisons & Crosfield purchased the bulk of the business from North American Philips. The company name was changed to Harcros Chemicals Inc. in 1988. In 2001, a management buyout resulted in the privatization of Harcros. It remains a privately held corporation today.

Harcros operates twenty-nine distribution locations in nineteen states and provides geographic coverage throughout much of the United States. The Harcros Manufacturing Division, headquartered in Kansas City, Kansas, with a second facility in Dalton, Georgia, is a niche producer of surfactants, emulsifiers, defoamers, and a myriad of specialty products, custom blends, and reaction chemistries. They also have expanded globally with growing teams and operations in India.

In January 2014, they made a bold move to become employee-owned (ESOP). Becoming an ESOP isn't necessarily bold; however, how Harcros approached it is. What is unique about the Harcros ESOP is that their CEO, Kevin Mirner, created it so that ownership is not based on tenure or position within the company; everyone is an equal owner. In the world of ESOPs, this structure is unheard of and provides a small glimpse of the humanistic mentality that makes Harcros unique. That said, the intention was not given to help people understand what it meant to shift from being an employee to an employee-owner; they needed help fostering a mindset shift and creating the conditions for everyone to show up thinking and acting like a business owner—to *show up as a leader*.

We began working with Harcros in 2017 to help them build a thriving culture and future. They have been doing incredible work to put the pillars of Conscious Capitalism into practice, including leveraging our Thriving Workplace Culture Survey™ to assess current state and measure progress, do in-depth development work with their people leaders, help them cocreate clarity of purpose and where they're headed as a company, and be conscious about their culture.

In late 2017, Harcros recruited a team of culture ambassadors to serve as the core of Harcros Impact (the name of their conscious culture efforts). This team of forty employee-owners represents every branch throughout the United States. They come together once per quarter for a full-day workshop to help equip them to be conduits of positive change throughout Harcros. Part of every workshop includes several hours of self/leadership development to support them in *showing up as leaders*. We include some of our core self-awareness exercises we outlined in chapter 7 as well as how to listen to their colleagues, role model the culture they're trying to create, and be an advocate for building a thriving future for the company.

When we first proposed work to help them *build a lighthouse*, we suggested using this group of ambassadors for a one-day workshop to help them find their **WHY** and **HOW**s, and to do culture-visioning work to guide next steps. However, Kevin Mirner said, "Everyone is an equal owner, why wouldn't we have everyone participate in this effort?" After the shock wore off (along with a few *holy crap* moments of trying to figure out the logistics), we embarked upon an amazing discovery journey with them. In March 2018, the marathon began; we conducted 16 workshops over 4 months in 6 different cities, reaching all 545 US employee-owners. Take in that magnitude for a moment!

Each full-day workshop (eight a.m. to four p.m.) included thirty to forty people split between three table groups. As prep, everyone was given a link to watch Simon Sinek's TED Talk; however, only two-thirds of people watched it prior to their workshop. The following outlines the flow and content of each workshop:

- We started out with ice-breaker exercises to get them warmed up to tell stories as part of the **WHY** discovery process and then followed the three conversation model from the book *Find Your WHY.*[162] We asked people to share specific stories of when they've been the most proud to work at Harcros.

- Each table group worked to come up with their table's **WHY** statement. Then we worked as a large group to come up with one final **WHY** statement as the output from the workshop.

- Once the **WHY** was determined, we moved into the **HOW** discussion. We teed it up by spending time making the distinction between being "just an employee" versus an employee-owner and what it means to *show up as a leader* and business owner. We then invited them to do some partner discussion on the Ingredients to Be My Best exercise (referenced in chapter 7) so they could put some intention to what they need to shift from being "just an employee" to a business owner.

- We likened the **HOW** for Harcros to the Ingredients to Be My Best exercise on an individual level; each table was tasked with coming up with the specific behaviors and actions taken in each of the stories that allowed them to live their **WHY**. We compiled them as a group and then narrowed by themes to finalize the five **HOW** statements from the workshop.

- Using the **WHY** and **HOW**s as a guide, we facilitated a culture-visioning discussion asking people to share what life would look like at Harcros when they are thriving . . . when they are able to bring their best selves to work and home each day and are consistently living their **WHY** via the discipline of **HOW**. Then, leveraging their thriving culture description along with the **WHY** and **HOW**s, we captured on flip charts what they collectively said they needed to start, stop, and continue doing in order for their vision to be a reality.

- We began wrapping up each workshop by encouraging them to not wait until some "magical" day in August when the ambassadors would finalize the **WHY** and **HOW**s; we encouraged them to start *showing up as a leader* and an owner by working to live the **WHY** via the discipline of **HOW** from their workshop and start holding themselves accountable to the "start and stop doing" lists.

- We then introduced Personal Recognition Messages using the F.B.I. formula from Barry-Wehmiller (which we will detail in chapter 10). Everyone was given an index card and shown an example of a recognition message. We demonstrated how to give one by publicly recognizing one to two people who stood out to us that day. We kept the room quiet for five minutes and asked everyone to write a message to someone in the room and then deliver it. We debriefed by asking what it was like to write a message; most said it felt really good. Then we asked what it was like to receive one. Many times, people were humbled and moved to tears. We challenged people to write one message per day (at a minimum, once per week) and suggested that they'd start to look for the good and would start moving Harcros forward toward its thriving future.

- The final component of each workshop was asking people to share their reflections on the day (either stating something they were taking away from the day or an intention they wanted to set). In each workshop, some employee-owners showed up crabby about being there. By the end, many of those people came up to us and said, "Thank you; this is better than I thought it would be." Many people also said how valuable it was to actually meet people from other branches and put faces with names. Here are just a few of the other reflections people provided:

  I'm grateful to be part of a company that invests so much time and energy in its culture.

  Not every day is rainbows and butterflies, and it's easy to lose sight of the big picture. I heard a lot of positive things about Harcros today. It was a great reminder of the great company we are a part of. Kevin's commitment to us as employee-owners is amazing.

  I will give more positive feedback to colleagues. And be more empathetic—more tolerant of people making mistakes, not be so quick to judge.

  I am inspired by everyone in this room. It is inspiring to hear about so many people sticking around Harcros through the good times and bad times. I am on my third company and Harcros is my home. This will be my last company.

  I came up here with a negative outlook on the day . . . thought it was a waste of time. I challenged myself to come in with an open mind, and it's been a motivational day for me. It'll carry on for me.

  If you are about to react negatively, or overreact, just pause. Take a breath and really think about the discipline of **HOW**. Think like an owner.

  Leadership is a behavior that really resonated with me. Just because you don't have a formal title doesn't mean you can't show up and act like a leader.

  Harcros impresses me with the commitment to invest in all of us with this initiative. Us "blue collar guys" don't normally get these types of opportunities to contribute.

> Raise your hand if this (the culture initiative) is one of the prouder moments of your time at Harcros. [The majority of the people raised their hands.]

Over the course of these sixteen workshops, we collected over four hundred and twenty amazing stories of examples of when employee-owners have been the most proud to work at the company. And guess what? None of them were about their products or services; they were all about their spirit and how they come together to make amazing things happen. We compiled the story summaries in a book called *The Heart of Harcros: A Collection of Stories of Us at Our Best.* We grouped the stories by the five main themes that emerged from the workshops:

1. **Truly Human Leadership: Stories about the incredible compassion and care from Kevin and various other people leaders.**

   One of the stories that was told at multiple workshops is such a great example of the humanistic approach Kevin embodies. Many years ago, one of Harcros's top salespeople, Preston, was in the hospital in Atlanta having quadruple bypass surgery. People were receiving emails from him and were confused; they said, "Why is he emailing and working? Didn't he just have surgery?" Without hesitation, Kevin hopped on a plane from Kansas City and flew to Atlanta. He showed up in the hospital and took away Preston's laptop and Blackberry and told him to just focus on his recovery.

2. **Caring for Each Other: Stories about how they support and rally around each other in times of need.**

   There were so many stories of amazing care and compassion Harcros employee-owners show each other in times of need. One of the stories that stood out (and was referenced at several workshops) involves Jay Walker. On January 26, 2005, Jay became a proud dad of twin boys, Kyle and Koby; at the age of three, his daughter, Anna Claire, became a big sister. Jay and his wife started noticing that Koby was not reaching milestones as quickly as Kyle. Koby also had trouble with fine motor skills and sitting up. They started going to different doctors to try to find some answers. After several months and several doctor visits,

Jay and his wife were referred to an orthopedic doctor to take a couple of X-rays of Koby's back and refer them to a genetic doctor.

Their first trip to the genetic doctor is a day Jay will never forget. The doctor came in the room with brochures and information about a rare genetic disorder. "Wait, hold up! What are you talking about?" Jay exclaimed. At this point, the doctor became upset because he thought Jay and his wife already knew why they were referred to him. The doctor told them that Koby had mucolipidosis II or I cell disease. The previous case was twenty-three years prior in the state of Mississippi. At that time, there were only about six other cases in the US. The doctor said that their only option to save Koby's life was for him to have a bone marrow transplant. Jay and his wife struggled as this hit them like a ton of bricks. Bone marrow transplant is a very dangerous process and could kill Koby; but if they didn't do it, he would be lucky to live to the age of five.

After much prayer and research, Jay and his wife decided that they wanted to do everything they could to give Koby the best chance at life. The process of selecting the facility to have the bone marrow transplant was not an easy task. They had a local hospital in Vicksburg, MS, that was capable but did not have experience with Koby's disease. Both MD Anderson in Texas and the University of Minnesota were also on the list as approved by their insurance. Jay spoke with the doctors in Minnesota; they had actually performed a couple of bone marrow transplants on patients with conditions similar to Koby. Jay wanted to use a facility that had experience with patients like Koby. However, Minnesota is a long way from Mississippi—especially when the procedure, plus the constant monitoring, could last up to three months.

So Jay and his wife started to lean toward a hospital in Jackson, MS, that was an hour from their home. Jay figured he could juggle work and being in and out of the hospital. Then another bombshell dropped; the insurance did not recognize Jackson Hospital's certification. They recommended Texas, Minnesota, or St. Jude's in Memphis. If they chose to have it in Jackson instead, it would likely bankrupt his family; procedures of this type could easily cost half a million dollars.

During all of this, Jay had been speaking with HR and his leaders at Harcros. He was only six years out of college and six years into his sales career. He felt tremendous pressure to take care of both his family and his job. Jay had a conversation with David Goode (who managed Harcros Memphis for years); his son worked at St. Jude's, so he put Jay in touch with a doctor to see if they would take his case. Jay expressed his concern over the length of time and distance, as St. Jude's was still four hours away. But they were able to get in for an initial visit.

Jay described that initial visit as a "God" thing! The doctor that was going to be taking care of Koby had just transferred from the University of Minnesota where he helped conduct bone marrow transplants. They knew right then that they had come to the right place.

Jay was worried about his job. And he found out that the housing provided by St. Jude's has a strict limit of four people; they have five in their family. Then, Jay received a phone call from David Goode. He said, "I talked to Kevin Mirner. We have arranged for your family to use an apartment while you have to be in Memphis. This will allow your family to be together. Work when you can on your phone, computer, and make calls when you can; don't worry about your job during this time. Take care of your family!" This was a huge relief—and blessing—for Jay and his family! This gesture is something that is unheard of in most businesses. Jay knew right then that Harcros was not like any other.

The next step was to find a bone marrow donor. They typically test family members first; Jay's three-year-old daughter was a perfect match. So Koby and Anna Claire went through the bone marrow transplant in April 2006. The procedure was tough, with long hours and many sleepless nights. But Jay felt blessed that he was able to work and had great support from his branch and many others during this time; and they didn't miss any orders. The Harcros family at all of the branches raised money for Koby. Jay received countless calls and emails checking on him. Anna Claire is now seventeen, and Kyle and Koby are fourteen and doing great. To this day, Jay's Harcros family continues to ask how Koby and his family are doing.

As Jay puts it, "To name a detailed list of everyone that helped me and my family during this time would be hard to do. To everyone who helped by prayer, phone call, email, card, or donation, I want you to know that I think about this every time I go to St. Jude's and when I think about Koby's journey. This was living the '**WHY**.' This is why I have such a deep respect and a sense of loyalty for Harcros Chemicals."

3. Going the Extra Mile for Our Customers: Stories about going above and beyond to service their customers . . . way above and beyond the call of duty.

   Part of what makes Harcros so unique in their industry is their care and pride when it comes to serving their customers. They don't even blink an eye at dropping everything to make what seems like the impossible happen. We heard countless stories of how people *showed up as leaders* to make a small miracle happen for their customers. One that stood out happened in Memphis. In the spring of 2011, the Mississippi River floods were among the largest and most damaging recorded in over a century. Thousands of homes were ordered to be evacuated, including thirteen hundred in Memphis.

   One of Harcros's customers, a large refinery, didn't know what to do. They called up the manager at the time and asked if he had any sandbags. Even though this is in no way in Harcros's wheelhouse of products and services, they quickly went to work to figure out a way to help. Next thing you know, they're getting ahold of giant super-sacks from one company and contacting a cement company. Within hours the Harcros team started filling two-thousand-pound super-sacks of sand. They delivered over eighty super-sacks of sand that were put in place via a forklift, saving the day and preventing the refinery from flooding. To this day, the customer still brings this up and values their relationship with Harcros.

4. Supporting Our Communities: Stories about the amazingly generous ways they give back and support their communities.

   Harcros is deeply invested in giving back to support their communities. Besides various charitable drives and events, each year each branch is given $10,000 to donate to local causes they choose to improve their communities—locally and abroad. The Harcros Charitable Fund was established to provide funding for projects where meeting basic needs is the fundamental criterion. The Fund, by way of example, will provide monetary support in the areas of medical care, nutrition, housing, education, and security of environment. It is intended that the money will be donated to charities in the local community of the Harcros branch.

   One story that was told several times is regarding their work in

South Africa. Harcros sponsors Lawrence Roundabouts Well Appeal, which is an organization set up to provide clean drinking water to schools in South Africa. The roundabout playpump (in the US we call a roundabout a *merry-go-round*) combines a children's roundabout with a water pump. The action of the children spinning the roundabout while playing pumps the water into an above-ground storage tank to be used later for drinking and washing. Harcros has sponsored the installation of two pumps per year around South Africa; to date, they have installed over fifty pumps.

5. The Resilient Harcros Spirit: Stories about how they rally and come back stronger in the face of adversity.

The date was Saturday March 10, 2001. There were two people working at the Nashua, New Hampshire, branch that morning, Jim Schlegel and Greg High. Jim was in to make a delivery to a customer and Greg was in to load him and do snow removal. At that time, they had several snowstorms (what seemed like every Friday), with one to three feet of heavy wet snow. The night before they received two to three feet of heavy, wet snow; Lucie Bergeron (a buyer) noticed some leaks in the warehouse but didn't think much of it. At 8:12 a.m. the roof collapsed (in Nashua there were three other roofs that collapsed within twelve hours of theirs); thankfully no one was hurt! Jim Grady (the manager of the Nashua branch) was at the scene within minutes and worked closely with emergency response personnel.

The next day (Sunday), the entire team met at a local restaurant to try to figure out what they were going to do. Several people were sent to their branch in Westbrook, ME (which is one hundred and ten miles away from Nashua); they decided to stock and move inventory from there. Michele Fontaine worked in sales and had a home office. She had previously worked in purchasing and customer service, so she opened up her home so she and Lucie could keep operations going. They worked out of her home for a month, doing all the purchasing and dispatching of delivery trucks. Jim Grady, Lisa Beaulieu (the office manager), and others also worked out of their houses for this month. In April 2001, they were able to rent a temporary office right near their building; so they moved their offices there and continued to stock and ship from Westbrook.

> Their drivers made deliveries out of Westbrook for about one year until their building was rebuilt. Jim Grady made arrangements with their suppliers and even some of their friendly competitors; they would package the chemicals that Harcros normally packaged in Nashua until further notice. Jim worked tirelessly to get the building cleared, cleaned out, and rebuilt. Their customers were aware of the situation and stood by Harcros; there was barely a hiccup in servicing them. They moved back into their original location just over one year later. In a nutshell, although it was a challenging year, they all rallied together to make this all work.

The next step was to bring the ambassadors together in August 2018 to take the WHY and HOW statements from all sixteen workshops and finalize them into one WHY statement and one set of HOWs. We were a little uncertain of the best way to do this, so we decided to reach out to David Mead (one of the authors of *Find Your WHY*). We didn't know if he'd respond or not but wanted to thank him for their work and let them know what it inspired in Harcros—and see if he had any pearls of wisdom as we brought together the ambassadors. David did respond, and I (Rosie) had a Zoom meeting with him. He said he was "blown away" by us taking this approach and that they've never tried to include all employees as part of the WHY process. He also loved the ambassador concept, provided some really important clarity about the components of the WHY statement, and gave us helpful ideas for finalizing the HOWs.

Being the first to take on a WHY journey of this magnitude, we weren't sure how (or if) it was going to work. We wondered if we'd really be able to help the ambassadors find consensus to create one WHY statement that could energize them. Not only did they find their WHY, but it was in action during this entire process. Harcros's WHY is "Working together, we create a positive impact and enrich the lives of others."

Their WHY (working together) was in action in creating the final WHY statement—including components from all but one workshop location:

- "Working together": Chicago workshop 2
- "Create a positive impact": Atlanta workshop 1, Kansas City workshop 5
- "Enrich the lives of others": Dallas workshop 1, Memphis workshop 1

As we connected back to all of the stories, they realized that each story of when they were the proudest to work at Harcros was a reflection of their WHY in action—who they are at their best. Next was clarifying their behavioral anchors of the HOWs—the actions they take that are essential for their WHY to be realized. Through a voting and ranking process, the ambassadors were able to reach consensus on their HOWs:

- Show up with a spirit of service
  - Go above and beyond
  - Do what's right
- Empower others
  - Respect, support, and encourage each other
- Lead by example
  - Think and act like an owner
  - Show up as our best
  - Maintain a positive attitude
  - Be solution-minded
- Be a team player
  - Communicate clearly
  - Trust each other
  - Actively listen to understand
- Show compassion in all we do

Once the WHY and HOWs were finalized, Kevin joined the group; in true Harcros spirit of working together, several ambassadors shared the responsibility of presenting the final WHY/HOWs to Kevin. We started with recapping the process for Kevin and sharing the five main themes of the stories that emerged. Five ambassadors shared a story from each category as examples of when they're at their best. Then a different ambassador presented the WHY and another presented the HOWs. Kevin's response was "this is us" and "we should be doing this all along" (a good sign that they landed on the right WHY and HOWs).

Harcros *built a lighthouse* by engaging everyone in the process to clarify their WHY and HOWs. The storytelling created the opportunity for people to see beyond their branch and functional area and feel more connected to the heart of the company. And they've kept the storytelling alive. Each time the leaders and ambassadors get together, we start with a new ten-minute round of storytelling of recent examples where they've seen their WHY realized. And we've encouraged them to build this as a deliberate practice during their huddles and meetings.

Of course, clarifying the **WHY** and **HOW**s and sharing stories is just the beginning; the real work comes with equipping everyone to intentionally and consistently *show up as a leader* and live their **WHY**. And that was the focus of 2019 (more details on that in chapter 10). This has infused a new sense of clarity, energy, and passion into a one-hundred-year-old company. In other words, it's never too late to focus on purpose and be intentional about your culture!

Nurturing Purpose and Fulfillment at the Individual Level

We've already seen that having clarity of purpose and a purpose mindset fosters fulfillment, leading to better business outcomes. It also makes a difference on the individual level. Imperative's research also suggests that employees clearly differentiate between engagement and fulfillment. We've previously stated how important language is in our meaning-making. Look at the difference between how people describe *engagement* versus *fulfillment* (the bold words are those most commonly used):

Engagement	Fulfillment
Busy	**Happy**
Active	**Love**
Interest	**Enjoy**
Hard	Difference
Like	Achieve
Challenges	Goals

In this context, it is not difficult to see how concerns about engagement and burnout might play out. Fulfilling work (jobs that not only keep employees interested and busy, but that also bring happiness and joy) can go a long way toward correcting for the burnout too often associated with high engagement. It makes sense because when we are fulfilled, we have a sense of purpose that provides us with the energy, passion, and meaning we need to *show up as leaders*; it fuels our Creative Mind and helps us operate with greater self-awareness and intentionality.

Besides, research has also found a clear link between having a sense of purpose and greater well-being, including being less prone to disease.[163] Additionally, people reporting a strong purpose in life:

- Live longer
- Have a 27 percent lower risk of heart attack
- Have a 22 percent lower risk of stroke
- Have a lower risk and slower progression of Alzheimer's disease
- Experience better sleep and better sex
- Are more relaxed and less likely to become depressed[164]

So if organizations operate with a clear purpose and foster environments where people can find fulfillment and contribute to that purpose, it's a win-win for the well-being of the organization and its people; the purpose and well-being of organizations is inextricably interconnected to the purpose and well-being of their people.

In fact, Imperative suggests that we have been living for decades with a "dangerous myth" about humans and work: that people can go to work and spend a large percentage of their waking hours in a toxic environment, where they don't feel trusted or safe to show up as their whole selves, and then they can go home and be the best family and community members they can be. The reality is that the likelihood of people being fulfilled in life if they are not fulfilled at work is a startling **1 percent**![165]

The good news is that **everyone** can find fulfillment in work—regardless of the type of work. Really! It seems pretty obvious to most people how doctors, lawyers, teachers, and so on might feel a special purpose to their work, something bigger than just clocking in and getting a paycheck. But how about people in what are generally considered more menial jobs?

Some fascinating research from Amy Wrzesniewski sheds light on this seeming dilemma. She asked the cleaning staff of a large Midwest university hospital how they felt about their jobs. Many in the group saw their jobs as not particularly satisfying; they were there primarily for the financial benefits of the work. However, she discovered a subset of the hospital's cleaners who felt like they were part of the professional care team and saw their work as deeply meaningful. From providing words of encouragement, a box of Kleenex, or a glass of water to patients and their caregivers to making sure the floors were clean, dry, and safe to rearranging pictures on the walls of comatose patients, hoping that perhaps the change might have a positive benefit, they saw themselves as an integral part of the healing staff of the hospital. Wrzesniewski and her colleagues labeled this phenomenon *job crafting*, which they described in this way: "What employees do to redesign their own jobs in ways that foster engagement at work, job satisfaction, resilience and thriving. Employees craft their jobs by changing cognitive, task, and/or relational boundaries to shape interactions and relationships with others at work."[166]

Their research uncovered that job crafting is positively associated with increased satisfaction, commitment, and attachment to job and organization.[167] Even more importantly, experimental research has confirmed that randomized assignment to job crafting leads to improved happiness, performance, and mobility to new roles—in other words, to increased fulfillment.[168]

In his insightful book *Why We Work*, psychologist Dr. Barry Schwartz sums up the possibilities for meaning and purpose for work: "Virtually every job has the potential to offer people satisfaction. Jobs can be organized to include variety, complexity, skill development, and growth. They can be organized to provide the people that do them with a measure of autonomy. And perhaps most important, they can be made meaningful by connecting them to the welfare of others."[169]

In other words, every single one of us has the opportunity to *show up as a leader* and find meaning, purpose, and fulfillment in our work and lives.

How to *Show Up as a Leader* and Influence Change at This Part of the Pyramid

Building a lighthouse cuts through the fog and creates clarity so people know where the organization is headed, believe in and are engaged in the cause, know how they can best contribute to furthering the cause, and are able to find fulfillment as they do so. Having a clear and engaging purpose alone is not enough; it's critical to also articulate clear behavioral anchors that serve as guiding principles and non-negotiables for your organization. They go hand in hand. Here are some ways you can advocate for and help bring greater purpose and fulfillment into your organization:

- **Start engaging others in purpose storytelling.** Stories connect people, elicit emotion, and help us feel like we're contributing to something greater than ourselves; stories illuminate the lighthouse and bring our WHY to life. Start asking others individually or in meetings to share stories of when they've been the proudest to work at your organization; listen for the themes that start to craft your WHY (*Find Your WHY* is a great reference for how to structure these). If your organization already has a clearly stated purpose, continue to engage people to tell stories about recent examples of your WHY being realized. Pride, energy, and passion result from our purpose being realized and us showing up as our best. Building a deliberate practice to keep your purpose at the forefront can help foster fulfillment and allow others to see how their work helps contribute and connect to the organization's purpose.

- Foster a Purpose Mindset. Purpose and fulfillment are not some far-out, grandiose things. They can be created in small moments. Start paying attention to what inspires, energizes, and fulfills you. Include those in your own Ingredients to Be My Best exercise, and nurture them. Proactively have conversations with your colleagues and leaders about what you need to find fulfillment in your work, and invite others to do the same. As you pay more attention to your own fulfillment, notice the impact it has on your life outside of work as well: are you a better spouse, parent, friend, community member, etc.?

- Move beyond engagement to fulfillment and the employee experience. Employee engagement is no longer enough—and can sometimes even come at the expense of our well-being. Move beyond what interests people and how busy and productive they are; start asking questions and engaging others in conversations about what brings them joy, happiness, and fulfillment in their work.

Chapter 9

TRUST, CONNECTION, AND SUPPORT

We are hardwired for connection. From our mirror neurons to language, we are a social species. In the absence of authentic connection, we suffer. And by authentic, I mean the kind of connection that doesn't require hustling for acceptance and changing who we are to fit in.

—BRENÉ BROWN, *Dare to Lead*[170]

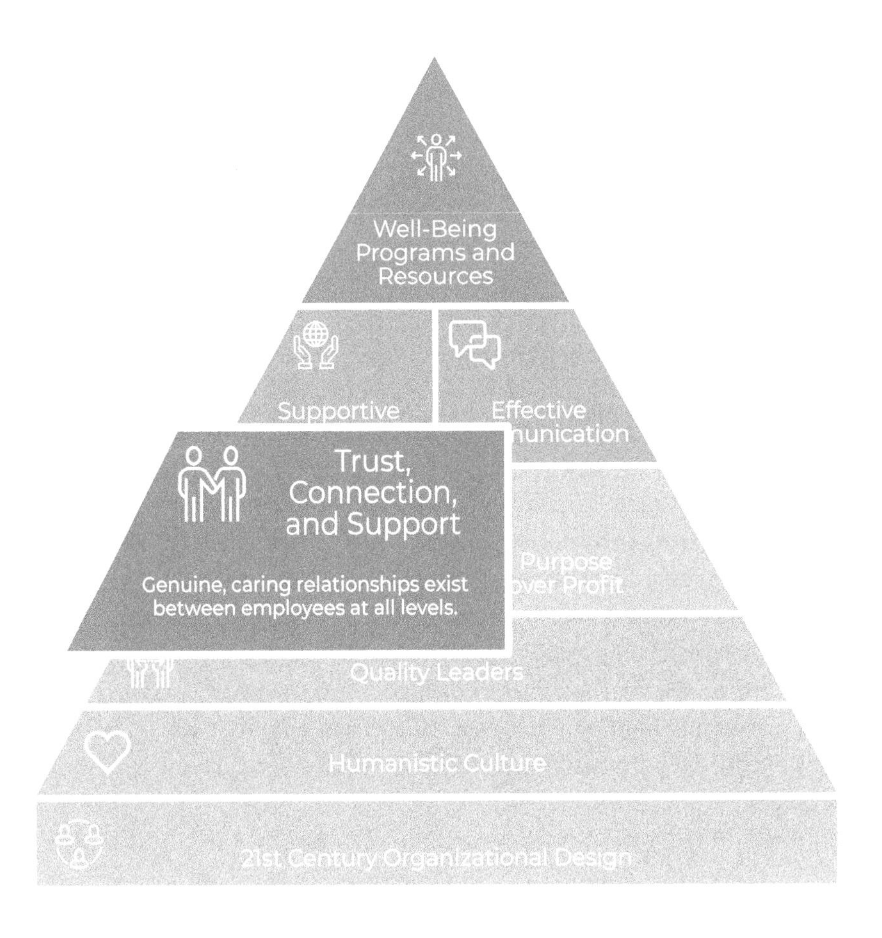

When life throws you curveballs, who are the people you trust and lean on for support? What if they weren't there and you were isolated and disconnected? As human beings, we are hardwired for connection; without it we suffer. Period. The sailors in our opening story had a high degree of trust, and supported one another as they weathered the storms of the VUCA seas and the uncertainty on the shipwrecked island. This allowed them to embrace the discomfort of their situation, *wade in the messy middle*, and *show up as leaders*. If they didn't have that foundation of trust, connection, and support, it would have been very difficult for them to organize and move forward toward a thriving future.

In order to truly find connection with others, we must be able to show up with authenticity (which requires us to be willing to be vulnerable and remove our own righteousness). Thriving, human workplaces foster our ability to show up authentically. With that, this part of the pyramid (trust, connection, and support) resides within the context of *creating fearless environments*. People must feel safe to show up authentically human and take interpersonal risks necessary to further the organization's purpose. We've already provided the expert definition of psychological safety. Just to expand upon it, we believe that employees feel psychologically safe at work when they know that their workplace will:

- acknowledge and celebrate their strengths and accomplishments **and**
- help them understand their weaknesses and learn from their mistakes

According to Amy Edmondson's research, in order for organizations to innovate and truly thrive in this VUCA world, hiring smart, motivated people is not enough. Even knowledgeable, skilled, and well-meaning people can't always contribute what they know if they're reluctant to stand out, be wrong, or offend someone. People have to be able to collaborate and work well together; they have to operate as a team. And when work environments have reasonably high psychological safety, not only do people contribute ideas but they report mistakes quickly so that prompt corrective action can be taken.[171]

The Key to Effective Teams

We already know that culture is ultimately built team-by-team and that psychological safety resides at the team level. So what are the ingredients that make up effective teams? In 2012, Google embarked upon a five-year study—code-named *Project Aristotle*—to examine hundreds of their teams to find out why some stumbled and others soared. They gathered statisticians, organizational psychologists, sociologists, engineers, and researchers to examine the literature and study behaviors and group norms.[172] They identified five key behaviors:

1. **Psychological safety:** People can take risks on this team without feeling insecure or embarrassed.
2. **Dependability:** People can count on each other to do high-quality work on time.
3. **Structure and clarity:** The goals, roles, and execution plans on their team are clear.
4. **Meaning of work:** They are working on something that is personally important for each of them.
5. **Impact of work:** They fundamentally believe that the work they're doing matters.

Of these behaviors, psychological safety is the most important dynamic that contributes to team effectiveness.[173] It's not surprising, as several other studies have found, that psychological safety is key to many organizational outcomes. It is critical to help foster employee engagement[174] and help people overcome the defensiveness and "learning anxiety" they face at work (especially when things don't go as planned, as is frequently the case in this VUCA world).[175]

When we *create fearless environments*, people believe that others will not react badly if they make a mistake or ask for help. In fact, candor is allowed and expected.[176] If we also want high performance, we must foster environments for people to feel connected to each other. In his book *The Culture Code*, Daniel Coyle states that "group performance depends on behavior that communicates one powerful overarching idea: *We are safe and connected*."[177] It is only within *fearless environments* that we are able to foster trust and human connection and create a space where people feel supported to learn, grow, and show up as their authentic selves.

The Trust and Psychological Safety Connection

Although psychological safety and trust are not the same thing, they are very much interconnected. Psychological safety is experienced at a group level and is a temporally immediate experience. Trust, on the other hand, involves interactions between two individuals or groups and whether we can be counted on to do what we promise in some future moment. So, when we trust people, we give them the benefit of the doubt; when we experience psychological safety, we believe others will give us the benefit of the doubt when we mess up, speak up, or ask for help.[178]

In other words, being able to collaborate and make the adaptive leaps necessary to be effective in the face of change requires that people trust themselves and each other. And high-trust organizations are three times more profitable than low-trust organizations.[179] It's also important to realize that trust is not some abstract concept. Just like leadership is ultimately a behavior, so is trust. It is built in very small moments; in every behavior and action we take, we either build or erode trust. In his book *The Thin Book of Trust*, Charles Feltman distinguishes between trust and distrust: "Trust is choosing to risk making something that you value vulnerable to the actions of another person."[180]

What we make vulnerable can range from concrete things (e.g., money, a job, a promotion, or a particular goal) to less tangible things (e.g., a belief we hold, a cherished way of doing things, our "good name," or even our sense of happiness and well-being). We choose to make these things vulnerable because we believe others will support it—or at least not harm it.

The flip side is distrust, which Feltman defines as "what I have shared with you that I value is not safe with you." When we don't feel that what we value is safe with another person (i.e., will be dismissed, shared with others, manipulated, etc.), we don't extend trust. And what typically gets in our way is our own instinct to look good and self-protect; so we end up operating from our Reactive Mind, which hinders connection and collaboration. As Feltman puts it, "The disaster of distrust in the workplace is that the strategies people use to protect themselves inevitably get in the way of their ability to effectively work with others."[181]

In order for teams to be effective, people have to feel safe with one another and trust one another completely so that they can speak straight, make effective decisions, and effectively support the purpose and goals of the organization. This requires *wading in the messy middle*; we need to be able to move away from self-protection to great courage—be willing to be vulnerable and show up and be seen as our authentic selves. When everyone on a team trusts one another, no one hides weaknesses or mistakes; people speak more freely and fearlessly with one another; and they don't waste time pretending to be something they're not.

Trust starts with self; this means doing our own work to own our inner narrative and actions and then show up with integrity and authenticity. In our work with teams, we leverage Brené Brown's BRAVING acronym to invite people into work to enhance their self-trust.[182]

- Boundaries: I respect my own boundaries. I'm clear about what's okay and not okay and ask if I'm not clear. I'm willing to say "no."
- Reliability: I'm reliable and do what I say I would do. This means staying aware of our competencies and limitations so we don't overpromise and are able to deliver on commitments and balance competing priorities.
- Accountability: I hold myself accountable; I own my mistakes, apologize, and make amends.
- Vault: I respect the vault and share appropriately; this means I don't share information or experiences that are not mine to share. We need to know that our confidences are kept, and that people aren't sharing with us any information about other people that should be confidential.
- Integrity: I act from my integrity by choosing courage over comfort; this means choosing what is right over what is fun, fast, or easy. And this also means choosing to practice our values rather than simply professing them.
- Nonjudgment: I ask for what I need. I'm nonjudgmental about needing help, and create a space for others to ask for what they need. We can talk about how we feel without judgment.
- Generosity: I'm generous toward myself; and I extend the most generous interpretation possible to the intentions, words, and actions of others.

It's likely becoming clearer how important *wading in the messy middle* is for being able to practice self-trust. Our own fear and self-protection can keep us from trusting ourselves. However, if we can practice self-trust, then we can move to relationship trust and then ultimately organizational trust. The key is putting intention toward the behaviors that build trust—and being keenly aware for those that erode it. In his bestselling book *The Speed of Trust*, Stephen M. R. Covey outlines thirteen core behaviors essential to building relationship trust; what erodes trust most often is not necessarily the opposite of these behaviors but what he refers to as *counterfeit behaviors*. The following table summarizes each behavior with its high trust and counterfeit behavior examples; the first five behaviors are character-based behaviors, the next five are competency-based behaviors, and the remaining are a combination of both:[183]

Behavior	High Trust	Counterfeit
1. Talk Straight	Telling the truth and demonstrating integrity. Communicating clearly so that you cannot be misunderstood. Prefacing discussions by declaring your intent, so you leave no doubt about what you are thinking.	Technically telling the truth, but leaving the wrong impression by withholding information, using flattery, manipulating people, distorting facts, "spinning" things, or leaving false impressions.
2. Demonstrate Respect	Exhibiting respect, fairness, kindness, love, and civility. Showing that you genuinely care, and showing kindness in little things.	Faking respect or concern. Or only showing respect and concern for those who can do something for you.
3. Create Transparency	Being real, genuine, open, and authentic. Erring on the side of disclosure, not having hidden agendas, and telling the truth in a way that people can verify.	Making things appear different than they are. Withholding information.
4. Right Wrongs	Apologizing quickly and taking action to make restitution. Demonstrating personal humility.	Justifying, disguising, or trying to hide mistakes instead of repairing them.
5. Show Loyalty	Freely giving credit to others. Being loyal to the absent and speaking about them as if they are present; don't badmouth people behind their backs, and don't disclose private information.	"Sweet-talking" people when they are present but talking negatively about them when they aren't. Appearing to share credit but then downplaying others' contributions when they are away.

6. Deliver Results	Taking the time upfront to define the results and then establishing a track record of delivering results, accomplishing what you are tasked to do, being on time and within budget, and not making excuses.	Delivering activities (busywork) instead of results (real work), or performing poorly.
7. Get Better	Continuously improving by learning, growing, and renewing yourself. Not being afraid to make mistakes and learn from them. Being thankful for feedback and acting upon it.	Being the eternal student—always learning but never producing. Or force-fitting everything into what you're good at doing—and becoming irrelevant.
8. Confront Reality	Meeting issues head-on; addressing the tough stuff directly.	Pretending to confront reality, but actually evading it or denying it.
9. Clarify Expectations	Creating a shared vision and agreement up front. Never assuming; always discussing and revealing expectations and renegotiating if necessary. But not violating expectations once they've been validated.	Being vague about specifics; failing to define results, deadlines, or resources that facilitate accountability.
10. Practice Accountability	Holding yourself and others accountable for results; not avoiding or shirking responsibility. Being clear on how you'll communicate progress.	Pointing fingers and blaming others. Failing to enforce consequences when expectations are not met.
11. Listen First	Genuinely listening to understand another person's thoughts and feelings before trying to diagnose or advise. Avoiding making assumptions.	Pretending to listen or listening only to formulate your reply—not to understand.
12. Keep Commitments	Stating your intent and then doing what you say you'll do. Don't break confidences.	Making vague, elusive commitments so you can't be pinned down.
13. Extend Trust	Not withholding trust because risk is involved. Extending trust conditionally to those who are earning your trust and abundantly to those who have earned it.	Acting like you trust someone but micromanaging his/her efforts; giving people responsibility but no authority or resources.

Another way to think about this is that high-trust behaviors stem from leveraging an outward mindset (where we are paying attention to the impact we have on others; seeing them as people with their own needs, objectives, and challenges; and then adjusting our efforts to be more helpful). Counterfeit behaviors usually fall in the realm of an inward mindset (where we are focusing only on how others impact us and seeing them as vehicles, obstacles, or irrelevant).

A great example of these trust behaviors in action is Ian Sohn, the president of Wunderman Chicago, a digital agency. In May of 2019, Ian wrote a post on LinkedIn that quickly went viral, with several media outlets who covered it suggesting that his "Never need to know" credo should become corporate policy. Here's what he wrote:

> I never need to know you'll be back online after dinner.
>
> I never need to know why you chose to watch season 1 of "Arrested Development" (for the 4th time) on your flight to LA instead of answering emails.
>
> I never need to know you'll be in late because of a dentist appointment. Or that you're leaving early for your kid's soccer game.
>
> I never need to know why you can't travel on a Sunday.
>
> I never need to know why you don't want to have dinner with me when I'm in your town on a Tuesday night.
>
> I never need to know that you're working from home today because you simply need the silence.
>
> I deeply resent how we've infantilized the workplace. How we feel we have to apologize for having lives. That we don't trust adults to make the right decisions. How constant connectivity/availability (or even the perception of it) has become a valued skill.
>
> I'm equally grateful for the trust/respect my peers, bosses and teams show me every day.

> Years ago a very senior colleague reacted with incredulity that I couldn't fly on 12 hours notice because I had my kids that night (and I'm a single dad. edit: divorced). I didn't feel the least bit guilty, which I could tell really bothered said colleague. But it still felt horrible.
>
> I never want you to feel horrible for being a human being.

Just think what this credo does for trust—and for people feeling valued as self-authoring human beings! In our work with teams, we teach them concrete examples of how to create their own version of a credo (i.e., what to say and what actions they can take that align with high-trust behaviors) as well as what to be aware of and avoid that falls into the counterfeit behavior category. We also encourage them to check in with each other and start owning where they've fallen short on any of the trust behaviors—creating a deliberate practice around owning their actions and how they're contributing to or detracting from team trust.

In order to *create fearless environments* for teams to be able to own their counterfeit behaviors and start being more authentic with one another, it's important to have agreed-upon "ground rules" or guiding principles. We like to use the Circle of Trust® Touchstones from the Center for Courage and Renewal (a nonprofit organization founded in 1997 by author, activist, and educator Parker J. Palmer).[184]

- **Give and receive welcome.** People learn best in hospitable spaces. In this circle we support each other's learning by giving and receiving hospitality.
- **Be present as fully as possible.** Be here with your doubts, fears, and failings as well as your convictions, joys, and successes, your listening as well as your speaking.
- **What is offered in the circle is by invitation, not demand.** This is not a "share or die" event! During this time together, do whatever your soul calls for, and know that you do it with our support. Your soul knows your needs better than we do.
- **Speak your truth in ways that respect other people's truth.** Our views of reality may differ, but speaking one's truth in a circle of trust

does not mean interpreting, correcting, or debating what others say. Speak from your center to the center of the circle, using "I" statements, trusting people to do their own sifting and winnowing.

- **No fixing, no saving, no advising, no correcting each other.** This is one of the hardest guidelines for those of us in the "helping professions." But it is vital to welcoming the soul, to making space for the inner teacher.

- **Learn to respond to others with honest, open questions.** Instead of counsel, corrections, etc. With such questions, we help "hear each other into deeper speech."

- **When the going gets rough, turn to wonder.** If you feel judgmental or defensive, ask yourself, "I wonder what brought her to this belief?" "I wonder what he's feeling right now?" "I wonder what my reaction teaches me about myself?" Set aside judgment to listen to others—and to yourself—more deeply.

- **Attend to your own inner teacher.** We learn from others, of course. But as we explore poems, stories, questions, and silence in a circle of trust, we have a special opportunity to learn from within. So pay close attention to your own reactions and responses, to your most important teacher.

- **Trust and learn from the silence.** Silence is a gift in our noisy world, and a way of knowing in itself. Treat silence as a member of the group. After someone has spoken, take time to reflect without immediately filling the space with words.

- **Observe deep confidentiality.** Nothing said in a circle of trust will be repeated to other people.

- **Know that it's possible to leave the circle with whatever it was that you needed** when you arrived, and that the seeds planted here can keep growing in the days ahead.

We give this list to people at the start of every core program, workshop, or retreat and invite them to read and note which Touchstones are resonating for them. Then we revisit this list at the start of each subsequent session and encourage them to use these as ongoing guiding principles for *creating a fearless environment.*

In our Building a Cohesive Leadership Team program (which we outlined in chapter 7), we ask each team to rate their current level of trust from two different vantage points on a continuum. On the far right is high trust and includes characteristics such as *I/our team speak(s) freely*, *I/our team admit(s) mistakes*, *I/our team admit(s) wrong-doing*, and *I/our team listen(s) to each other without judgment*. On the far left is low trust and includes characteristics such as *I/our team do(es) not speak freely*, *I/our team hide(s) mistakes*, *I/our team do(es) not admit wrong-doing*, and *I/our team do(es) not fully listen to each other*. We ask them to put an "X" on the continuum where their current level of trust is with the team and an "O" where they think the trust with the team is in general. We do this assessment in session 1 and again at the end of session 7. The image below represents a composite of the "before" assessments for three different teams.

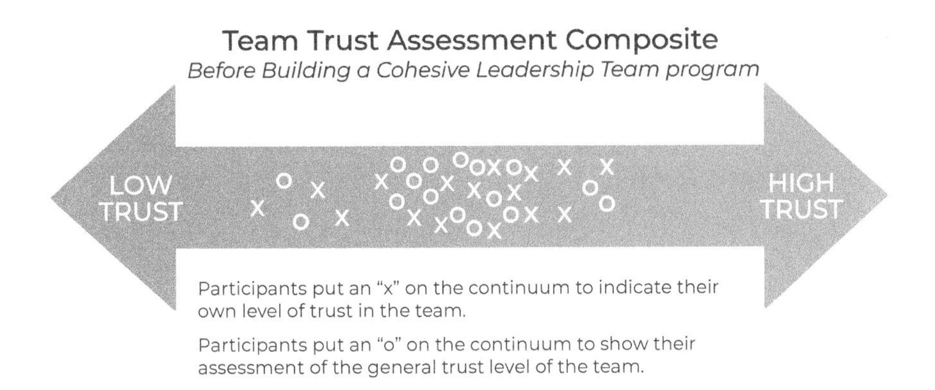

This is commonly what we see for most teams—a significantly varied assessment of trust. By grounding our work with them in the Circle of Trust Touchstones and trust behaviors, we are helping them build a deliberate practice around trust. Then, these leaders *wade in the messy middle* to identify their triggers, Big Assumptions, and Reactive Mind and then do the work to upgrade their inner game so they can leverage more of their

Creative Mind. In doing so, they *create a fearless environment* with each other so they can each show up authentically. And with greater trust comes greater cohesion, effectiveness, and performance. The image below represents a composite of the "after" assessments for these same three teams.

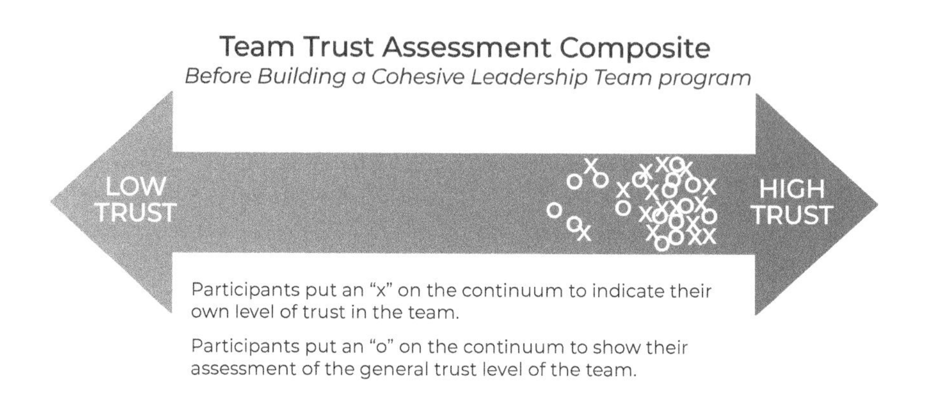

This shift is profound! And when we reassess team effectiveness, we see their scores also dramatically improve. As leaders are able to create greater trust, connection, and support amongst themselves, they are also better equipped to foster that with the teams they serve. Teams can also improve cohesiveness and collaboration by *showing up as leaders* and focusing on self and relationship trust; the formal people leader doesn't need to be the one guiding efforts.

The *Six Hands Story*: Elevating the Impact of IT by Fostering Trust

Improving is a leading software development company that offers technology management, consulting, and training services across ten locations throughout the United States and Canada. They believe companies flourish when they establish environments of trust. To bring value to their stakeholders, they consider it their first job every day to build that trust by creating transparency, delivering results, practicing accountability, and demonstrating respect. With this as their focus, they hope to elevate the perception and impact of the IT professional within their own organization, their customers, and the community in general. As a result of their dedication to establishing ongoing trust and a strong culture, they have created one of the best places to work for nearly five hundred employees and have grown to $100 million in revenue per year.

Their CEO, Curtis Hite, started Improving based on a previous difficult experience where he and several colleagues were taken advantage of, resulting in a lot of hurt for him and many of those people who had trusted him. He thought, "I never want to be a person who takes advantage of other people; nor do I ever want to be part of a group who would do the same." Luckily, many of the people who were affected in the process gave him a second chance. So in 2007, when Curtis had the opportunity to start a new business, he built the business on this trust extended to him.

Curtis belongs to a group in Dallas called YPO (Young Presidents Organization). One of his YPO colleagues invited him to attend a Conscious Capitalism CEO Summit in 2010; Curtis was thrilled with the prospect of finding other people who thought about business like he did. He said,

> I fundamentally believe that capitalism is one of the greatest forces of good in this world. I know that's not a popular thing to say these days. But what really frustrates me is, like most things that are good, a few highly visible bad examples can overshadow the overarching good of something. Should those few instances overshadow the whole? No. I'm extremely passionate about business being this force of good for humanity and what it can do for us, and all the stats behind that exist.
>
> So, I'm at the CEO Summit with these like-minded people. Then I learned about the four pillars of Conscious Capitalism and realized that at Improving, we already do those things; I just didn't have this language for it. We already had a purpose beyond profits, a huge stakeholder model, and focus on conscious leadership with a relentless pursuit of self-awareness; because self-awareness (especially around feelings) leads to empathy, and I believe that empathy is one of the greatest tools that a leader can have.
>
> For the opening keynote, I end up sitting next to Doug Rauch, former president of Trader Joe's. Being a little intimidated, I turn to talk to the guy on the other side of me. It turns out he was an acting president at Starbucks. I thought, "Wow, this is both exciting and scary at the same time." Anyway, the first keynote speaker asks for a show of hands in response to his question, "How many of you have had a great experience with either your IT team or your IT partner—and

> it's great enough that you're actually willing to share a good thing that has happened with your IT partner?" My hand went up, and I started looking around the room. Neither of the gentlemen next to me had their hands up. I'm like, "Uh-oh." In this entire room of about two hundred people, only six had their hands up. And I call this our "six hands story."
>
> The presenter said he wasn't surprised that there were so few hands up. Apparently, amongst CEOs, IT professionals have the second worst perception of all professional groups. And apparently the worst perception belongs to sales teams. Again, I thought to myself, "Ugh! I'm a tech guy and a sales guy!" At first I was extremely defensive and started to rationalize why the perception was inaccurate. However, when my emotions settled, it was clear that the industry had earned much of its reputation. I then started a list of why IT professionals may have earned their bad perception, and the list was significant. I don't even remember the rest of the keynote presentation; I heard the first three minutes, and that thought-provoked me into journaling, and turned into the ambition of our company today.

Curtis was on a mission to disrupt this negative perception and the IT industry. After all, there is not a business in the Western world right now where technology is not at the basis of their company; they run on it and need it, yet IT is not in the boardrooms due to having a bad perception. So Improving talks about it; it has become the ambition of their company. About a year later, Curtis realized that their main challenge was rooted in the concept of trust. "As a profession, we have great intent, but we break trust over and over and over. We have fears and don't talk straight, or we make excuses and practice little accountability."

Curtis leveraged Covey's thirteen trust behaviors to evolve Improving's purpose. They view that their first job every day is to establish environments of trust—not to build software for people or to build a new website. In doing so, they can live into their ambition and purpose. Curtis has become passionate about Conscious Capitalism, and everything about Improving is firmly rooted in the four pillars. He says,

> When businesses first start, their purpose is really to survive. If we don't make a profit, we die. I know it doesn't sound so good because there isn't a social cause, but you are irrelevant if you don't survive.

> A company doesn't live to make a profit, but it must make profit. Then you shift. After about year two, we shifted from survive to grow. Then we were in growth mode for three years. Growth creates excitement for a while, but even that eventually wears out. And that was right at the time that I was introduced to Conscious Capitalism. We had good values; we just didn't have a clear purpose.

With ten office locations, Improving takes great intention to *build a lighthouse* and *create a fearless environment* to ensure that they are deliberately living the tenets of Conscious Capitalism. They have helped start many local chapters; and each office has objectives for how many people will participate, and they will recruit for local Conscious Capitalism events—essentially how they are sharing the message of elevating humanity through business. Curtis explains it this way: "We paint the picture of what people are doing for Conscious Capitalism, and then we measure against it. Big surprise—when you measure people on their performance, results happen. And we do the same thing with trust." In every town hall meeting Improving has, Curtis speaks about both Conscious Capitalism and trust; as he puts it, "There's no escaping it."

Improving does not leave trust to chance. They have a two-hour Improving University trust course. In the first year when they launched the course, more than 90 percent of people were expected to complete it. Then they moved to "The 20 Days of Trust," which is rooted in Covey's thirteen trust behaviors. In each office, groups of five to eight people come together for a two-week period ("sprints"). During each sprint, every person on the team is expected to post four journal entries per week (they use Basecamp to host this shared journaling environment). Basically, it's an online shared portal where people can start threads. So every day someone is responsible to start a thread focused on one of the trust behaviors for the day. Then everybody is expected to post their reply; in each entry they write about what they consider to be their three individual strengths in trust and what their three areas of weakness are. It's all rooted in self-awareness and self-reflection.

So if you have a team of eight people who are all expected to do four posts a week for the first two weeks, you get a hundred or so posts of people saying, "I struggle with practicing accountability" or "I struggle with listening first" or "You know what? I don't talk straight. I get in a meeting and I'm thinking something, and I never talk out loud. I don't have the courage to talk out loud." These real conversations start happening. Last year they had over three thousand internal trust journal posts. There are so many trust posts that Curtis has to select only five or ten to read each day. And these trust behaviors start to become part of people's daily lives. Curtis explains how the benefits reach home as well:

> It becomes inevitable that these values then bleed over into your personal life. I was driving home one day, and you think things like "You know what? I missed my commitment with my kid" or "Okay, I need to right that wrong and I need to practice that accountability and get better at this." I'm using the language of the trust behaviors. Thousands of times I'm reading these now. They're out in front of everyone. We even did this same exercise with a client. As an example, we might say, "Today, we're going to focus on XYZ behavior. What's one five-minute thing you can do to show loyalty or demonstrate respect today?" Then everybody posts what they're going to do by the stand-up the next day. These are deliberate practices. How many companies have deliberate practice around their purpose or around their culture?

Think about it: how many companies have deliberate practices around their purpose or culture? And how many technology companies that do what Improving does are deliberately having a positive influence on all of their stakeholders, including their employees, families, and broader communities? We would say that Improving is definitely breaking the mold of "business as usual" and accomplishing their goal to change the perception of the IT professional. And through their efforts, they are fostering fulfillment and greater connection between people.

The Importance of Fostering Authentic Human Connection

When we feel safe, have a high degree of trust, and are able to shift from self-protection to self-reflection and collaboration, we are better able to honor our hardwired need for connecting and being in relationship with others; we are able to *find our tribe*. It's imperative for our health and well-being as well. A meta-analysis of studies on loneliness (which results when we feel isolated and disconnected) found that living with loneliness increases our odds of dying prematurely by 45 percent.[185] So just what does it mean to be connected to others? Brené Brown defines connection as "the energy that exists between people when they feel seen, heard, and valued; when they can give and receive without judgment; and when they derive sustenance and strength from the relationship."[186]

In the movie *Bad Moms*, Amy Mitchell ends up rebelling against the mean girl president of the PTA, Gwendolyn James, and runs against her. Toward the end of the movie, Amy is giving her candidate statement, which results in a thunderous standing ovation and cheers from the gymnasium full of moms. She starts out by being vulnerable and sharing her struggles as a mom and how she has no clue what she's doing. Then she challenges the audience by saying, "I think we're all *bad moms*, and you know why? Because being a mom today is impossible!" Then she continues with her plea:

> Can we all just please stop pretending like we have it all figured out and stop judging each other for once? I'm running for PTA president because I want our school to be a place where you can make mistakes, where you can be yourself. Where you're being judged on how hard you work and not what you bring to the f^*%ng bake sale. I want our school to be a place where it's okay to be a "bad mom." . . . If you're a perfect mom who's got this whole parenting thing figured out, then you should probably vote for Gwendolyn 'cause she's amazing. But if you're a bad mom like me and you have no f%^*ng clue what you're doing, or you're just sick of being judged all the time, then please vote for me.

Amy *found her tribe*; people felt connected to her because she was advocating for a *fearless environment* where they could feel seen, heard, and valued without judgment. Connection fosters a sense of belonging—an innate biological need and key to effective, cohesive teams. Yet we can't truly connect with others when we don't feel safe and are in self-protection mode. However, when we receive various belonging cues (such as eye contact, open body language, people giving one another full attention and taking turns, the tone of our voice, and everyone being included and having an opportunity for their voices to be heard), the amygdala calms down and no longer sends alarms that trigger our fight-or-flight response. These cues tell us we're safe with these people, and the amygdala instead supports us in building and sustaining social bonds. And when people receive clear, steady signals of safe connection, teams become cohesive.[187]

In other words, we need to embrace the discomfort and *wade in the messy middle* so that we can move from our Reactive Mind to our Creative Mind; we need to rewrite our inner narrative that keeps us self-protected and disconnected and be courageous enough to show up as our authentic selves. We need to learn to pause and be curious rather than judgmental so we can create a safe space for others to do the same.

How to *Show Up as a Leader* and Influence Change at This Part of the Pyramid

Psychological safety, trust, and connection go hand in hand to *create fearless environments* where people feel supported in showing up as their authentic selves. And they don't happen by accident; they happen with intention. Here are some ways you can advocate for and help foster greater trust, connection, and support within your organization:

- **Practice high-trust behaviors.** Pay attention to your own self-trust behaviors. Use the BRAVING checklist each week to see how you did and where you want to pay more attention. When you hold yourself in integrity by practicing high-trust behaviors, you lead by example and are better able to call others to greatness to do the same.

- **Create a deliberate practice for trust.** Take a cue from Improving; engage others to create deliberate, consistent practices to keep trust behaviors at the forefront. Start small; perhaps just engage a couple of coworkers and pick one or two trust behaviors per week to highlight. Before you know it, you'll be "hard-wiring" trust behaviors into your day-to-day operations and will build momentum to include more people and broaden your scope of influence.

- **Find your tribe; move from self-protection to authentic connection.** Be aware of your own triggers to self-protect. Practice pausing and reaching out when your inner narrative wants to withdraw. When you notice others self-protecting, make it safe for them to set down their masks and armor by showing up curious and with nonjudgment. Acknowledge and celebrate others' strengths and accomplishments; and be understanding and help them with their weaknesses and mistakes.

Chapter 10

EFFECTIVE COMMUNICATION

Authentic listening is the soul of growing others.
—KEVIN CASHMAN, *The Pause Principle*[188]

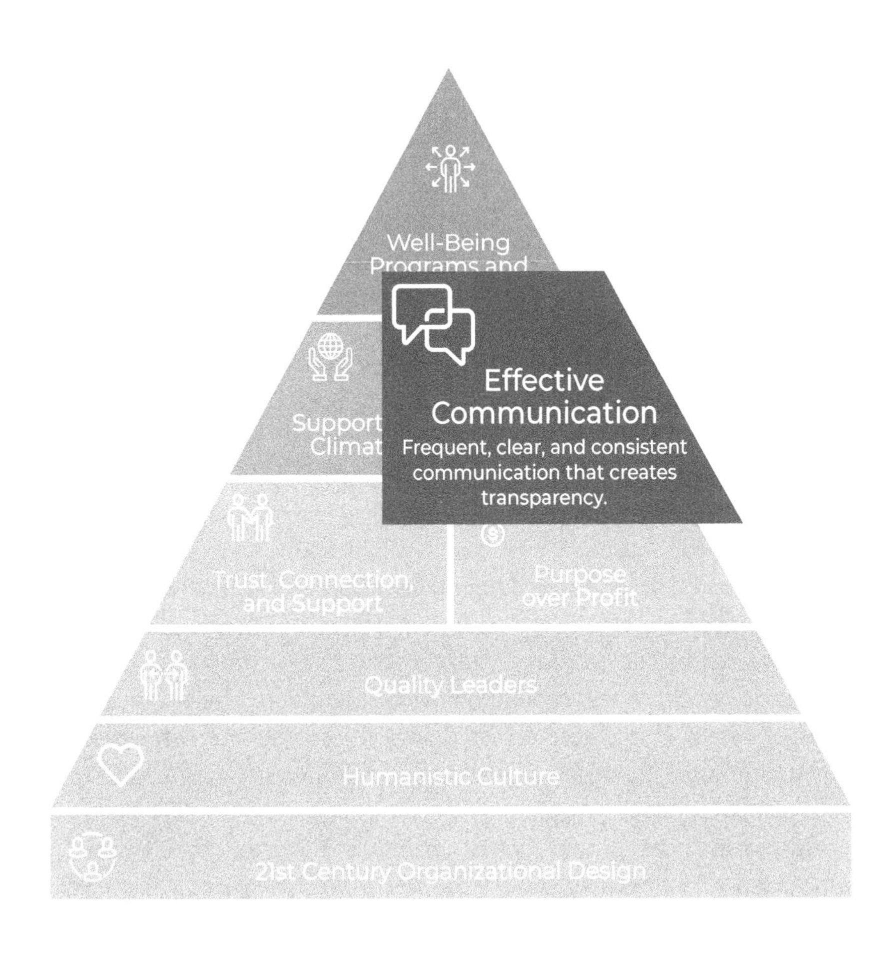

In stressful situations, our higher-level brain functioning essentially shuts down, and we revert to instincts and habits. Imagine if our shipwrecked sailors tried to proceed with their survival plans and new life from a triggered, self-protective place. Instead of the new-paradigm group listening to each other and leveraging everyone's input and ideas, they would have been frustrated. There would have been greater conflict as people shut down due to not feeling heard or talked over one another—only contributing to more stress and anxiety. Not only would they have a hard time thriving on the island, but their ability to even survive would be compromised. Now let's bring this scenario closer to home . . .

How often do you find yourself feeling frustrated due to not feeling heard . . . because someone isn't fully listening to you? How often do you hear people say that they don't bother bringing forward ideas because their ideas won't be considered? How often do you hear people at work complain about lack of clarity or transparency with company communication? If you're like the majority of people, our guess is that you just answered these questions with "a lot." We frequently hear that ineffective communication is the root of most interpersonal conflict and one of the most frequent complaints within workplaces. And hopefully by now you are seeing that how we communicate largely depends on our mindset, inner narrative, and whether or not we feel safe. Add in the adaptive challenges our VUCA world inherently brings, and our instincts to self-protect only get stronger. So when we receive requests to facilitate "better communication" workshops, we know there is usually a much deeper issue further down the pyramid.

Common sense teaches us that *finding your tribe* is impossible without being able to communicate effectively. Additionally, as we learned in the previous chapter, several of the high-trust behaviors also relate to our ability to communicate effectively—and it starts with **listening**. Let's face it, most of us tend to listen to reply rather than to fully understand another person; we are listening through our inward mindset filters and then formulating a reply in our head rather than setting aside our own ideas, judgments, and inner dialogue to turn up the volume of the other person. It never fails; every time we engage groups in exercises to help them see how poorly we usually listen, and then equip them to listen authentically, people are amazed at just how much work they have to do in order to listen well.

In his book *The Pause Principle*, Kevin Cashman outlines three listening pitfalls that inhibit people from authentic listening:[189]

1. Hyper Self-Confidence: This occurs when we move too quickly to our own perceived "right" answer and are attached to being "right." Not surprisingly, this is the kiss of death for collaboration, connection, and innovation.
2. Impatience and Boredom: This occurs when our inner voice of judgment (e.g., "They're not getting it!" or "Get to the point, already!") starts to drown out other voices in the room.
3. Bias for Action: This occurs when we want to DO something, not just hear about it. Our impulse is to act because we assume we know the solution.

In all of these listening pitfalls, the conversation stems from an inward rather than an outward mindset. It becomes all about us, our ego, and what we care about or what we can contribute to the conversation and situation; and it completely ignores the other person's experience, needs, objectives, and challenges. If we want to have true connection and collaboration, and be able to innovate and grow, we need to be able to fully listen to all of our stakeholders. And we can't do that without incredible self-awareness and then leveraging our ability to pause.

How Well Do You Really Listen?

One of the listening exercises we do with groups is to pair up people. Person A's job is to sit and listen to Person B for sixty seconds and not say a word while Person B complains about something. Then they switch, and it's Person B's turn to listen to Person A complain. When they're done, we ask them what it was like to sit there and listen. Most people say it's difficult or frustrating. Then we debrief about where they get sucked into listening to reply rather than listening to understand:

- As you were listening, if you found yourself either wanting to jump in and commiserate with the person and validate their frustration, or you found yourself thinking, "Seriously? Why are you complaining about that?" you were listening to assess or listening with judgment. You were listening for whether or not you agreed with the other person. So the conversation ends up being completely **me**-focused and about what you think is "right." This also is an example of what listening with hyper self-confidence and/or impatience and boredom can look like.

- As you were listening, if you found yourself wanting to jump in and share a similar story or experience or offer ideas and solutions, you were listening for an opening to insert yourself into the conversation—a bias for action. When we jump in and start sharing our own ideas and experiences, it diminishes the other person and makes the conversation **me**-focused. Think about it: have you ever experienced unsolicited advice or someone who essentially takes over a conversation with something like "I know exactly how you feel; one time I . . ." while you're sitting there frustrated thinking, "You don't have a clue; this is not the same as your situation."

Most people realize they've been listening from one of these **me**-focused perspectives; and when we listen from more of an inward mindset, we miss so much. Even if we're facing a situation where our ideas and expertise are needed, we can't effectively offer our input or a relevant solution without fully understanding what is important to the other person, group, or situation. However, when we can notice our initial reaction to make the conversation about ourselves and then pause, remind ourselves to be curious, and seek to understand as best as we can what the other person's experience is, we are not only honoring a core human need to feel heard and valued, but we are better able to offer relevant input.

Being able to listen well (i.e., authentically and focused on understanding) is an incredible strength; it's more like a superpower! When we can give someone the gift of being fully present, hold a safe space for them to share, allow them to be heard, and focus our energy on simply understanding them, it's truly transformative. Not only does it quickly build trust and connection, but it actually helps *build a lighthouse* so we're working with greater clarity and what actually matters. As a result, we become smarter with our contributions to conversations.

In their book *Get to What Matters*, Wendy Lynch and Clydette de Groot discuss some key tools for transforming conversations at work so that we are actually addressing what matters most to people. One of their tools we leverage in our work with groups is the power of setting intentions—for the other person and for ourselves.[190] We have the Person A/Person B pairs practice listening with setting intentions to feel the difference between two different conversations. In both conversations, the person talking is asked to offer ideas and suggestions for an improvement at the organization. The first conversation reflects more typical listening to reply and how we listen when we're operating from an inward mindset and in self-protection mode. The second conversation reflects authentic listening when we're operating from a place of self-awareness and an outward mindset.

Conversation 1

- Intention for the other person: Dismiss them because they don't know the situation or have the expertise like you do
- Intention for yourself: Assert your rightness and how smart you are

Conversation 2

- Intention for the other person: Help them feel valued and heard
- Intention for yourself: Pause, let go of needing to be "right" and be curious

When we debrief conversation 1, the people bringing forward the ideas describe being frustrated, wanting to shut down, and feeling like they were going in circles and that the conversation was useless. When we debrief conversation 2, people describe feeling heard, energized, connected, and collaborative. This is why it is so important to pay attention to our inner narrative, know when we're triggered to self-protect, and be able to pause. It makes a profound difference when we can set aside our own stuff, choose to *create a fearless environment* for other people, and give them the gift of our presence. Imagine if before every important conversation, you were to make a conscious decision to be fully present, hold back and be curious, learn as much as you can, and find some common ground.

Andrew was a member of one of the teams we were working with. He never realized how poorly he listened to people and how much that was actually costing him. Andrew saw himself as a "doer" and was always pushing himself to have an immediate answer; he thought he was disappointing people if he didn't quickly reply with his thoughts or fix things. As we worked through the self-reflection and listening exercises, he felt a pit in his stomach. He started realizing how little he really knew about his coworkers, his wife, and even his kids. His interactions had become more about transactions than connections.

Although he wasn't sure he could really change after all these years, Andrew decided to humor us and try putting some of the concepts into practice. He started paying attention to how often his inner narrative was focused on being "right," and practiced setting an intention for himself to pause, be curious, and make the conversation about the other person rather than him. He also practiced pausing for five seconds before jumping in to offer his thoughts. And when he did contribute to the conversation, Andrew asked more questions to try to understand the other person's experience.

It didn't take long before Andrew became emotional—with both sadness and regret and love and excitement. He said, "I can't believe how much time I've wasted! How frustrating must it be for people to be around me. Here I thought I was being helpful, and instead I've been railroading people. I feel like a jackass; my own kids have probably been thinking I don't really care. At the same time, I feel like I'm getting to know them again. We're having better conversations and more quality time. My wife even thanked me the other day for listening and not trying to be 'the fixer' all the time. Maybe there's something to this stuff after all."

Being self-aware, pausing, setting clear intentions, and holding back are all critical aspects of authentic listening. If we are going to shift from listening to reply to listening to understand, we need to also be able to ask open and honest questions that help foster greater clarity and understanding. Open and honest questions are those that are designed to elicit broader thinking in others, that we could not predict the answer to, and that help us better understand what it's like to be the other person in any given situation. Here are some sample questions that can be helpful:

- What was that like for you?
- What is the impact that had on you?
- What are you wanting for yourself in all of this?
- What did that prevent you from doing? And what's important about that?
- Given what you experienced, what is feeling really important to you right now?
- Given what transpired, what are you wanting more of for yourself? . . . Less of?
- What will tell you you're headed in the right direction?
- How will you know what's the "right" decision or next step?

When we ask open and honest questions, not only does it help us and the other person(s) gain more clarity about what really matters, but it sends a clear message to others that they are valued as people.

The Power of Hosting Listening Sessions

One of the most powerful ways to understand other people's experience is to hold listening sessions. Just as the name implies, these are for asking open and honest questions, listening, and taking in feedback to understand what is important to your colleagues and what their experience is like. Barry-Wehmiller has a deliberate practice of holding listening sessions at all of their locations. I (Rosie) have personally observed Bob Chapman host a listening session about their well-being efforts, and it was truly extraordinary. To have the CEO take the time and intention to be fully present and simply ask questions designed to understand what his employees care about and elicit their ideas sends a clear message: *you matter.*

We've taken a cue from them and provide a framework, training, and practice for all teams we work with so they can leverage the power of dedicated, focused time to listen to people. Listening sessions are a way to bring together small groups of people around a focused topic to understand their experience and what matters to them, and to elicit their ideas and feedback.

The ideal format is a small group for approximately forty-five to sixty minutes; however, listening sessions can be abbreviated and be held on a one-on-one basis and be just as effective. We suggest anchoring them on a specific topic to keep the sessions relevant and to reduce the risk of "recreational complaining" tangents. We also suggest letting people know what the topic is when scheduling the session; and we even consider providing some prep questions ahead of time so that people are able to give some thought and intention to the topic and show up ready to contribute. It is helpful to have another person available to take notes during the session so the facilitator can focus on listening and facilitating. Much like the process we described in chapter 7, we suggest categorizing any improvement suggestions that arise during the session into short-, medium-, and long-term improvement opportunities and circling back with participants so they know what became of their feedback.

Listening sessions can be centered on any topic that is relevant and important to have input from multiple perspectives. We've seen them focused on everything from specific strategic objectives, communication, safety, well-being, benefits, learning and development needs and interests, purpose, and more. The following is a sample outline of sixty-minute listening sessions for one of our clients who was working to understand where they were and were not aligned with living their purpose (i.e., their **WHY** and **HOWS**):

- Introduction/Welcome (five minutes). Thank everyone for coming, and explain the purpose of the session (i.e., to understand their experience and provide them an opportunity to help show up as leaders and shape the experience at our company).

- Introduce Topic (five minutes). Where we are and are not living our **WHY** via the discipline of **HOW**.

- Questions (forty-five minutes):
  - Tell me a story of when/how you've seen us effectively living our **WHY** and **HOW**s recently. **What's the IMPACT that has on you?**
  - Tell me a story of when/how we have **not** been effectively living our **WHY** and **HOW**s recently. **What's the IMPACT that has on you?**
  - If we could change one thing that would help you show up as a leader, be the best version of you, and live our **WHY** and **HOW**s, what would that be?

As you're listening to people's stories and experiences, make sure to ask open and honest questions that help you understand the **impact** these situations have had on their lives. This is critically important for understanding their experience and also for pivoting away from "recreational complaining." Depending on the topic, this can also be a place to add in start, stop, and continue feedback questions:

- What should we continue doing that is helpful in supporting you to live our **WHY** and **HOW**s?

- What should we start doing that will help you more effectively and consistently live our **WHY** and **HOW**s?

- What should we stop doing that would remove barriers to you being able to effectively and consistently live our **WHY**s and **HOW**s? . . . And how would that help you show up as the best version of yourself so you can maximize your positive impact on others (i.e., show up as a leader)?

Facilitating listening sessions is not the sole responsibility for the CEO, executives, or formal people leaders. Certainly, having leaders take the time to hold a listening session sets the tone for the culture and communicates how valued people really are; and the organization can benefit from others hosting these sessions as well. As part of our Building a Cohesive Leadership Team program, we include a session where we train people how to host listening sessions. We also go beyond the leadership team with organizations to help them leverage their culture ambassadors to hold listening sessions (which we'll detail more in the next chapter). Many of them now regularly hold listening sessions or have a "listening tour" so they can deliberately collect feedback that includes the human context and helps them stay on the leading edge (something that is very helpful in navigating the VUCA waters).

The Ultimate "Listening Tour": When a Company Supports Its People in Dreaming

Intentional, deliberate listening not only helps the organization adapt, but it *creates a fearless environment* for people to *show up as leaders*. Miron Construction Co., Inc. is a remarkable organization that is putting listening at the forefront—to help foster people's ability to dream.

Miron is a unique, family-owned construction company that has been in business for more than one hundred years. Headquartered in Neenah, WI, they also have offices in Eau Claire, Madison, Milwaukee, and Wausau, WI, and Cedar Rapids, Iowa. As one of the nation's premier construction firms, with more than fifteen hundred employees, Miron strives to exceed client expectations and bring their dreams to life by building strong relationships, creating innovative solutions, serving the community, and focusing on the health and well-being of employees. They provide pre-construction, construction management, design-build, industrial, and general construction services nationwide.

Miron is a forward-thinking, fast-growing private company with a rich history of reaching beyond construction to understand client stories and translate them into the built environment. Miron has experienced tremendous growth in the past decade, from approximately $450 million in revenue in 2007 to $1 billion in 2018, and is considered an industry leader. Their vision is this: "At Miron Construction, our commitment reaches beyond construction; our passion brings dreams to life!"[191] And they have six key corporate drivers that guide them in realizing their mission to:

- Create relationships built on honesty and integrity, with clients, partners, and employees. At Miron, people come first.
- Fulfill dreams and assist our clients in turning their visions into realities.
- Promote innovation and be the leader in providing and utilizing the best tools, processes, and safety measures.
- Develop solutions that exceed the needs and requirements of our clients, partners, and employees.
- Integrate sustainability to enhance health and well-being and reduce our environmental impacts.
- Serve the communities in which we live and work, giving back whenever and wherever we can.[192]

Not unlike most companies, the economic downturn of 2008 impacted Miron; they had to call on employees to take on more work. They asked themselves, "How do we repay our employees and offer them something unique that doesn't involve more vacation time or more money?" Tonya Dittman started working at Miron in 2007 as a marketing specialist. She is a wonderful example of *showing up as a leader* rather than being defined by a job title or description. Tonya is very passionate and engaged about what makes Miron unique, and saw that there were gaps, so she started inviting herself to be involved in various initiatives. She said, "Here I am out marketing our work; but I want to make sure that we're taking care of our people to deliver on what we're promising." And because Miron worked to *create a fearless environment*, Tonya regularly shared her ideas.

In 2012, Tonya attended a local conference where she heard two people from Goodwill speak about their cultural journey. She was intrigued and wanted to learn more, so she began meeting monthly with Goodwill's COO of people for coffee and to share ideas and book recommendations. One of the books Tonya learned about and ultimately read was *The Dream Manager* by Matthew Kelly.[193] After all, *dreams* are a part of Miron's vision statement (which is unique for a construction company).

It just so happens that Tonya plans Miron's annual summits. Each year, the company hosts employees at an off-site meeting where information is shared about the previous year's successes and initiatives for the upcoming year, and where employees participate in team-building activities. They host one summit for office employees and a separate one for field employees. Tonya approached Miron's owners and began to *build a lighthouse* for them: "You know, I love the idea that we're expecting our employees to bring our clients' dreams to life. Why couldn't we have that same thought for our employees? How do we help them bring their dreams to life? And what if we had a speaker, Matthew Kelly, come and talk at our summit about that concept?" One of the owners, David G. Voss Jr., really liked the idea. Tonya gave Dave and the entire senior executive team a copy of *The Dream Manager*, and they became excited about having Matthew Kelly speak at the event and about the possibility of creating their own internal Dream Manager resource to support their employees. They really believe in their vision statement, and, as Dave said, "If we're honest with ourselves, how do we expect our employees to bring our clients' dreams to life if we are unable to offer them something to help them experience that for themselves?"

Dave began tough conversations with the executive team about what it might look like if they started a program and brought in a resource to help put the principles of *The Dream Manager* into action at Miron. *Was this the right place to invest resources, given the growing pains they were experiencing? Should we be focusing on other things instead?* At the end of the day, the executives realized this program aligns with the company's drivers of *relationships* and *dreams* and would be a way to give back to employees; so the process began to bring this initiative to life.

This program was designed to be about personal rather than professional development; and yet it is something employees can do on work time. It was important to create "rules of engagement" to ensure participants were protected and the program remained confidential and ultimately would be a benefit that people would use. Next, the team created a job description for their Dream Coach and went to work to hire the right person for the role.

In 2013, Miron's Dream Project officially kicked off with Matthew Kelly speaking at the summit. He shared the concept of "dream-storming," where he asked people to write down different dreams in different areas of their lives. Miron connected it to their vision statement, and then when Matthew was done speaking, the company's owners announced that they were going to be hiring a Dream Coach and provided some highlights of the new program. Miron's first Dream Coach was Carrie Garczynski; then in 2015, Eric Marcoe took over, *creating a fearless environment* for Miron employees to *wade in the messy middle* and *show up as leaders* in their lives. As Eric puts it,

> So much of the time, we're focusing on what we're doing and what we have versus who we're **being** and how we can actually "being" now,

which will help us get to the doing and the having. It's just—it's our society, it's our world, it's our industry. Most of the people at Miron have never spent that much time just focusing on themselves; and not necessarily on the things they're checking off their list or are getting done, but to truly look at themselves in the mirror. And that can be hard for people. If you're "checking a box," then you're not really present. Self-work doesn't really end, so there's no destination. It's increasing your ability to be present. And that's what I work with a lot of people on—increasing their own awareness to see what's there and how their thoughts and feelings are serving them.

It did take a bit of time for the Dream Project to gain momentum. People initially treated it like a covert operation, wanting to meet in a private meeting room or offsite rather than in Eric's glass office. There was a stigma attached to the program, like they only met with Eric if they were in trouble or needed help. But now that stigma has subsided, and there's never been a time when leaders questioned the coaching or said, "Hurry up and get your work done and then maybe you can meet with Eric." Instead, Miron's leaders are more likely to be heard saying, "Go meet with Eric. Don't miss this opportunity." Although it's completely confidential, more and more people are sharing their stories, so the value of *wading in the messy middle* is being seen. But it took a while for them to come around.

When the program first began, some executive group members and key leaders weren't necessarily supportive of the idea of the Dream Project. In fact, some thought it was downright ridiculous, including Jason Fuhrmann, Miron's vice president of estimating. Eric was only in his role for two or three weeks when he introduced himself to Jason, who presented to the group during new hire orientation. Jason said to Eric, "Hey, if you have any feedback for me in regards to my presentation, I'd be open to it." Eric was excited and called Jason the next day to set up some time to talk. Jason said he was available, so Eric went to meet with him. The conversation started off great as they discussed the training piece and where there were opportunities to enhance the new hire orientation program.

Then Jason started shaking his head and said, "I don't get it. You seem like a nice guy and a smart guy. What are you doing in this role? You realize this is a joke, don't you? The only way you get ahead in this company is to work your tail off. You don't sit here and dream, Eric. There's no time for that." Eric was taken aback and thought, "Oh my goodness, what have I done? I don't know if I can still get my old job back." But then he just moved into a coaching role. A forty-five-minute conversation transpired, during which Jason vented and shared that he didn't have a real connection with his family anymore, due to his never-ending workload.

ERIC: Let's just take a timeout.

JASON: A timeout?

ERIC: Yeah, let's just take a timeout. What are you feeling right now?

JASON: What am I feeling?

ERIC: (*thinking to himself*) *Oh no, wrong word for this situation, but decided to trust the process and go with it*. Yeah, what are you feeling?

JASON: (*looks down, shakes his head, and then looks up with a half-smile*) I don't know how to explain this, but for some reason I feel better after this conversation.

ERIC: That's because I'm coaching.

At that point, Eric decided to put it all out on the table and said, "Here's what I want to do, Jason. I want to challenge you to meet with me six times. You said you feel a little bit better. Meet with me six times. If it doesn't change your life, tell anybody anything you want about this coaching program. Are you willing to do that?" Jason agreed. By the third time they met, Jason said, "Before we get started, I have to ask you, did so-and-so come talk to you yet? Because I told them they need to meet with you." Then he looked at Eric and said, "Oh, never mind, you aren't able to share who you meet with, are you?" Not only had Jason started to see the difference the meetings were making for him, but he was so thrilled with the results that he started promoting the program without any prompting.

Six months later, as planning was underway for Miron's annual summit, Jason asked Eric, "Do you think it would help if I shared my story at the summit? It's going to be hard and extremely humbling, but if you think it would change someone's life the way it's changed mine and the way I now interact with my family, I'd be willing to be vulnerable and share my story."

At the summit, Eric shared a little bit about the Dream Project, introduced himself, and said, "Rather than hear from me, I'm going to let Jason Fuhrmann tell you about his experience." Looking around the room, all you could see were expressions of surprise. Jason took the stage and shared his story. Afterward, more people approached Eric than during his entire first six months with the organization, individuals who were curious about the coaching process. By sharing his story, Jason broke the stigma. By two months later, Eric's client load had doubled from twenty to forty people. He now maintains a consistent client base between forty and fifty people.

Jason is a great success story—not only because he moved from critic to champion, but because he transformed by *wading in the messy middle*. He used to be challenging to work with; his way was the "right" way. Jason has since transformed into a better, more humane leader and one who people look to for ideas. He began giving team members opportunities to step up (where in the past he might have feared letting go). People now respect him and want to work for him. In fact, Jason's department has one of the lowest turnover rates in the company. He's making an incredible impact—not just in his department but across the organization. He's also creating a better life for his family, and said, "It's really hard to describe how cool it feels to come home and have my kids run to the door to say, 'Daddy's home,' versus when I used to come home and nobody would say a word." Jason is finally becoming the dad he always wanted to be.

Miron leaders are often asked by other organizations, "What's the ROI on this program?" They admit that it's hard to measure but share that it's easy to see the impact, such as when one watches Jason working with individuals throughout the company. And he's just one powerful example. The impact is evident. One of Miron's owners explained, "If one person per year becomes more engaged, decides to remain in our organization, and/or finds their purpose, the program has more than paid for itself."

Miron Construction's opportunity moving forward is to *create more fearless environments* in all relationships within the organization, environments that encourage coach-like behavior and push people to get uncomfortable, *wade in the messy middle*, and grow. As much as Eric loves his work, he views ultimate success as the day he's no longer needed at Miron. At that point, the coaching mentality will have fully permeated the organization. Miron recently developed a new role, director of culture, and the company is doing more intentional work to fill in the gaps toward the base of the pyramid.

Organizations like Miron Construction and Barry-Wehmiller understand the importance of listening well, and they intentionally nurture it. And listening is only part of what comprises effective communication. Being able to be authentic, clear, and transparent is also essential—especially when it comes to providing people with feedback.

The Gift of Clear, Transparent Feedback

By starting with authentic listening, the foundation is set to practice more trust behaviors while providing clear, transparent communication and feedback. People like to feel successful; and, as we noted in chapter 8, part of feeling fulfilled is knowing that our work is meaningful and making a difference. If no one tells us when we are making a difference, or lets us know where and how we're getting in our own way of being able to make a difference, it's pretty impossible to find fulfillment. We cannot support one another in making the adaptive leaps necessary to thrive in a VUCA world if we're not willing to be real with each other. As Daniel Coyle writes in *The Culture Code*, "One misconception about highly successful cultures is that they are happy, lighthearted places. This is mostly not the case. They are energized and engaged, but at their core their members are oriented less around achieving happiness than around solving hard problems together. This task involves many moments of high-candor feedback, uncomfortable truth-telling, then they confront the gap between where the group is, and where it ought to be."[194]

High-candor feedback can only occur when we *create fearless environments* where people feel safe giving the feedback. And because feedback inherently sparks the threat response in our brains, we also need to *wade in the messy middle* so we are able to accept and leverage the gift of feedback when it's given to us. In her book *Radical Candor*, Kim Scott describes a simple yet powerful formula needed for building trust and having open and direct communication that helps achieve results: the intersection of caring personally and challenging directly.[195]

- Care Personally: Means being curious and seeing others as human beings. In other words, we need to be able to embrace an outward mindset to see people as unique individuals with needs, objectives, and challenges and truly care about their well-being and success. It's caring enough about people to let go of our own vanity and worries of what they'll think of us—because it isn't about us.

- **Challenge Directly:** Involves providing personal and specific feedback and recognition. This is not a license to be harsh or insulting, and it is not an invitation to nitpick. Challenging directly recognizes that we all have blind spots. It involves telling people when their work isn't good enough and when it is; when they're not going to get the job they wanted; when the project they've been working on isn't getting the results desired and will be redirected. Challenging also means delivering the hard feedback and making the difficult decisions that are necessary for the organization to live its purpose and achieve real results.

One humorous example that comes to mind of caring personally and challenging directly is a Snickers commercial. In the commercial, two guys who have been friends since third grade are at a party talking to two gals. Brad (being played by Joe Pesci) is acting like his common hot-headed gangster characters and starts yelling at the gals. His friend pulls him aside and gives him a Snickers bar:

FRIEND: Brad, eat a Snickers.

BRAD: (*as Joe Pesci*) Why?

FRIEND: Because you get a little angry when you're hungry.

(*Brad starts to eat the Snickers bar; the camera goes back to Friend.*)

FRIEND: Better?

BRAD: (*as himself*) Better.

Besides being a damn funny commercial, it shows Radical Candor. Brad's friend cares enough about him to pull him aside, give him feedback, and even help him improve to get back to his best self. As simple as it sounds, the majority of people fall short of being able to operate from a space of caring personally and challenging directly; most of the time it's due to our own inner narrative keeping us in self-protective mode due to bumping up against our own Big Assumptions and adaptive challenges. Instead, we end up operating from one of three other quadrants:

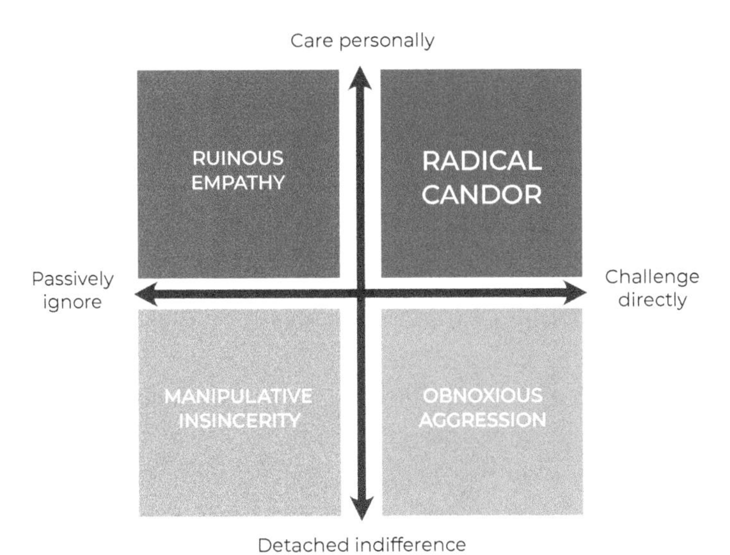

- Obnoxious Aggression: We affectionately call this the *asshole quadrant*—criticizing people without even taking two seconds to show we care (and not providing any guidance for how to improve). This might sound like "Why did you do that?" or "This is unacceptable and subpar performance" or "You suck at that." It can become easy to revert to this style when we're stressed and overwhelmed, *below the line*, operating from our Reactive Mind, and not tending to what we need to be our best.

- Manipulative Insincerity: We refer to this as the *schmoozy politician quadrant*—worrying more about how people perceive us, resulting in being ungenuine and more political. This might sound like "I think there may have been some concerns with how you handled that, but I didn't really catch what they were and haven't heard anything."

- Ruinous Empathy: We refer to this as the *passive aggressive quadrant*—being overly invested in everyone getting along; this can result in not soliciting or delivering criticism, thinking it helps build trusting relationships. In addition to avoiding giving feedback altogether, this might sound like "I think you did fine on that project" or "I think you handled that well" or "I don't have an issue with it."

We usually say that operating out of any of these three quadrants is actually completely selfish and driven by an inward mindset; it's really more about *us* protecting ourselves than caring about the other person. And we rob people of the opportunity to learn and grow when we are unwilling to care enough to give them clear feedback; they have no opportunity to develop and improve.

Kim Scott suggests that the best way to start to move toward a culture where people are showing up authentically and aligning with the organization's purpose via the principles of Radical Candor is to ask people to be Radically Candid with *you*; start by *receiving* feedback. Then, when you do start giving feedback, start with genuine praise and recognition, not criticism.[196] We share her model with all of our groups. It also helps give them a common language; we will hear people say, "I'd like to request some Radical Candor feedback from you" or "I need to have a Radical Candor conversation with you," or call each other to greatness to say, "It sounds like you need to have a Radical Candor conversation with that person."

To further enhance the effectiveness of Radical Candor conversations, we have also been using the F.B.I. formula for giving feedback from our friends at Barry-Wehmiller and the Chapman and Co. Leadership Institute, and it has been transformative. The F.B.I. formula is a way to be relevant and meaningful by being as clear and specific as possible to help the recipient understand the impact of his or her behavior. It stands for: **F**eelings, **B**ehavior, **I**mpact.

- F: This part of the message includes your feelings about the other person's behavior. The more you can focus on how you feel (vs. how you perceive the other person feels), the more impactful the feedback is.

- B: This is where you are specific about what the person actually did. The recipient of the feedback needs to know what he/she did that led to you feeling a certain way; the more specific you can be, the better.

- I: Most of us have blind spots and may not be fully aware of the impact we have on others or the organization. By including this in the feedback, it helps connect the dots for people so they see the results of their behavior—the impact it has on you, others, customers, their team, or the broader organization.

It's also important to realize that **everyone** can *show up as a leader* and leverage Radical Candor and the F.B.I. formula. Let's say one of your colleagues has been showing up in hyper self-protective mode, hasn't been very collaborative, and then dropped the ball on something important. You could say, "I really care about you and have noticed something's been off with you lately. I'm worried about you, as you've been short, distant, and uncollaborative with the team. And now, with missing this critical deadline, I feel disappointed and frustrated. The impact on me is that it hinders my ability to trust and rely on you. And the impact on the team is that we've all had to jump in and work extra to make up for this. I want us all to be successful. Can you give me some insight into what is going on with you?"

With this approach, we're not shaming anyone. We're showing we care and being specific about the behaviors, our concerns, and the impact. It helps *create a fearless environment* where others can hopefully let go of defensiveness and self-protection, be authentically human, and admit and learn from their mistakes. If we want people to grow and develop, we need to *build a lighthouse* to help provide clarity of expectations and then be willing to care personally and challenge directly to help them see their path for success.

We would be remiss in discussing clear, transparent feedback without addressing one of the most dehumanizing approaches to feedback. One of the old-school feedback models we need to be aware of and stay far, far away from is the *shit sandwich*. We've all probably received one of these at some point:

Half-ass compliment + critical feedback + disingenuous praise

Here's an example: "Becky, I really appreciate how hard you work and think you're doing great on most things. BUT . . . [I need you to be more detailed on XYZ; you need to improve on QRS; etc.]. Other than that, you're doing great."

We frequently hear people say they were taught to start with something good before giving critical feedback. Who in the world thought this approach was a good idea? When we do this, we've just negated everything before the BUT; the compliment is now seen as disingenuous. And the same goes for any half-hearted praise after the criticism. The criticism also fails to be direct and clear by being "watered down" on either side. Additionally, chances are that anytime in the future when we want to genuinely recognize people, they will be skeptical and waiting for the other shoe to drop.

Let recognition and praise stand on their own. And use Radical Candor and the F.B.I. formula to have effective corrective conversations; drop the *BUT* and don't combine them. Please, please, please . . . no more shit sandwiches!

Reframing and Leveraging Conflict to Strengthen Relationships

We also can't talk about effective communication without addressing what will inevitably emerge at some point—conflict. Most people tend to view conflict as something that is negative; however, when approached effectively, it's an extremely useful tool that can actually strengthen relationships.

When we work with groups on effectively leveraging conflict, we always go back to The Frame that we introduced in chapter 7.

The Frame

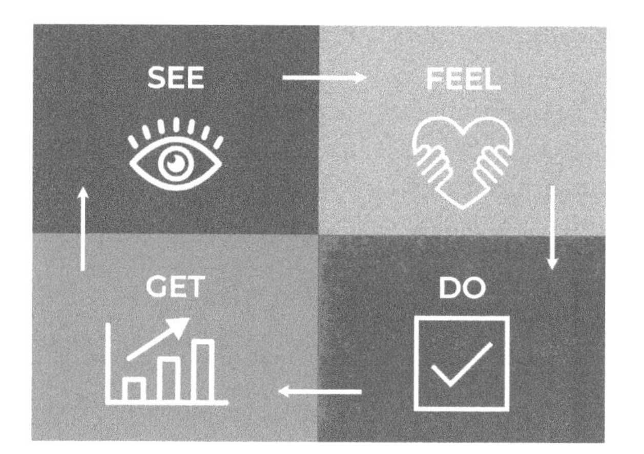

It always starts with how we **see** things, not how we **feel**. This is important because feelings are really nothing more than our body's manifestation of our thinking and inner narrative. If we're telling ourselves stories that are negative and self-limiting, we're going to experience more negative feelings. So we view feelings as a really useful self-awareness tool; they're an invitation to look inward and pay attention to the stories we're telling ourselves, and to get curious about why we're feeling the way we are and what our needs are.

Another important consideration is that we usually end up in conflict because we are seeing things from an inward mindset and end up with a win-lose orientation. With that, we tend to get into conflict about *strategies* for meeting our needs rather than discussing our actual needs; we become attached to our stories and then get married to a specific strategy—as if that's the only strategy that will work for meeting our needs. Yet there are likely many different strategies that can work to meet our needs.

However, if we can move to more of an outward mindset approach, we can shift from a win-lose to a win-win orientation—where both parties can have their needs met. *What am I needing, and what are you needing?* From this perspective, conflict becomes nothing more than a call to creativity to find a find a sustainable solution recognizing everyone's needs. But, in order to do this, we have to start with identifying and naming our needs.

When we feel anger or other negative feelings, it's usually a sign we have an unmet need. So it's important to first identify what need was *not* met that resulted in the feeling. We give teams a page full of words describing basic human needs. We also give them a list of feelings segmented by whether they are categorized as positive or negative. We ask people to think of a time at work that they would describe as negative and then ask them to note which of the feelings best describe what they experienced. From there, we ask them to identify what needs they have that were not being met in the situation that resulted in those negative feelings.

When people gain more clarity about what needs are important, they can start to look for a variety of strategies that will help meet them. And conflict conversations can shift from a repetitive cycle of:

> YOU: I feel ______ .
>
> OTHER PERSON: Well, I feel ______ .
>
> (*With each person working harder to justify being right about his/her feelings.*)

to something more like:

> YOU: I feel ______ ; and I realized I have core needs of XYZ. What are you needing, and how can we work to find a win-win so we both can have our needs met?

Something we always ask people to consider:

Is being ***right*** more important than the quality of this relationship?

Would you rather be ***right*** or ***wildly successful***?

One of the exercises we invite people to complete is called My Top 3 "Button Pushers." We ask them to list the top three things at work that push their buttons and drive them bananas. Then, for each button-pusher, we ask them to challenge their assumptions and then reframe and rewrite their narrative by reflecting on the following:

- My button pusher is ______ .
- My assumptions going into this situation are ______ .
- The story I'm telling myself about this is ______ .
- What I'm noticing about myself in this situation is ______ .
- Other ways I could try **see**ing this situation are ______ .

Most people realize just how married to their stories they really are and how much they're assuming without really knowing. We encourage people to practice using this language: "The story I'm telling myself right now/in this situation is . . ." This helps them start to own that their reaction is based on the story they're holding as true. And when people start to try on more of an outward mindset, the strength of their button-pushers diminishes and becomes much less triggering. We also challenge people to call themselves and others to greatness and *show up as leaders* by asking:

- What is the next action I/you could take that would add value?
- What can I/you do to help?

When we can learn to effectively listen, give feedback, and reframe conflict and leverage it in a productive way, relationships improve. If we want to foster fulfillment and people feeling valued, we also need to be intentional about recognizing others in a meaningful, effective way.

Recognizing Others in a Meaningful Way

We've spent quite a bit of time discussing the harder, sometimes negative aspects of providing clear communication. This is because these are the areas we collectively need to improve upon in order to move from self-protection to authenticity and connection. We must *create fearless environments* so people feel heard and can speak up and provide candid feedback in a supportive way. And we must support people to *wade in the messy middle* to address and overcome their own inner narrative that keeps them from entering into feedback and conflict conversations in a productive way.

That said, another part of fostering trust, communication, and connection is building a deliberate practice around recognition. The WorkHuman Research Institute's data indicates that "for people to find meaning in their work, they need frequent validation and recognition that what they do day-to-day matters in the context of the greater goals of the organization." Yet we are deprived of recognition; 45 percent of workers report not receiving any recognition within the past six months.[197] When done in a meaningful way, recognition is a powerful tool for connection—for *finding your tribe*.

You might be familiar with the chicken-and-egg dilemma but may not be familiar with the analogy of the chicken and the pig. However, Tom Schoen from BTM Global enlightened us. Let's say when you have breakfast in the morning, you're eating bacon and eggs. You know the chicken contributed to the process, but the pig was fully committed!

BTM uses this analogy as the center for one of their recognition programs; their MVP stands for Most Valuable Pig. They literally reward people for being "pigs" because they want people to actually take ownership and do something—to own a problem and take initiative to find solutions. BTM leaders make sure to explain the MVP to people who are new so they don't think it's considered an insult to be referred to as "pigs." Without the humorous context behind the program, it could be considered insulting or dehumanizing. But it is embraced and is part of the ownership culture at BTM.

We like to take a simple, yet impactful approach to recognition by applying the same F.B.I. formula we do for feedback. Let's say I (Rosie) wanted to acknowledge Jon for something he did. I could do what most of us typically do and just say "thanks" or "I appreciate you" or "nicely done." However, by using the F.B.I. approach, I am giving him a gift—fostering his sense of feeling valued and potentially creating energy for him to want to engage in similar behavior in the future to keep having the impact he desires.

"Jon, I appreciate the effort, follow-up emails, and phone calls you did to secure some of the interviews for this book. It's energizing for me to be able to add more stories to help inspire others. Your efforts not only strengthened the quality of this book, they will help others see more of what is possible and hopefully advocate for more humanized workplaces."

Imagine if you were on the receiving end of thoughtful, specific feedback like that. During the last session of our Developing a Leadership Mindset and Building a Cohesive Leadership Team programs, we introduce the F.B.I. formula for both feedback and recognition. Just like we described in chapter 8 as part of the WHY discovery workshops with Harcros, we give everyone a three-by-five-inch index card and ask them to write an F.B.I. recognition message to someone in the room. We keep the room quiet for about five minutes and then ask them to deliver the message. When we debrief, we consistently hear from people how great it felt to write one and that it was touching, humbling, and impactful to receive one. We see this over and over; if you challenge yourself and others to write an authentic F.B.I. recognition message each day, you will start to look for and appreciate the good; and people will feel valued and know they matter.

How to *Show Up as a Leader* and Influence Change at This Part of the Pyramid

Effective communication—starting with authentic listening—is a gift that builds trust and fosters greater connection; it allows you to *find your tribe.* Lack of effective communication is one of the most commonly cited sources of frustration in workplaces and leads to a sense of dehumanization. That's because communicating well takes intention, practice, and ongoing commitment. Here are some ways you can advocate for and help foster more effective communication within your organization:

- **Strengthen your own listening skills.** Pay attention to how you listen, and watch out for the listening pitfalls. Create a deliberate practice for setting clear intentions before important conversations (with individuals or groups) to stay curious and nonjudgmental, pause, and be fully present. Start using open and honest questions; and challenge yourself to not jump in to offer thoughts, ideas, or suggestions until you've asked at least two or three questions and have a greater sense of clarity about what's important to the person(s).

- **Challenge your colleagues to practice authentic listening.** Use some of the exercises we described with your colleagues, and initiate dialogue about the importance of strengthening how well we listen. If you don't already have one, suggest that your teams and workgroups create an agreement to not have cell phones in meetings so people are fully present.

- **Leverage listening sessions.** Pull together some of your colleagues and host a listening session around a current issue or initiative you're working on together. Start small and make it relevant to core business functions and operations. As you start to see the benefit and get more comfortable, you can invite others to facilitate and start broadening your scope of topics.

- **Reframe conflict and practice Radical Candor.** Notice which quadrant (other than Radical Candor) you find yourself in most often. Pay attention to your triggers and the stories you tell yourself that keep you from practicing Radical Candor. Pause, leverage an outward mindset, and rewrite your narrative to one that supports the value of caring deeply enough about people to give them clear, direct feedback.

- **Use the F.B.I. formula.** Whether it's for the purposes of feedback or recognition, the F.B.I. formula makes a profound difference for people. It's hard for people to *show up as leaders* when they don't know what's expected of them or what impact they're having. The F.B.I. formula also helps *build a lighthouse*, highlighting what's possible and the difference others can make while also bringing some clarity and calm to the VUCA storm.

Chapter 11

SUPPORTIVE CLIMATE

We have no choice but to figure out how to invite in everybody who is to be affected by change. Those that we fail to invite into the process will surely show up as resistors and saboteurs . . . We can't see what's meaningful to people or even understand how they get work done. We have no option but to invite them into the design process. —MARGARET WHEATLEY[198]

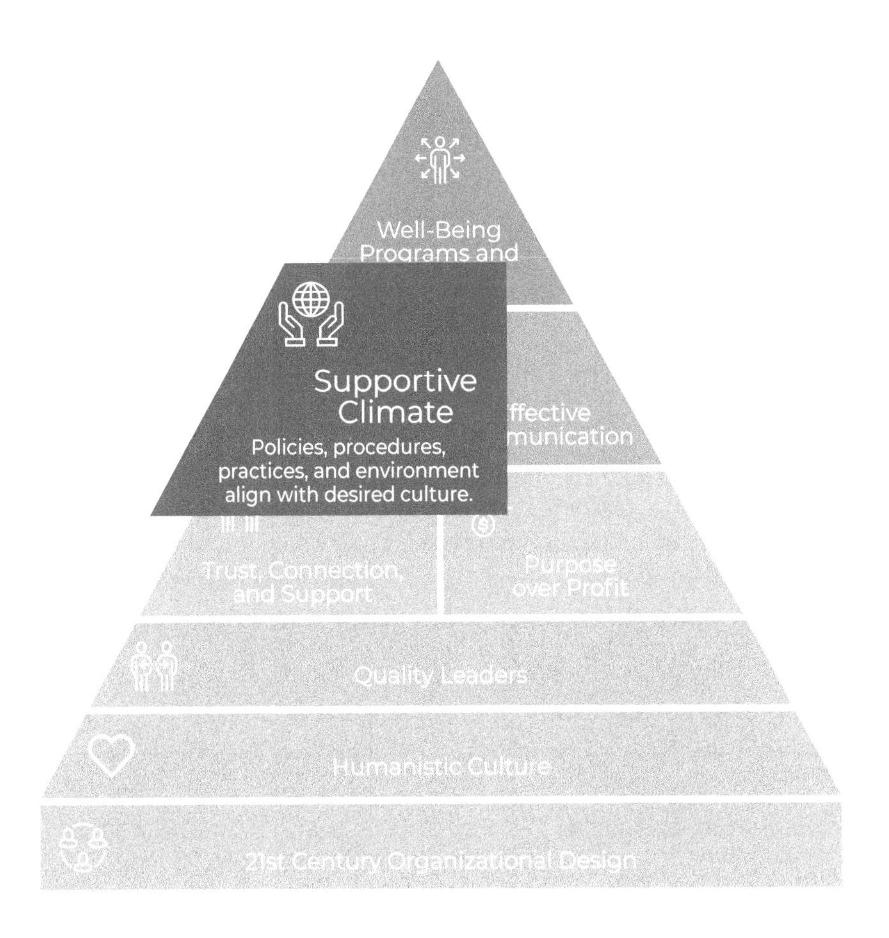

The new-paradigm team of shipwrecked sailors invited everyone to *show up as a leader* and contribute to their plans for surviving and thriving life on the island. They were intentional about *creating a fearless environment* so that people could speak up and share ideas and concerns. How each tribe member behaved reinforced the group's underlying culture; everyone knew and felt that they mattered and were valued. As time on the island went on, they didn't leave things to chance. They collectively created agreed-upon guiding principles for how to behave and treat one another. Not knowing if or when they might be rescued, and knowing the unpredictability of the VUCA seas, the sailors wanted to create clear guidelines that fostered their ability to thrive. They knew that they needed something to refer back to when people's humanity takes over and they show up triggered. And they figured this would help them orient any new tribe members should another group find themselves shipwrecked on the same island.

Unlike the shipwrecked sailors, too often companies leave their culture to chance and don't create a structure to nurture it. Or they think they can improve their culture by focusing on aspects of climate. Neither is effective in the long run.

The Conscious Capitalism tenet of Conscious Culture largely influences this part of the pyramid. Every organization has a culture (and many subcultures, built team-by-team). The question becomes whether we simply work with an *accidental culture* (what has evolved over time on its own) or nurture an *intentional culture.* **Thriving, human, future-ready organizations operate with an intentional culture and align their climate to support it.** They *build a lighthouse* by taking the time to identify the behaviors that are consistent with their purpose and core values and then use them as non-negotiable guiding principles. As a result, they create the conditions that free, fuel, and inspire people to bring their best selves to work each day.

INTENTIONAL CULTURE (actively nurturing a thriving, human workplace)	ACCIDENTAL CULTURE (letting culture evolve on its own)
Core values clearly identified, operationalized, and used as Guiding Principles for everything	Core values not clearly identified or operationalized
Behaviors inconsistent with Guiding Principles promptly addressed	Behaviors inconsistent with Guiding Principles frequently ignored

Hire for cultural fit/enhancement first	Hire for competencies first
Deliberate practices to keep purpose and core values at forefront	No deliberate practices for purpose and core values
Culture is a standing agenda item at all meetings/huddles	Culture is rarely, if ever, discussed
Generously support professional AND personal development	Mediocre support of professional development
EVERYONE is included in discussions and works to shape the culture	Culture is isolated as an HR initiative
Physical and mental space provided to pause, rest, and recharge	Physical space might be provided, but people don't feel they can take time to recharge

As we look at the differences between an intentional and accidental culture, we can see that we must be deliberate in our efforts to foster purpose, fulfillment, and a humanistic culture. It's not actually that hard to do; however, it requires awareness and intentionality.

Creating Deliberate Practices to Support Purpose and Culture

As we saw in an earlier chapter, Improving is not only deliberate about their trust practices, but they also are deliberate about their culture. They leverage their daily stand-up meetings as a conduit for deliberate practices around their culture and core values so that everyone can *show up as a leader*. For example, every week for the past two years their practice on Wednesdays is to focus on one of their values. So if the focus one week is on *excellence*, people will be asked to give an example of somebody who exemplified that value. This allows their values to be a consistent habit rather than an occasional act. How many people can say that they talk about their core values at their company every week?

As another example, in the Dallas office, every Tuesday, the stand-up meetings have shifted from focusing on "what did you do?" or "what are you going to do?" to gratitude day. Everybody comes in and shares the reasons why they are grateful for somebody that works at Improving. Someone might share, "I'm grateful for Marcus because this weekend he came over to my house and helped me move, and I didn't have anybody else." Then someone else might share, "I am grateful for Bethany because she stayed late two times to host the user groups that we're in." It only takes fifteen minutes; and it lifts people up and becomes a big energizing boost during the week.

Another deliberate practice Improving has helps them *grow and find their tribe* and nourishes the Stakeholder Orientation pillar of Conscious Capitalism. Each of their offices opens up their space at night to local professional groups. Many of these groups need places to meet, such as the American Marketing Association, .Net Users Group, Agile for Patriots, and more. So Improving opens up their classrooms at night to these professionals, all free of charge to the attendees and organizers. Last year alone they had over twenty thousand people use their space across all of their office locations. In Dallas, they have become the meeting place with over forty groups that use their space every month. In Columbus, OH, they even had the mayor use their space. This means that someone from Improving needs to volunteer to be present to host these groups and be an ambassador for the company. And they do it because these professional groups are a key stakeholder of Improving's community.

Improving is a great example of not leaving culture to chance. By building in deliberate practices, they are "hard-wiring" their purpose and values into daily operations. Building deliberate practices to help people embody core values and further the organization's purpose helps create an intentional culture. And, if we want to have self-aware, human workplaces, we also need to go beyond daily behaviors and practices to build deliberate practices around how we develop people.

Nurturing a Climate to Support Personal and Professional Development

People are looking for organizations that truly value them not just as cogs in the wheel of the company machine but as self-authoring human beings who are thinking, evolving, and complex-systems capable. As detailed in chapter 7, we need to approach development more intentionally—starting from the inside out, *wading in the messy middle*, and helping people upgrade their IOS. This is the only way to equip people to be able to make the adaptive leaps necessary to thrive in our VUCA world.

Some organizations that are great examples of creating an intentional culture via deliberate support of personal and professional development are Deliberately Developmental Organizations (DDOs). Bob Kegan and Lisa

Lahey have found that human potential and organizational potential are interconnected. There is no bigger cost to an organization than the time and intention spent managing other people's favorable impression of us (i.e., trying to look good); we need to quit this second job of *impression management*. They see DDOs as a cornerstone for high potential and performance by leveraging adaptive change work and supporting people in turning personal struggles into growth opportunities.[199]

These organizations represent a series of departures from typical, business-as-usual principles and practices. It's a mindset shift from work as *performance* to work as *practicing*. In DDOs, people are expected to be working on identifying and overcoming self-defeating patterns of thinking and behavior as part of doing their job well; so how do they do it?

- DDOs *create fearless environments* in which people embrace their vulnerabilities as prime opportunities for personal growth; they are committed to developing *every single* person by weaving personal growth into daily work.
- They operate on the assumption that personal growth of employees and the bottom line are interdependent.
- The personal development that is the key to a DDO is profound adaptive change work; people are challenged and supported via coaching to recognize and transcend their blind spots and "stuck" thinking that has them resisting change. They focus on *wading in the messy middle*.
- DDOs go beyond simply accepting employees' inadequacies; they cultivate them as part of the journey toward organizational transformation.
- In DDOs, employees feel valuable even when they're messing up because they are able to see their limitations as their "growing edge" on a path to the next level of performance rather than as failures.

DDOs are a relatively new phenomenon but stem from years of work by Kegan and colleagues. Three companies that have been operating as DDOs for more than ten years, and seeing great success, are:

- Bridgewater Associates (the world's best performing hedge-fund). The heart of Bridgewater's culture, and the reason for their success, is their search for radical truth and radical transparency. They embrace the discomfort of adaptive challenges, and see that getting uncomfortable, combined with reflection and learning, is what guides progress. This is manifested in everything they do, from intentionally stretching people who become comfortable in their position to how they approach leadership practices. Bridgewater believes that if a job is easy and comfortable, you've outgrown it; they look at roles like a towrope that's pulling you uphill, and they expect people to fail a lot in the beginning. *Wading in the messy middle* is the essence of who they are as a company.

- Decurion Corporation (a California real estate and property management company). Decurion's portfolio of companies has won numerous awards while benefiting from consistent, profound growth during the past few years. They have established axioms (fundamental beliefs about people and work) that provide a common language and touchstone for the company's bedrock principles. While no member (they prefer *member* rather than *employee*) is required to believe the axioms are true, they are expected to act in accordance with them as part of their job responsibilities. They *create fearless environments* with a built-in practice in all meetings called check-ins and check-outs that ensures that focusing on individual mindsets and growth becomes a habit.

- Next Jump (an e-commerce technology company). Next Jump fiercely nurtures and protects its culture and recognizes that sustained happiness can only come from a culture that makes work meaningful. From how they recruit and onboard to daily practices like expecting people to acknowledge their "backhands" (weaknesses that usually lead to trying to overcompensate), leveraging candor, and operating from a mindset of failing frequently, fast and forward (i.e., learning from it), they put adaptive change work front and center. They help people *find their tribe* and never feel alone because they are constantly practicing candor with each other. Their motto is: **Better Me + Better You = Better Us**

All three of these DDOs are doing what the science of human development recommends—in innovative and effective ways. They take these concepts to scale so everyone in the organization has an opportunity to grow and develop. And they intentionally and continuously nourish a culture that puts business and personal development front and center every day. As a result, they experience:

- Increased profitability
- Increased employee retention
- Better error detection
- Reduction in employee disengagement
- More creative solutions to problems[200]

While it may not be the goal or desire for every organization to aspire to become a DDO, there are many great lessons that can be learned from them—including how the intentional integration and alignment of people's personal and professional lives (i.e., *The Fusion*), and *creating fearless environments* that support this work, result in high levels of organizational performance.

Establishing a Structure of Support

Establishing and nurturing deliberate practices that allow organizations to live their purpose and align culture and climate requires *building a lighthouse* to foster clarity of purpose and expectations. It also requires *finding your tribe* and supporting development so that everyone can *show up as a leader*. Because people tend to only support what they've helped to create, it's important to establish a structure that gives everyone a voice and an opportunity to contribute to furthering purpose and close the gaps to living the company purpose and core values.

We have found that one of the most effective ways to do this is by creating a hub-and-spoke model. The hub is a smaller, core team focused on coordinating culture efforts; and the spokes are a broad network of culture ambassadors representing every key area within the company. Ambassadors serve as a two-way source of communication, listening, and bringing feedback to the core team from their colleagues, and sharing clear, transparent communication from the core team and leadership. They serve as a critical conduit for positive change and help keep culture, purpose, and core values at the forefront of day-to-day operations.

Harcros has taken the role of their ambassadors to heart. They launched their ambassador program in the fall of 2017, with forty employee-owners representing each branch location. Since this was a new initiative, people were admittedly a little uncertain and confused about what their role was. We anchored our work with them on the premise of leadership being a **behavior**, not a role, and what it actually takes to show up as the best version of ourselves (a.k.a. *show up as a leader*). We started with many of the core self-reflection exercises we mentioned in chapter 7 and gave them the tools to go back and engage their colleagues in some of those principles. The initial feedback was positive; however, the ambassadors were going back to branches with varying levels of support.

So Harcros began bringing the ambassadors together quarterly for full-day workshops to continue to not only develop them to *show up as leaders* but to also make sure their culture efforts (Harcros Impact) are relevant to the employee-owners. We practiced listening and taught them how to hold listening sessions, how to move from an inward to an outward mindset, how to leverage the F.B.I. formula for feedback and recognition, and how to leverage process-mapping to engage others in identifying system-level improvements and reducing work-arounds. In February 2018, they collectively created their "Ambassador Guiding Principles," which were laminated and distributed to everyone:

- **Be Your Best Self.** Be the change you wish to see, and work to be a leader.
- **Listen.** Listen with a spirit of service; then ask open and honest questions to try to understand what the experience is like for others. *When others feel heard, you're in a good position to leverage the remaining steps.*
- **Be a Conduit for Positive Change.** Focus on creating the conditions where others feel safe and heard and can be part of the change. Focus on the Innovators and Early Adopters and gain traction; don't let the detractors (i.e., naysayers) drag you down and halt progress.
- **Leverage Process Maps.** Pull out those Post-it notes and include people in the process to help identify gaps and areas for alignment and improvement.
- **Embrace an Outward Mindset.** Get curious about your stakeholders and colleagues in other areas/locations.
- **Use Personal Recognition Messages (F.B.I.).** Whether it's a written index card, email, or in person, use the formula provided and commit to giving at least one recognition message each day.

Eventually, we created a *Harcros Ambassador Guide* to serve as an onboarding and reference manual for this group. It includes the various exercises we did with them during their workshops as well as tips for how to engage their fellow employee-owners in being part of the change and Harcros

Impact efforts. The ambassadors now serve a critical role; they were tasked with finalizing Harcros's **WHY** and **HOW** and distilling the Start and Stop feedback from all employee-owners into priorities to guide 2019 efforts. They have begun partnering with the people leaders to have time during safety huddles to discuss aspects related to Harcros Impact. And, for 2020, they are creating subgroups to tackle key organizational issues in a more focused way.

One of the concepts we've used that has been really helpful for Harcros Ambassadors is anchoring their work as conduits of positive change in the law of diffusion of innovation (DOI), based on a theory developed by E. M. Rogers in 1962. It explains how an idea or product gains momentum over time and diffuses (spreads) throughout a population or social system. Adoption means that people are doing something differently than they had previously (e.g., using a new product, adopting a new idea, behaving in a new way). For a new idea, product, or service to take hold, we must move from engaging only the left side of the curve (Innovators and Early Adopters) to the middle and beyond.[201] So the key is to engage the left side, as these people help us *find our tribe* and build a foundation of followers/believers who can influence others.

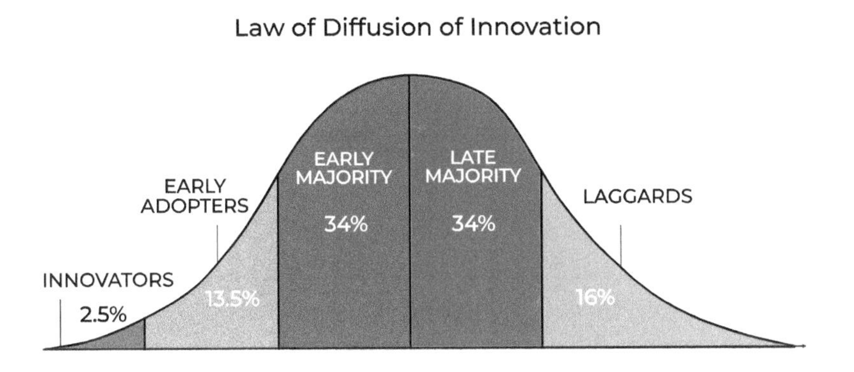

As the Harcros Ambassadors would experience push-back from some of their skeptical colleagues (i.e., Laggards), we continued to leverage the DOI model and encouraged them to focus their efforts on the left side—to *find their tribe* and use that energy to build momentum rather than getting sucked in and trying to convert the skeptics. In October 2018, we decided to take a quick pulse on the adoption of Harcros Impact (their culture efforts). We created a large DOI curve and asked each ambassador to post where they are with their teams and branches in terms of adoption. The left side represents low adoption (i.e., only engaging a small minority), and the right side represents broad-spread adoption. As you can see from the photo below, they were making some progress but still had a long way to go. They had less than 50 percent adoption with twenty-three locations being on the left half of the curve and fifteen locations being on the right half.

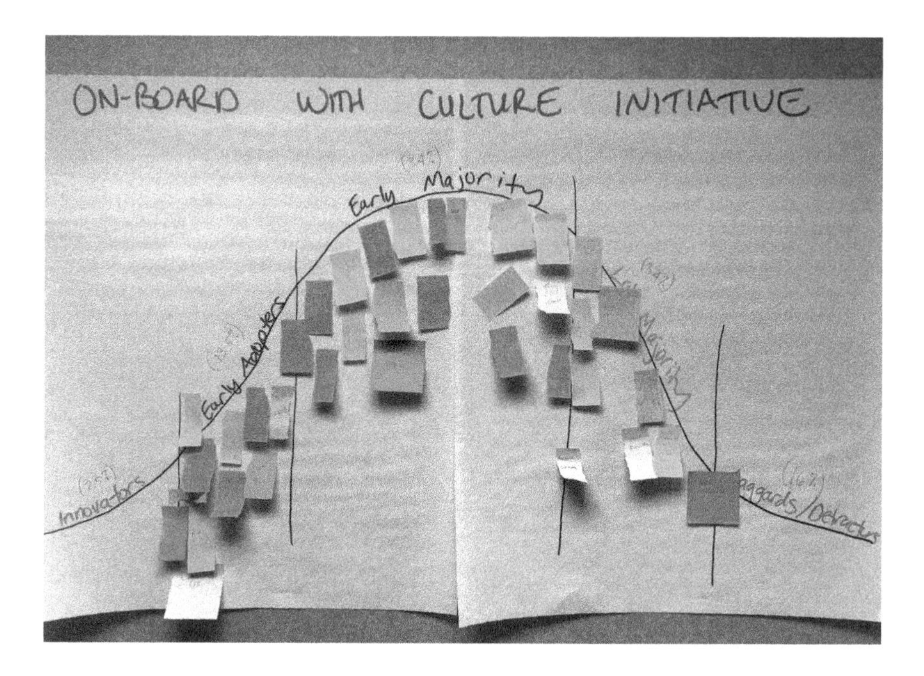

Considering this was only one year into their efforts, they were encouraged. Between October 2018 and May 2019, we had completed initial development work with all one hundred and ten people leaders (leveraging core principles from our Building a Cohesive Leadership Team and Developing a Leadership Mindset programs) and had begun facilitating the Living the WHY Workshops (more on these later in this chapter). We also continued to develop and support the ambassadors to show up as leaders and help engage others in being part of the change by owning their part in the 2019 improvement plan.

We decided to reassess where they were in terms of adoption of Harcros Impact. Once again we created a large DOI curve and asked each ambassador to post where they are with their teams and branches in terms of adoption. As you can see from the photo below, they made incredible strides over that seven-month time period. They had shifted to greater than 50 percent adoption, with twenty-six locations being on the right half of the curve and fourteen locations being on the left half.

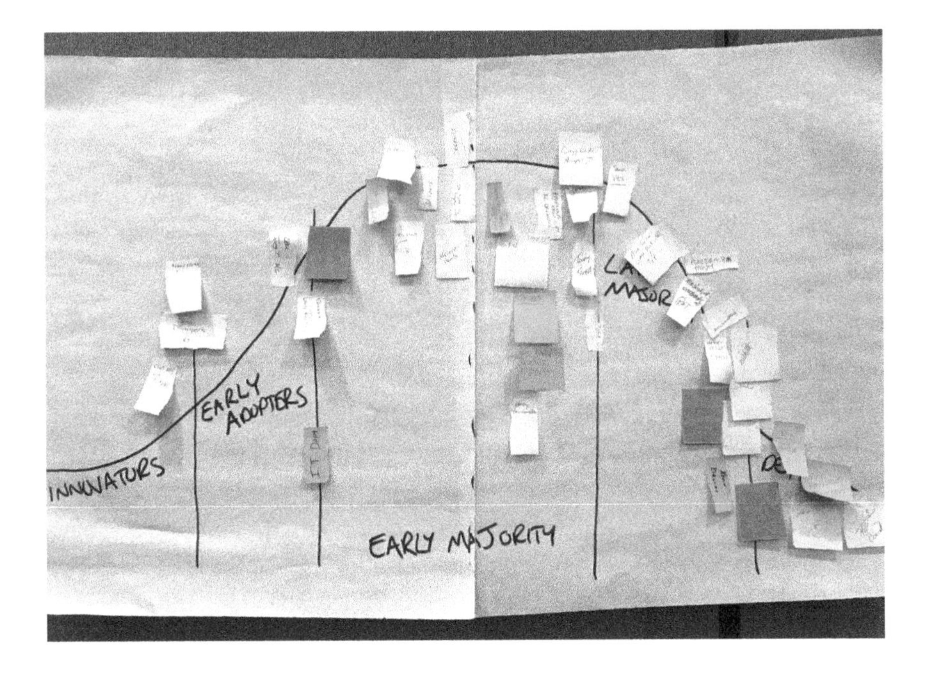

Seeing their progress helped further reenergize the ambassadors. And we shared the progress with the people leaders—which also helped strengthen their energy and support. Establishing this structure to provide ongoing support and intentionality to their culture has been critical to Harcros's success in rehumanizing their workplace.

As Harcros continues to expand and refine their efforts to nurture an intentional culture, they've begun paying attention to their hiring and onboarding. When companies *build a lighthouse*, it becomes easier to be more purposeful about who they hire and how they onboard people to effectively contribute to the organization's success.

Developing a Supportive Climate through Purposeful Hiring

Y Scouts doesn't do placements; it matches leaders and work by "hiring on purpose." Max Hansen and Brian Mohr founded Y Scouts in March 2012 in Scottsdale, Arizona. They wanted to radicalize executive search by placing purpose and values first. Y Scouts takes the broken vertical model of placement and flips it on its side to create horizontal alignment between a leader and an organization. They are transforming how people and organizations connect to work that matters.

Y Scouts provides retained search services for leadership and executive roles for organizations with strong purpose, mission, and values. Many of their clients are part of the Conscious Capitalism movement or are Certified B Corporations (a new kind of business that balances purpose and profit and is legally required to consider the impact of their decisions on all stakeholders). Y Scouts is also a Certified B Corporation, which allows them to engage in a really productively disruptive approach to talent acquisition that better serves their clients and the candidates to whom they also have responsibility.

In order to disrupt the executive search space, Max and Brian knew they had to redefine one simple but gargantuan question: *What defines an exceptional leader?* To best address this question, they enlisted the help of Dr. Robert Cooper, a neuroscientist and strategic advisor to CEOs who has been recognized for his pioneering work on the practical application of emotional intelligence. They enrolled in Dr. Cooper's renowned *12 Leader Program*, an intensive fifty-two-week course. From learning gained during the program, Max, Brian, and Dr. Cooper identified six elements of exceptional leadership, but Max said, "It felt too complex, so we boiled it down to three. That felt like the magic number." Essentially, Max and Brian combined all six into three major themes: *learns relentlessly*, *develops others*, and *drives results*.

Y Scouts defines exceptional leaders as those who understand learning is more valuable than knowing, especially now that the world constantly changes at a progressively faster pace. These individuals demonstrate innate curiosity and insatiable thirst for knowledge. The best leaders have the capacity to inspire and improve the lives and performance of those around them. Exceptional leaders invest in their direct reports, provide coaching, mentoring, and guidance, and truly relish in the success of a unified team. Lastly, memorable leaders are those who get things done. The right leaders possess grit and are inevitably known for their work ethic. They have the stamina to work diligently until they reach their goals.

The Y Scouts process is very intentional and thorough. They work in deep consultation with their clients to understand their organizational DNA—their core values demonstrated through behaviors. This is critical to help them find someone who is aligned to that organizational DNA and who can help move it forward. And because purpose and values can sometimes feel "pretty squishy," Y Scouts also works with their clients to make sure that they are building organizations that can be successful, which means profitable and financially stable. From their perspective, life is always growing, shifting, and shaping; if an organization's culture isn't doing that, it is dying. Y Scouts' process also allows them to provide amazing transparency to the candidates about what it's actually like in the organization. Tasha Hock, one of their practice directors, describes why this is so important:

> So often agencies or search partners do a grave disservice to their candidates and their clients. They buff everything up. They coach the candidates to be who they think the client wants. They make the client organization look like Shangri-La, not realizing that diminishing authenticity, transparency, and candor damages the search process and weakens the hiring match, because ten days or two weeks into this honeymoon, everybody is going to wake up and say, "Holy whoa! This is the real world, and this person isn't perfect; they've got their development opportunities. And this organization isn't perfect; they've got lots of challenges and problems to solve."
>
> When we're really transparent about those problems and those challenges in the organization, it will actually be energizing to the right candidate. That person will raise their hand and say, "Yes, please. That's exactly what I want to do." They'll come into their new role and organization prepared to really engage with those things. It's the same thing on the candidate's side. We work to not overcoach our candidates. Through our covert approach, we are able to discover who that candidate really is; how their purpose and passion can align to help them create positive impact. Then, if Y Scouts sees alignment between what the candidate is looking for and their client is offering, we can put them together to investigate each other. By letting people be their authentic selves, really demonstrating trust and vulnerability around what their development opportunities are, we can help

prepare their new organization to support them in that. Hiding those things helps no one, and so let's just be open about that.

Another element that differentiates Y Scouts is that they're finding candidates who are first a fit for values and purpose as well as key functional skills and the Y Scouts model of exceptional leadership. Y Scouts also connects with potential candidates through their leadership community. The Y Scouts team gets to have conversations with these people, without a specific role in mind, to simply understand who they are and what they care about. It's a really unique experience because it's not transactional. It's not about "What do I need to know about you in order to plug you in against this requisition that we're trying to fill?" Y Scouts has even counseled candidates who were excited about a particular role that is not a good fit for them. Y Scouts has a responsibility to put people in an environment where "their heart is going to sing and they're going to face the kind of challenges that they need to grow as a leader to drive organizational success."

Y Scouts definitely walks the talk. They implement their Exceptional Leadership Model into many facets of their organization and have adopted the model as part of their own core values. This helps to *build a lighthouse* for their internal team, with clear parameters on how to demonstrate values through behaviors. Each core value (*learns relentlessly*, *drives results*, and *develops others*) is accompanied by clear behaviors, and it rotates around a nucleus of "be grateful." Each month, they celebrate the ways in which they live their values because they believe everyone has the capability to be an exceptional leader, regardless of their title or reporting structure. They also work to *create a fearless environment* so their value of *learns relentlessly* can be put into practice; this value is the heart of allowing people to be their authentic self. People can admit when they're struggling and partner with each other.

Interviewer training, custom interview guides, and feedback collection tools are another way Y Scouts makes a difference for their clients. Y Scouts understands talent as the differentiator for organizations, so it doesn't make sense to put assessment and selection into the hands of people who they haven't prepared to do that. The conversion of an offer to an acceptance starts in the first conversation with a candidate. Y Scouts makes sure to spend time to teach people how to be expert assessors and help them understand their role in the assessment process. They want to ensure that everyone who touches a potential employee or a candidate is giving that person an exceptional experience that reinforces their employment brand and mission. They make sure the internal hiring teams are being transparent about the opportunities within the organization and being authentic about themselves while representing their organization as joyous ambassadors. So, even if a candidate who goes through the process isn't the person that they've selected, it still ends up being an exceptional experience full of gaining self-knowledge and growing just by participating in the process.

Y Scouts' intentional human approach provides a competitive advantage for their clients in the talent market because they can reach candidates that other recruiters can't. Unlike most search firms, Y Scouts offers a one-year guarantee on all of their placements because they know their approach yields different results for the bottom line; and they even offer an unheard of one-year guarantee on executive placement! They also try to protect their clients' time by making sure they're spending their time in conversations with the right people. With that, Y Scouts aspires to a five-to-one ratio; for every five finalists they present, their client will make one hire. Currently they're doing even better than that with a four-to-one ratio.

In true outward mindset fashion, Y Scouts gathers impact statements from every candidate they place. Recently they partnered with the American College of Education, a B Corporation whose mission is *to provide accessible, affordable, high-quality higher education*. They engaged Y Scouts to bring onboard a chief marketing officer. As they moved through the search, Y Scouts ended up presenting four strong finalists to them who were all exceptional people—aligned in values, aligned in purpose, and with exceptional functional skills and experience running successful organizations. The American College of Education ended up hiring not only an exceptional chief marketing officer in a pretty short amount of time (seventy-two days), but they accelerated their timeline to bring on a chief innovation and strategy officer because one of the other candidates was so powerful and so well-positioned for that role. Because they really felt the impact of Y Scouts understanding their organization and who was needed to lead that success forward, the HR leader said, "This is going to be my favorite check I write all year."

In an industry where talent acquisition can become a numbers game and robotic rather than a thoughtful, intentional, and humane experience, Y Scouts is a breath of fresh air! It is not uncommon for them to hear from a candidate, "You know, I get hundreds of emails a month from recruiters, but nobody has ever reached out to me speaking a language of humanity around what matters to me." And they are such a great example of starting with purpose and having the discipline to live it. A far cry from the video-based hiring Donna experienced in our introduction!

Leveraging Deliberate Practices to Further Purpose and Unleash Human Potential

As we've seen, being intentional about aligning your culture and climate doesn't happen by accident. When it comes to *building a lighthouse*, it's one thing to find our **WHY** (purpose); it's another to *live* it. Establishing deliberate practices to nourish humanity and further the organization's purpose requires having discipline and accountability around the **HOW**s (operationalizing core values) and being clear about the non-negotiables.

We knew when we helped Harcros find its **WHY** after one hundred years that it was just the beginning. Unless we work to equip every employee-owner to be able to truly *live* their **WHY**, our 2018 work would be in vain. Harcros leaders saw the value in bringing all of the employee-owners together; it helped cultivate community and *build a lighthouse*, with everyone receiving the same tools, language, and experience. So in 2019, once again all employee-owners came together during one of six full-day Living the WHY Workshops. Each full-day workshop (eight a.m. to four p.m.) included eighty to one hundred people. The following outlines the flow and content of each workshop:

- We started out with ice-breaker exercises to help them connect and build relationships. Then we recapped the process and journey that got them to this point, shared the *Heart of Harcros* book with the more than four hundred and twenty stories of them at their best, and revisited how the **WHY** and **HOW**s came to be. That led into a new round of storytelling at their tables. We asked people to share specific stories of recent examples when they've experienced their **WHY** being realized and the impact it had on them. We heard more and more stories of branches reaching out and collaborating and starting to operate more as "one Harcros" (as opposed to separate locations). And with Mother Nature being extra difficult in 2019, they were finding even more of their resilient Harcros spirit!

- The majority of the workshop focused on specific exercises and tools to help employee-owners understand what it actually means to live their **WHY** via the **HOW**s and to truly *show up as leaders*. We prefaced the work by letting them know that the exercises would benefit them as much in their personal lives as their work lives and would give them a common way of showing up and a common language. Then we walked people through our core self-awareness and reflection exercises (The Frame, The Choice Line, and inward vs. outward mindset), and had them practice listening and reframing conflict (as we detailed in chapter 10).

- The afternoon focused on guiding them through some fun, illustrative consensus-building exercises. Then we reviewed how the 2019 Improvement Plan came to be (i.e., a result of the collective Stop and Start doing feedback from the 2018 workshops and then the ambassadors classifying each item as a behavior or system and whether it was a short-, medium-, or long-term improvement). Part of *showing up as a leader* and as an owner requires everyone to take initiative and own their improvement plan (versus sitting back and waiting for someone else to take the lead). We asked people to discuss at their tables key actions they could take to help move forward each of the six improvement plan priorities, and encouraged them to start taking action when they went back to their respective locations.

- We then reminded people about using Personal Recognition Messages, leveraging the F.B.I. formula. We asked who had been using them; although the adoption was not as great as we had hoped, those that were being more intentional about recognition reported how helpful it has been to usher in more positivity and foster connection. Others appreciated the reminder and stated they were going to start using them. Once again, we challenged everyone to go back and write at least one F.B.I. recognition message to someone in their location.

- Just like with every workshop we facilitate, the final component of the workshop was asking for people to share their reflections on the day (either stating something they were taking away from the day or an intention they wanted to set). Here are just a few of the other reflections people provided:

> Your strongest negative emotion is equal to your greatest unmet need. We get in this rut of self-loathing and self-pity. I am now equipped to identify the needs that are not being met . . . that will help me stay above the line and continue to develop and grow.

> "When we have an inward mindset, we become self-focused." It's not about me. I am taking away an intention to have an outward mindset.

> Introspection . . . I need to look within. I need to work on myself; I need to do my part so that we help each other out at any time.

> I came to this workshop feeling negative . . . I had great discussions about issues. It was great to hash it out. We don't totally see eye-to-eye, but we have a mutual respect for one another. My negativity went away. Great reminder to look in the mirror and ask, "What can I do?"

> "Listening to understand" was a good takeaway. Allow myself to pause and really listen to understand.

> Breaking the Cycle of Collusion. I need to improve on my ability to cooperate. Doing that exercise was a nice eye-opener for me.

> I noticed in the **HOW**s we've been given permission to recognize when we don't show up as our best and how to cope with it. It's hard to admit that, but we need to embrace that we are human and have bad days.

> I'm a new hire, and this work/workshop gives us a nice template; it's also helpful to be able to put names with faces. I am inspired and grateful. Harcros has a family feel. We pick each other up.

> These workshops make me very proud to work here at Harcros. I love the team-building and investment Harcros is making in us. I appreciate the culture and the work we are committed to as a company.

To further *build a lighthouse* and create a structure to support the ambassadors, people leaders, and the work the employee-owners did during the Living the WHY Workshops, Harcros has now created an *Owners Manual* that all new hires receive. It includes content about the ESOP, what it means to be an owner, what Harcros Impact is, information about the ambassador program, a brief recap of the **WHY** journey and the **WHY** and

HOWs, and some of the key self-awareness exercises all employee-owners completed (The Frame, The Choice Line, and inward vs outward mindset). And to further model a conscious culture, Harcros now conducts a monthly full-day new-hire orientation; so all new employee-owners are brought up to speed and learn from the start about key aspects of Harcros, its culture, expectations, and more.

Other Ways to Intentionally Align Culture and Climate

In addition to the examples we've provided of how Harcros, Improving, and Y Scouts are intentionally creating a conscious culture via a supportive climate, we can't say enough about Chapman and Co. Leadership Institute's alignment process (detailed in chapter 7 under step 4 of our leadership/people development framework for growing the organization) and how much it has helped our clients.

1. Start with WHY

2. Engage the Organization

LISTEN to Identify Themes and Understand Gaps (not to problem-solve)

"How does that impact you?"

3. Bring your WHY to Life

We consistently come back to this process and encourage everyone to use it as a guide for meetings and discussions within the organizations. Not only does it keep the culture and purpose at the forefront, but it helps encourage people to operate from more of a Creative Mind (fueled by purpose, vision, and passion).

Student Maid is another great example about fostering an intentional culture. They live and breathe their core values. They have turned down contracts and "rightsized" their company to ensure they aren't putting their people in toxic environments. And they are also very intentional about *building a lighthouse* and aligning how they hire people. They want to make sure they find people who want to be part of the team and are energized by their company purpose. Yet they didn't have the financial means to take an approach like Zappos (an online shoe and clothing retailer) takes. Zappos's CEO, Tony Hsieh, is known for implementing their orientation program where everyone (regardless of position) spends weeks taking phone calls and is then paid $3,000 to quit. This is to ensure they're keeping people who truly believe their core values and are able to further their purpose. Student Maid founder, Kristen Hadeed, describes her approach: "When your hiring pool isn't made up of broke students who donate plasma to pay for their textbooks, I'm sure Hsieh's plan probably works. But we needed a way to identify new hires who really wanted to be part of a team without forking over any cash . . . that's how we came up with The Scoop, a document that gave potential team members an inside look at what working at Student Maid and being part of our culture was really like."[202]

Another organization that is intentionally creating a supportive climate is Silberstein Insurance Group (SIG), an employee benefits consulting firm located in Baltimore, MD. Richard Silberstein founded SIG in 1999, and it has steadily grown to become one of the leading employee benefits brokers and consultants in the United States. SIG is known for its thriving workplace culture, which nurtures well-being and humanity. This is reflected in their emphasis on nurturing a truly flexible work environment. SIG trusts and treats its people like adults. They have people working wherever they want to work, however they want to work, as long as they achieve their outcomes. As Richard puts it, "If you're a millennial, who wants to sit in a cube for eight hours a day doing what you don't want to do, right?" Richard also asked their employees what they wanted in their environment. They said they wanted tall cubicles, not low ones; they wanted inside offices and smoked glass so they're not in a fishbowl. SIG embraces what their employees want in terms of the physical environment because they're the ones who have to live with it. Richard says, "Who better to decide than the people working primarily in the office? The leaders and salespeople are running around visiting clients most of the time, anyway." Not surprising, SIG regularly wins Top Workplaces awards.

We can learn a great deal from the deliberate practices of Barry-Wehmiller, Improving, Y Scouts, Harcros, Student Maid, SIG, and Deliberately Developmental Organizations. **Human, thriving workplaces don't happen by accident; they happen with intention and care.** And they happen when **everyone** *shows up as a leader* and takes responsibility for culture.

How to *Show Up as a Leader* and Influence Change at This Part of the Pyramid

Part of *building a lighthouse* is establishing a sustainable structure to nourish purpose, effective communication, and connection. It's being intentional and conscious about aligning culture and climate through deliberate practices—not leaving them to chance. Here are some ways you can advocate for and help foster a more supportive climate within your organization:

- Create deliberate practices to intentionally support your organization's culture and purpose. Take a clue from *Improving*; ask for a few minutes at your next team meeting to engage others in a gratitude practice. Expand from there to discuss where you collectively are and are not aligned with the company's core values; focus on specific behaviors to make the culture and purpose real and tangible.

- Review your hiring and onboarding practices. If this isn't in your wheelhouse, build relationships with others within your organization; start having discussions about where you could be more deliberate and intentional to hire people who will enhance your culture and set them up for success.

- Establish a network of culture ambassadors. Look for opportunities to potentially repurpose various committees (i.e., well-being, recognition, safety, engagement, etc.) that play a key role in the employee experience but may be siloed. Take a cue from Harcros and leverage your ambassadors to create momentum and a critical mass to foster adoption of initiatives. In this VUCA world, it's essential to have people and systems in place that can help navigate the waters of adaptive change.

- **Follow the law of diffusion of innovation.** Whenever you're challenging the status quo or trying to gain support for a new approach, there will be naysayers. Ignore the haters! *Find your tribe* and build energy with the innovators and early adopters. Just like Harcros, you will build momentum and support; it just takes patience and persistence.

Chapter 12

WELL-BEING PROGRAMS AND RESOURCES

There is a huge difference between aspiring to be our best selves and claiming to be perfect. One is a journey of fulfillment. The other is a lie we tell ourselves and others. —SIMON SINEK[203]

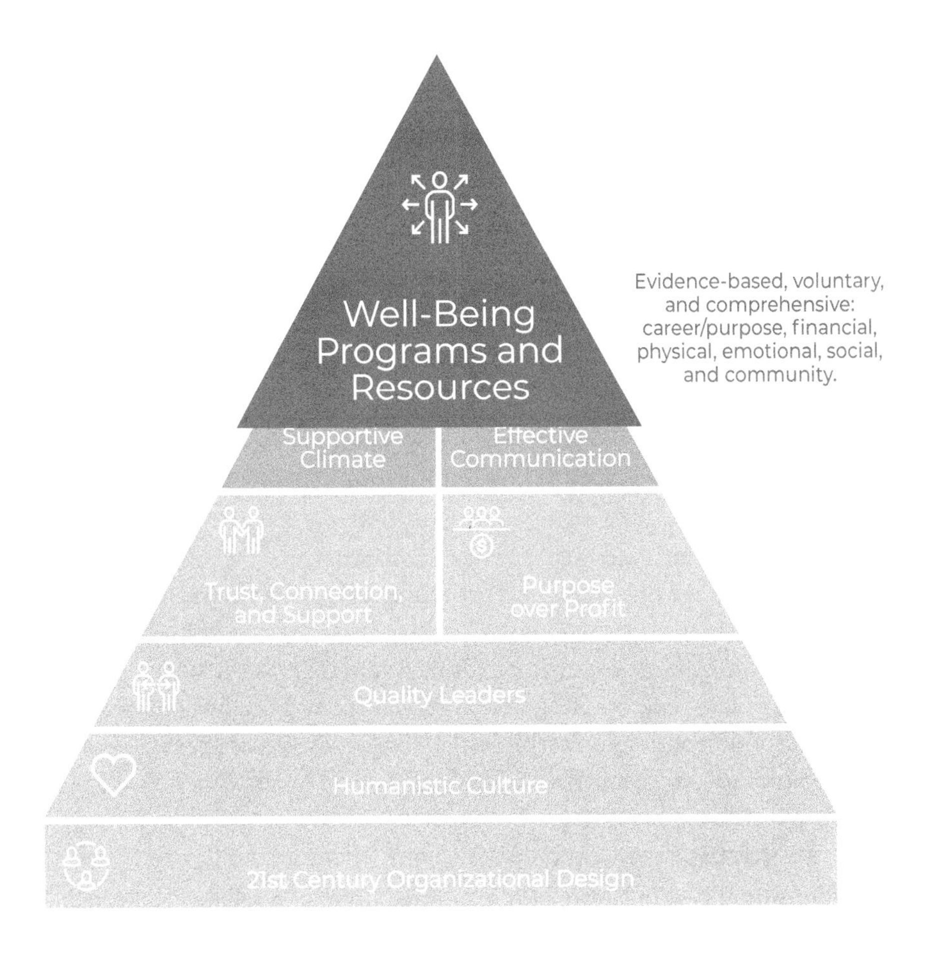

What the shipwrecked sailors needed to be the best version of themselves evolved once they found themselves on the island. They had to focus on different aspects of their well-being, as life on the island was not anything like life onboard the ship. In order for them to *show up as leaders*, they had to clarify what they needed; then they could support one another so they could all tend to the ingredients required to show up as their best selves—despite the circumstances.

This brings us to the top of the pyramid—*Well-Being Programs and Resources*. Given what you have read so far, we are hoping you already see that employee well-being really starts at the base of the pyramid, not at the top. Without a humanistic culture, servant leadership, and physical and psychological safety, these programs and resources are unlikely to make much of a difference. If good work is done in these other areas, however, properly implemented well-being initiatives can bring additional benefits—perhaps as the icing on the cake, so to speak. Anyway, before we can talk about employee well-being, we need to clarify our understanding of what it actually means to be *healthy* or *well*.

In the early 2000s, my (Jon) career was progressing nicely, and I was doing a lot of presenting (and loving it). Then at age fifty-four, I experienced a catastrophic interruption. I had arthroscopic surgery on my right knee to fix a painful torn meniscus incurred playing competitive racquetball. The doctor told me he could fix the problem but that I might consider taking up a different sport. I went home the day of the surgery with my knee wrapped and pain medication built into the dressing so it could be delivered continually. A few days later, scooting up the stairs to our bedroom, I accidently pulled out the tube delivering the pain medication.

We called the doc and found out that it was too late to reattach the tube and that I should continue with oral pain meds. It was excruciatingly painful even though I was eating opioids like candy. It was getting progressively more, not less, painful and difficult to walk until I finally could not get to the bathroom without my wife's help. My neurologist suggested I go to the hospital and get treated for an MS (multiple sclerosis) attack that she said had likely been provoked by the surgery.

The treatment was multiple days of one-thousand-milligram IV steroids. She warned that, although the treatment could stop the attack (which it thankfully did), it could also cause serious side effects (daily steroid production in the average adult male is about twenty milligrams). She suggested that we notify our neighbors so that our ten-year-old son, Joshua, would have a place to go in case I became suicidal or homicidal. Though I was lucky not to suffer from the worst of the potential side effects, the treatment left me manic depressive, unable to walk, and with severe knee pain and even more debilitating muscle spasms, particularly in the leg that had not yet fully healed. Both Joshua and Jerilyn had to live for many weeks with my nightly screams from the combination of the still unhealed knee and the debilitating muscle spasms.

It is amazing how crisis can bring out the humanity in people! Our neighbors directly behind us, who we barely knew, stepped up far beyond anything we could have anticipated. Aside from offering to provide a safe haven for our son, Ron and Natalie regularly brought us food—shrimp dinners and fresh salads; and they mowed the lawn and shoveled the snow for many months so that Jerilyn could take care of me and Joshua. We are forever in their debt for their kindness and compassion.

It took almost six months to teach myself how to walk again. I fought with my insurance company for months and finally convinced them to approve a very expensive electronic device that helped eliminate the "foot drop" in my right leg that kept me from being able to walk safely. Being on that side of the health care space taught me volumes about how important it is to have the knowledge and ability to advocate for yourself in a system that is often stacked against doing so.

I was committed (perhaps a bit obsessively) to showing Joshua that I was not going to let this horror take me away from the people I loved. At age ten he was a gifted athlete and in love with the game of *fútbol* (what us Americans call *soccer*). He had games almost every week, and there was one scheduled shortly after the MS treatment. I insisted that my wife and I attend, even though I was still in a wheelchair. When we got to the game, we discovered that the field was fenced; the only way in was through a turnstile, which would not accommodate a wheelchair. Again, friends and strangers alike stepped up. Some helped me navigate the turnstile while others elevated the wheelchair over the fence. I know now that, at the time, this was a very difficult spectacle for Joshua to watch. I also know that now, as a twenty-four-year-old young man, he is able to understand why I felt it was so important for me to be there.

To this day, I still have to pay attention to every step I take and, though I ride a recumbent trike and swim almost every day, my walking is severely limited to short distances and only on solid, flat ground—no grass, no beaches, and no stairs!

It took more than five years for me to return to the work that I love, and my remaining disabilities continue to make that pursuit quite difficult. Just as I was getting back to some semblance of normalcy, a second catastrophe occurred. I had begun spending the coldest months of the winter away from our home in Michigan and down in the warmth of Fort Myers, Florida. Unlike most people with MS who are heat sensitive, my disease left me cold sensitive; existence in the winter in Michigan was debilitating, making it very difficult and dangerous for me to go outside at all, and making my spasticity much worse. At this time my wife, Jerilyn, was still working in Michigan as a trauma specialist—which she had been doing for nearly forty years.

On her way back to Michigan from visiting me in Florida on Saint Patrick's Day 2015, she decided to take a taxi home from the airport to avoid the potential drinkers out late celebrating the holiday. About two miles from our home, her cab driver ran a red light. Jerilyn was T-boned by a four-thousand-pound car going at sixty miles per hour—a direct hit! The cab was totaled, and they had to extricate her from the vehicle with the "jaws of life." By the time our son, Joshua, and I got home from Florida (he was visiting me as well to celebrate "gotcha day"—we adopted him on St. Paddy's day years earlier), Jerilyn had undergone a number of surgeries, and with dozens of broken bones, a lacerated liver, detached lungs, and traumatic brain injuries, was given a 30 percent chance of surviving.

After almost three weeks in a coma and months and months in rehabilitation, Jerilyn did indeed survive and, to everyone's (including her doctor's) delighted amazement, gradually made a truly miraculous recovery. She did have to give up her beloved profession due to the brain injury, but she was able to move down to Florida with me where she now swims, plays on the neighborhood travel tennis team, and dances to her heart's delight. It has now been four years; as I retell this still so painful, and almost surreal, story, Jerilyn is actually considering returning to work as a therapist, though her damaged short-term memory will make that more difficult.

My experiences as her advocate and caregiver during these past years (as well as those being on the receiving end of her caregiving after my attack and continued disability) have given me perspectives on health that I never would have had without them. And although I would not wish these experiences on anyone, I believe they have made me more compassionate and more understanding of the complexities of the human condition.

Rethinking and Redefining *Health* and *Well-Being*

This brings us to the fundamental question at hand: **What does it mean to be healthy or well?** Perhaps the most popular conceptualization comes from the 1946 World Health Organization proclamation that defined health as "a state of complete physical, mental and social well-being and not merely the absence of disease or infirmity."[204]

Let's examine this widely adopted definition for a moment. According to this, in order to call yourself *healthy*, you would need to have no diseases of any kind, no infirmities, and complete well-being in all of the elements or dimensions of wellness or well-being. Just the thought of that makes us anxious; we both certainly have a number of *infirmities* (defined as bodily ailments or weaknesses, especially those brought on by old age, and/or any failings or defects in a person's character). And neither of us is free from diseases of any kind. At the age of 68, I (Jon), in addition to MS, have early prostate cancer. And I (Rosie) have had Hashimoto's hypothyroidism since I was twenty-seven years old—and will have it for the rest of my life; yet my primary care doctor and endocrinologist will tell you they consider me to be very healthy.

So while a machine could perhaps fit the World Health Organization description, it is woefully lacking when applied to real human beings. We can also clearly see the problem when we look at the *Illness-Wellness Continuum* below, adapted from similar ones dating back to the early 1970s (and repeated in numerous forms over the past four decades).

Illness and Health Continuum

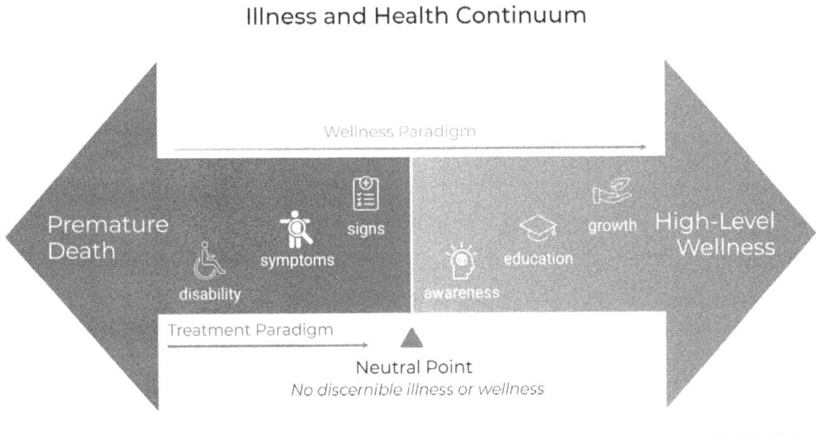

So many confusing conclusions and unanswered questions come to mind immediately when looking at this linear model of health. Using ourselves as an example, we wonder:

- Can we not be on the wellness side of the continuum because of our disease states, which likely have no relationship to personal health behaviors?

- In fact, given that I (Jon) have signs, symptoms, and lots of disabilities, am I about to experience premature death? Or when I (Rosie) experience symptoms related to my thyroid condition (which usually warrants a medication adjustment), am I quickly headed toward premature death as well?

- Are we not able to experience awareness, education, and growth because of our position on the continuum?

- And what the heck is this *Neutral Point* anyway—in the middle of the graphic—a place where there is supposedly no illness or wellness? It's hard to imagine how this could represent any human—or life form for that matter; perhaps a rock!

We would argue that this characterization of health is at best dehumanizing and at worst misleading and confusing enough to recommend being ignored all together. In fact, my (Jon's) illness has encouraged and motivated me to reach what feels like a fairly high level of wellness; I exercise for two hours every day, eat a wide-reaching and nourishing diet, am sure I get the sleep I need, and focus on enhancing my relationships and purpose in my life's work.

So what conceptualization better represents a starting point for understanding the realities of health, wellness, or well-being for *human beings*? First, given the always messy imperfections of being human, we find it instructive to think of the relationship between health and illness as described by David B. Morris: "Health is something that happens not so much in the absence of illness as in its presence."[205]

As for a more precise definition of health that fits with this perspective, there are a number of candidates. Our favorite one comes from Ivan Illich: **"Health is not freedom from the inevitability of death, disease, unhappiness and stress but rather the ability to cope with them in a competent way."**[206]

Like life in general, health is messy, chaotic, and unpredictable. Linear, machine-like, compartmentalized representations (like the one we showed earlier) do nothing to accurately reflect these realities. Besides, as the subtitle of my (Jon's) first book suggests, the real causes of poor health have very little to do with broccoli, jogging, and bottled water anyway.

The Real Causes of Poor Health

There has been a tremendous amount of discussion recently about the sorry state of health in the United States. We are constantly being told that we are in the midst of a number of devastating epidemics (obesity, diabetes, etc.) and that, as a result, our children are not going to live as long as their parents. Regularly scolded by prevention experts, health professionals, and just about anyone else who has a computer and an internet hookup, we are told (often in quite demeaning tones) that we are simply too fat, too sedentary, and eating all the wrong foods.

The solution according to these folks? If we would just exercise and eat the way they say we should, it would fix our broken health care system, prevent 80–90 percent of chronic diseases, and maybe even save the planet. Hardly a day goes by without hearing claims that these unhealthy behaviors lead to chronic diseases that account for the majority of our health care costs. In fact, this inaccurate conclusion ushered in the era of "wellness or else." Interestingly, this whole mess is falsely blamed on four misguided assumptions about our nation's health.

- **Misguided Assumption 1: We should all be frightened that 80 percent of our population dies from a chronic disease.** Given that the death rate for humans is 100 percent, from what (other than chronic diseases) would we prefer to have people die: Malaria, dysentery, famine, or saber-toothed tigers? We are among the privileged nations of the world where these conditions have been largely eliminated, allowing us to live long enough to die from the chronic conditions of old age.

  On a related note, it is instructive that some of these chronic diseases that are almost always attributed to lack of exercise and "unhealthy" eating ("diseases of civilization") actually have much more complex etiologies. Meet Otzi. He lived at the foot of the Alps in Italy more than five thousand years ago and was unearthed recently in almost perfect shape, frozen in the ice. Keep in mind that this was long before fast food, cigarettes, or cars. As a result, although he only stood five foot three and weighed about one hundred and ten pounds, he was lean, very active, and probably ate a plant-based diet, with any meat consumed being wild and low in fat. Researchers were able to determine that he died around the age of forty-five as the result of a spear wound.

The startling finding, however, is that Otzi had significant coronary atherosclerosis, even with all of his "healthy" lifestyle behaviors and even though he was only in his mid-forties. According to the researchers, this is hardly an isolated finding, as it turns out that "heart disease and atherosclerosis were prevalent throughout antiquity, in people who had dramatically different diets and lifestyles."[207] So while individual health behaviors can exacerbate or ameliorate the likelihood of acquiring diseases, there is more to their etiology than just personal responsibility.

- **Misguided Assumption 2: Addressing individual health behaviors is likely the most powerful way to impact population health disparities.** The mantra for health promotion, wellness, and well-being alike has always been that individual health behaviors are the key to improving the health of Americans. However, we know from the Centers for Disease Control and Prevention that these personal behaviors account for only about 25 percent of the disparities in health across our country. The Social Determinants of Health (SDOH) (the economic and social conditions that influence the health of people and communities) play a much larger role.[208]

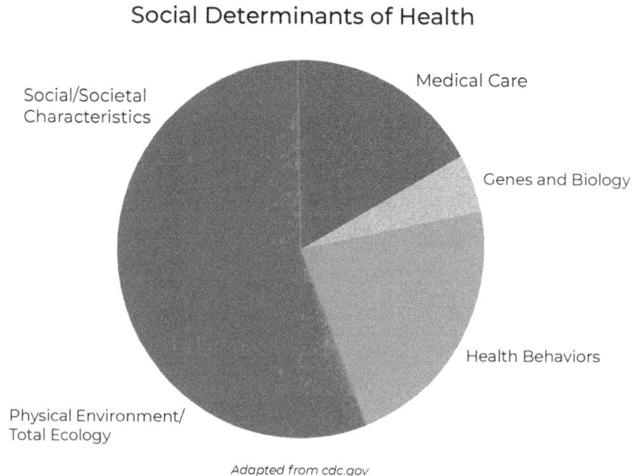

In his book *The Status Syndrome: How Social Standing Affects Health and Longevity*, Dr. Michael Marmot (the world's leading researcher on the SDOH) reviews the evidence in detail. In addition to exploring how significantly our longevity is impacted by where we live, he sums up what really matters when it comes to well-being: "For people above a certain threshold of material well-being, another kind of well-being is central. Autonomy—how much control you have over your life—and the opportunities you have for full social engagement and participation are crucial for health, well-being and longevity."[209]

In his book *The Last Well Person*, Dr. Nortin Hadler also describes the importance of these social determinants of health: "At least 75 percent of the hazard to longevity can be captured with measures of socioeconomic status and job satisfaction. Socioeconomic status overwhelms and subsumes all the measured biological risk factors for all-cause mortality as well as most other mortal and illness end-points."[210]

Consider these statistics:

- Seventy-eight percent of full-time workers live paycheck to paycheck.[211]
- Forty percent of adults cannot cover a $400 emergency expense.[212]
- Forty million people are currently living in poverty in the United States.[213]
- We have the highest income inequality in the Western world.[214]

The reality is that the major causes of health disparities across our population have more to do with income and wealth gaps and the SDOH than they do with individual health behaviors. If we want to address health disparities, we must move beyond kale and CrossFit and start focusing on equity and social justice.

- **Misguided Assumption 3: Medicalizing the workplace and shuffling people into behavior change programs will improve employees' health and the organization's bottom line.** We already established in chapter 2 how "wellness or else" programs not only don't work but they further dehumanize the workplace. Just to refresh our memories:
  - There is no evidence that these programs save money or reduce health care costs.

- Behavior change programs that rely on extrinsic motivation rarely produce sustainable change, especially for adaptive challenges; and they can engender a whole host of iatrogenic consequences.

- **Misguided Assumption 4: Health care costs for Americans (employees) can be significantly reduced by a focus on individual health behaviors.** Our exorbitant health care costs have little to do with what diseases we are contracting, how many fruits and vegetables we eat, or how many times a week we go to the gym. They have everything to do with a system that is set up to make some people rich at the expense of almost everyone else. In his book *How We Do Harm*, Dr. Otis Brawley (the chief medical and scientific officer of the American Cancer Society) exposes the deep systemic issues with our health care system. He says, "The system is not failing. It's functioning exactly as designed. It's designed to run up health-care costs."[215]

  Dave Chase, health care expert and author of the book *The CEO's Guide to Restoring the American Dream: How to Deliver World Class Health Care to Your Employees at Half the Cost*, echoes this sentiment: "The problem isn't the people, it's systemic: our health care system is crushing the altruism right out of physicians and nurses. At the same time, it's crushing the hopes and dreams of middle-income families."[216]

  Think about it. If forty million Americans are living in poverty, that means a family of four has to get by on less than $26,000 per year. Given that the average worker is paying around $7,000 per year for health insurance (or $20,000 for family coverage), it is no wonder that people's health is suffering, as they are constantly having to make decisions about whether to pay for food or medicine. So how do we actually address this problem?

Addressing Rising Health Care Costs While Enhancing the Social Determinants of Health

We know that the cost of health care in the United States is out of control. We spend, on average, twice as much per person on health care as other wealthy countries. This is a major concern for all. The money has to come from somewhere; so the more we need to increase spending on health care, the less money there is available for public health, mental health, infrastructure (housing and economic development), education, human services, local aid, law, and public safety.

The good news is that we now know what to do to substantially lower health care costs for organizations and employees alike. Health Rosetta is a nonprofit organization pushing back against more than fifty years of hyperinflating health care costs. They are a collective group of experts who have "cracked the code" to the health care crisis and are working to build an ecosystem to scale these health care fixes. They have helped numerous public and private employers and unions provide better care while reducing health benefits spending by 20–40 percent.[217] Really!

One example they share is Rosen Hotels. The majority of people working in the hospitality industry make pretty low wages. Additionally, profit margins are pretty low in this industry. So when health care costs increase, it's incredibly problematic. Rosen decided to tackle the health care issue head-on while also protecting and enhancing their benefits—but not by reducing benefits and cost-shifting to their employees. Today they spend 55 percent less per capita while maintaining one of the best benefits packages in the country (which is especially unheard of in their industry). For example, employees can go to a primary care clinic on the clock, and Rosen provides them with free transportation to get there and back if needed.

All of this is despite the fact that 56 percent of Rosen's pregnancies are categorized as high risk, and they have many other high-risk conditions commonly found in large immigrant populations. And with saving money by managing their health benefits well, Rosen reinvests back into their employees—helping with social determinants of health factors:

- They pay for college for their employees after five years of service and for their employees' children after three years of service. As you can imagine, their turnover is way below other employers.

- They also help build up their surrounding communities. They adopted a nearby neighborhood, investing in funding daycare, pre-K, and after-school programs.

- So far, Rosen has paid for over four hundred and fifty college educations. Crime is down 62 percent in the surrounding neighborhood; and high school graduation rates have improved from around 45 percent to nearly 100 percent.

What makes this even more remarkable is that the cost for them investing in their employees, surrounding community, and helping improve the social determinants of health is less than 5 percent of the amount they save compared to other employers. And they continue to pay it forward and have adopted a neighborhood five times that size. Imagine what might be possible if more employers stopped wasting resources on mismatched strategies, actually implemented solutions to help with health care costs, and then were able to reinvest in their employees and community stakeholders!

Humanistic Alternatives to "Wellness or Else" Programs

Let's recap for a moment . . . We know that health care costs are impeding organizations and their people; and it's not primarily due to individual lifestyle behaviors. We know that money doesn't grow on trees and that organizations need to be profitable to be in business; so we need to do something to address the escalating costs. And we now know that we can help solve this crisis by following the great work of Health Rosetta and taking a lead from Rosen Hotels.

We also know that "wellness or else" programs are not a part of the solution to rising health care costs and can lead to further dehumanization within organizations. However, we can't ignore individual health and well-being; it matters profoundly and is significantly impacted by organizational health. So how do you reposition your wellness/well-being strategy so both the organization and your people benefit?

- First, though we have said it before, it bears repeating that employee well-being begins at the bottom, not the top of the pyramid. Without considerable focus on creating the necessary conditions for employees to thrive, add-on wellness programs will do little to improve health or the employee experience.

- Secondly, and just as importantly, remove the carrots and sticks and stop using technical fixes for what are adaptive challenges. Rather than behavior modification, focus instead on supporting better thinking, navigating adaptive change, and overcoming psychological *Immunity to Change*. After all, behaviors are fundamentally the outward manifestation of how we think.

- Next, uncouple wellness from the health plan altogether, because it is not a cost-savings strategy. With the exception of some good health care consumerism and literacy initiatives, it doesn't belong there at all.

- Shift from offering wellness programs to installing employee well-being as part of your cultural brand—an overarching umbrella that encompasses everything you do to support employees in bringing their best selves to work and home each day. Consider embedding it within your leadership and people development strategy instead.

With all of this context serving as an overarching guide, we want to provide some effective, humanistic alternatives to better support people in tending to their well-being. And before we do that, we need to first address the critical, underlying need to bring some ethics and common sense back to how we support health and well-being.

Bringing Ethics and Sanity Back to Health and Wellness Programs

In 2017, we partnered with WELCOA (the Wellness Council of America), the National Wellness Institute, and Quizzify (a health literacy company) to develop the nonprofit Ethical Wellness (www.ethicalwellness.org) and create *The Employee Health and Wellness Program Code of Conduct.*

According to dictionary definitions, placing the word *ethical* before a noun like *workplace wellness* implies that industry policies and procedures should focus on:

- Involving questions of right and wrong
- Being in accordance with the rules or standards for right conduct or practice, especially the standards of a profession

Unfortunately, to date there are no "standards for right conduct or practice" for workplace wellness. *The Code of Conduct* is meant as a first step toward developing guidelines for the ethical promotion of wellness in general and, specifically, wellness in the workplace. Derived from the Latin maxim "*primum non nocere*," meaning "first, do no harm," it is based on the concept of *nonmalfeasance*, which is one of the principles and fundamental precepts of bioethics that all health care practitioners throughout the world are taught. It is a necessary reminder that any provider must consider the possible harm their intervention might do so that "given an existing problem, it may be better not to do something, or even to do nothing, than to risk causing more harm than good."

The Code of Conduct consists of three basic components:

1. Avoiding physical, emotional, and economic harm by implementing only safe, proven, science-based interventions and being transparent about the likely outcomes and risks of those interventions
2. Protecting employees from the misuse of identifiable personal data
3. Making a firm commitment to employ only valid, transparent, and plausible outcomes measurement, including full disclosure of all research limitations

The first two components of *The Code of Conduct* are necessary to protect the health, safety, and privacy of people subjected to these programs. The third component is essential to avoid false, improbable claims. Unfortunately, the use of invalid methodologies in the wellness industry is rampant. Bear with us, as we have found this is critically important to help move beyond our attraction to "wellness or else" programs prevent our good intentions from producing (or engendering) unintended negative consequences. Without getting too far into the weeds, here are some key red flags to watch out for when reviewing any outcome claims:

- **Comparing participants to nonparticipants.** Participants always do better than nonparticipants (largely why they are participating); therefore, any benefits cannot actually be attributed to the intervention. Imagine splitting a group of one hundred smokers into fifty who want to quit and fifty who don't, and then claiming the invariably higher quit rate in the first group is due to the program, not the preexisting desire to quit.

- **Ignoring the natural ebb and flow of risk factors (regression to the mean).** People's risk factors can fluctuate in both directions even when no intervention is present. When evaluating the impact of an intervention, you must consider the changes in both directions. Imagine if you flip ten quarters and get ten heads. Then you gather them up, say a magic word or sprinkle some fairy dust, and flip them again. This time you get five heads and claim it was your "magic" that caused the dramatic change. Of course, this is nonsense, as the likelihood of getting two flips with all ten being heads is astronomically low! This is referred to as *regression to the mean*. You can see this creates confusion in studies when researchers use a relatively low-risk group as control for a high-risk group—almost assuring that the intervention will show changes in risk in a positive direction for the experimental group.

- **Not including dropouts in the data.** This is extremely common, especially in weight-loss research. Imagine a two-year study that claims that 25 percent of participants lost and kept off at least five pounds. This would be an earth-shattering result, as the research is consistent that no more than 5 percent are able to accomplish this. However, reading between the lines you discover that, of the initial one thousand participants, only one hundred were still available at the two-year weigh-in. So the claim that 25 percent (25/100) succeeded in the weight-loss goal is not correct. The correct success statistic is 25/1,000 or 2.5 percent!

- **Claiming impossible outcomes.** Although it may be hard to believe, some have claimed that as a result of their program:
  - Participants were 300 percent less likely to be absent due to illness.
  - There was a 350 percent decrease in appointment waiting time.
  - There was a 240 percent decline in the number of people on disability.

  Just in case your statistics training didn't take you far enough, the problem here is that no matter how powerful your intervention, it is *mathematically impossible* to decrease a number by more than 100 percent. And unfortunately, this true in both the Northern **and** the Southern hemispheres!

- **Inferring Causation from Correlation.** Last but not least, this is perhaps the most common but also the easiest red flag to spot. For the purposes of this discussion, there are basically two general types of research designs—observational and experimental. In an observational design, there is no intervention. Researchers study collected data and try to discern patterns about, for instance, the relationship between various lifestyle behaviors and the prevalence of disease in a particular population. Because there is no intervention, these studies cannot determine cause and effect; their conclusions produce correlations, which merely tell us something about the strength of the relationship between two variables. This leads to creating a hypothesis that still needs to be tested to see if that relationship is actually causal.

In experimental research, an intervention is the purpose of the study—to prove or disprove a hypothesis. It involves applying some intervention to an *experimental* group that is not applied to a *control* group, which is similar to the experimental group in as many ways as possible.

Unfortunately, people regularly take observational studies and claim causality—which is rare appropriate. If there is no intervention (observational study) and the researchers or reporters claim that one variable influences (increases, decreases, is linked to, etc.) another, your red flags should be flying high!

The initial feedback on *The Code of Conduct* from wellness practitioners has been very positive, although some industry leaders have balked, either ignoring the invitation as unnecessary or suggesting that acceptance of *The Code of Conduct* would imply that harm has already been done. Since its initial launch, we have grown a workgroup of professionals who have a desire to help organizations know what to look for to separate the ethical vendors from those who continue to perpetuate outdated, harmful wellness programs and services. Organizations can sign on to endorse *The Code of Conduct* and also embed the language in their contracts; doing so means taking a stand for humanity and not supporting harming employees with misguided interventions and programs.

We hope, with the help of other industry professionals, to continue the process by building out more definitions, examples, practice and program standards, and the like. At an even more basic level, to assist in rehumanizing our organizations, we simply must stop doing things to employees that have a high likelihood of harming them. We invite all interested parties to take part in this important undertaking. In addition to bringing more ethics to well-being programs and resources, we also need to remove the most common dehumanizing approaches to wellness and replace them with more effective, humanistic alternatives.

From "The War on Obesity" to Inclusivity, Self-Acceptance, and Well-Being

Speaking of moving away from programs and interventions that harm people, we need to address one of the most common, shame-triggering, ineffective, and dehumanized approaches to supporting well-being—weight-loss programs. Although many workplaces may implement them from a place of good intent, they cause more harm than good. Instead, we need to shift to health-focused programs that help people make peace with their bodies and their food. A 2014 comprehensive review published in the *Journal of Obesity* concluded that no weight-loss initiatives to date have generated positive long-term results for the majority of participants.[218] And a more recent comprehensive review of decades of research further supports these findings.[219]

Regardless of the population, the length and intensity of the program, the type of intervention, the credentials of the people running the program, and every other variable imaginable, the results of weight-focused interventions are remarkably consistent:

- Many people lose weight during the programs.
- The vast majority gain the weight back once the program is over.
- One to two thirds eventually gain back more than they lose.
- The resulting weight cycling may be detrimental to participants' health.

Given the decades of dismal results from these programs, it is hard to justify continuing to foist them on employees at the workplace, without at the very least presenting upfront the most likely outcomes and potential negative consequences. In fact, it's unethical. *The Employee Health and Wellness Program Code of Conduct* suggests that the following declaration (a.k.a. warning label) should be mandatory for all weight-loss programs: "Research shows that the vast majority of people who participate in weight-loss programs will eventually gain their weight back after the program ends. Many will also gain back more than they lose. The weight cycling that occurs with repeated participation in weight-loss programs may have negative effects on their health."

It is long past time to put these archaic and potentially harmful approaches behind us. The good news is that there are more effective, safer, evidence-based approaches for helping people who are struggling with weight-related concerns.[220]

The Humanistic Alternative: Health at Every Size/ Health for Every Body®

Rather than focusing on weight, approaches that embrace the Health at Every Size (HAES) philosophy have been shown to improve people's health, regardless of their weight, while minimizing the likelihood of weight cycling and the negative consequences that often follow participation in weight-focused programs.[221] By altering the focus from weight to well-being, these approaches can help people develop sustainable self-care behaviors, regardless of size, by honoring and caring for the bodies they have—right now!

The basic conceptual framework of the HAES philosophy includes the following five principles:[222]

- **Weight Inclusivity:** Accept and respect the inherent diversity of body shapes and sizes and reject the idealizing or pathologizing of specific weights.

- **Health Enhancement:** Support health policies that improve and equalize access to information and services, and personal practices that improve human well-being, including attention to individual physical, economic, social, spiritual, emotional, and other needs.

- **Respectful Care:** Acknowledge our biases, and work to end weight discrimination, weight stigma, and weight bias. Provide information and services from an understanding that socioeconomic status, race, gender, sexual orientation, age, and other identities impact weight stigma, and support environments that address these factors.

- **Eating for Well-Being:** Promote flexible, individualized eating based on hunger, satiety, nutritional needs, and pleasure rather than any externally regulated eating plan focused on weight control.

- **Life-Enhancing Movement:** Support physical activities that allow people of all sizes, abilities, and interests to engage in enjoyable movement, to the degree which they are able.

Here's an example of why the shift from weight to HAES is so important. Several years ago, I (Jon) was asked to speak to a group of fitness professionals at a large health insurance company in Tennessee. The nutrition professional who invited me was leaning in the direction of Health at Every Size and wanted me to speak with the fitness staff of their on-site gym who were responsible for running their weight-loss program. When I arrived at the facility, I was led into the fitness conference room and introduced to the staff, led by a young man with a master's degree in exercise physiology.

I was prepared to do a presentation explaining the futility and dangers of weight-loss programs and the benefits of Health at Every Size. As I was about to begin, I noticed that adorning the walls all around the room were a series of *before and after* pictures of men and women who had gone through their weight-loss program. They were typical; the *before* photo showing a rather frumpy, unhappy-looking person, and the *after* photo showing a much, much thinner, well-dressed, happy-looking individual. There were eleven or twelve sets of such pictures. I turned to the group and asked them two questions:

1. How many of these employees still work here?
2. Where are they now in terms of their weight?

A general silence fell over the room. After a brief pause, one of the fitness staff said, "All but one of these employees still works for the company; and I never really thought about how they are doing now with their weight." We went around the room and one-by-one addressed the pictures. Aside from the individual who had left the company, they realized that every other employee had gained back most, or all, of their weight since the pictures had been taken. As I looked around the room, the surprise and dismal reality was clearly evident on their faces and was probably more impactful than anything I had to say in the ensuing training.

There is so much shame and self-limiting inner narrative that surrounds food and weight that is frequently often ignored. Years ago, my colleague Laura McKibbin developed a HAES-oriented workplace program called Health for Every Body that we have implemented in numerous worksites throughout the US. When we first began implementing the program, I (Jon) contacted professionals I knew in the HAES community to facilitate the program wherever it was requested. As we received more and more requests, we decided to create a training program for facilitators.

The Health for Every Body Facilitator Training is a live, online twelve-week course that provides participants with the skills and confidence to help people develop positive self-care behaviors regardless of size, while making peace with their bodies and their food. After completing the training, graduates have everything they need to deliver a turnkey ten-week program at their workplace or in their community. One really nice feature of the program is that facilitating it is not confined to just nutrition professionals. Here is what two graduates of the training had to say about their experiences:

> I went into this course knowing I was going to learn about helping individuals make peace with their bodies and their food regardless of their size. What I didn't know is that I would also learn about myself and be able to use the course to live my life in a different way. The concepts, ideas, and information presented in this course will forever change my views not just as a health professional but as an individual. (Megan, Senior Benefits Analyst/Well-Being)

> One of the most valuable things I learned is that I need to be kinder to myself. I have realized just because I am a health professional in this area, I still am human, so our messed-up culture is bound to affect my thinking. I have learned valuable strategies, activities, and resources that will improve my teaching. (Alison, Dietetic Internship Faculty)

Ours is not the only approach that helps people improve the quality of their lives without a weight-loss focus. Am I Hungry?® (https://amihungry.com/) is a wonderful program, created by Dr. Michelle May, that teaches mindful eating (something we introduce in HFEB but don't have time to spend practicing in a way that will actually alter behavior sustainably). The underlying principle of mindful eating is that people can learn (actually relearn, since children are brought into this world knowing how to do this) to eat according to internal signals of hunger, appetite, and satiety. The program helps people to reduce anxiety around weight and food. I (Jon) like to say that it helps people to decide for themselves what and how much to eat without having to pay someone else to decide for them.

In 2017, we partnered with Am I Hungry? for a pilot program at Michigan's largest health care system, Beaumont Health. The workplace intervention consisted of two components: part 1 was a ten-session in-person Health for Every Body program; and part 2 was an eight-session in-person Am I Hungry? mindful eating program.[223] We saw positive changes in a wide variety of health and eating-related behaviors, including improvements in body appreciation, intuitive eating, positive emotions, relationships, accomplishments, and perceived health. Participants' reflections on the class experience were overwhelmingly positive, and the programs are now in their third iteration at the hospital system.

We encourage any workplace considering supporting employees who are struggling with weight and eating to avoid weight-loss programs and instead consider one of these humanistic alternatives. And while weight tends to be one of the most common focuses of traditional employee well-being efforts, there are multiple aspects of well-being that organizations would benefit far more from by supporting. If we want to support people in thriving in their well-being and *showing up as leaders*, we need to make sure programs and resources that are offered are effective, ethical, holistic, voluntary, and honoring what it means to be human.

Leveraging Well-Being to *Build a Lighthouse* and Boost Community Well-Being

We spent a great deal of time in our first book highlighting specific alternatives to common stuck wellness program components; if this is of interest to you, we encourage you to read it. Our hope for this book is to highlight what is possible when we move from control-oriented "wellness or else" programs to those that nurture and support people in their well-being and becoming the best version of themselves.

One organization that is fostering purpose along with well-being is Silberstein Insurance Group (SIG). Giving back and supporting their community has become a staple of SIG's humanistic culture. A few years ago, Richard Silberstein saw something on television that gave him the idea to do a *pay-it-forward* program. He was at the beach where he saw this man named Scotty who was a veteran. Scotty was the local town vet who everyone thought was a crazy loner. Richard would go into Starbucks on the weekend and sit with him. After a while, Scotty told Richard he was his therapist, and they became friends. Every Saturday or Sunday Richard would spend about an hour with Scotty.

Richard saw Scotty on Christmas and gave him $100. He told Scotty that his office was doing this pay-it-forward initiative. Scotty said he was going to take three other vets out for Christmas dinner at $25 each. It moved Richard to tears. So he went to the bank and came back to the office with $9,000 ($200 for each of the forty-five people in his firm); everyone needed to use the money to pay it forward.

They started having meetings every month, where Richard would ask if anybody wanted to talk about their pay-it-forward, and they had people telling their stories with lots of tears of joy and feeling great. One woman went to the airport wanting to give the money to a Marine. She waited two and a half hours. Then she saw a man in uniform and asked, "Are you a vet?" He replied, "Yes." "Are you a Marine?" she asked. "No; Air Force." He was paraplegic. She spent an hour with him, and then gave him the money. His mom ended up calling her to tell her how much her kindness meant.

Another woman working at SIG created a nonprofit, Blankets for Baltimore; they put together care packages for people to take to people living on the streets. SIG holds HR roundtable events and has now encouraged their HR community to bring old blankets; they're now engaging their clients to also pay it forward. At one of their roundtables, they had speakers from Habitat for Humanity, Ulman Cancer, and Conscious Venture Lab (to name a few) talking to HR people about the importance of social impact. They *built a lighthouse* to show what is possible with a little effort and care, and they are engaging others and *finding their tribe* to continue to grow their collective impact.

Nurturing Well-Being in Every Area of the Pyramid

An organization that is effectively supporting well-being from the bottom of the pyramid and enhancing it at the top is Envision IT. Their business model supports "whole life." And it starts with their conscious, humanistic culture. They don't have a big product line to sell, so there's no temptation for typical industry bad behavior. They've *built a lighthouse* so everyone shares the same interest in making sure they are living their purpose, helping other people have a great day at work, and making sure they can effectively contribute by making technology work for them. Envision doesn't push any of their consultants to work crazy hours, and they reinvest their profits into improving the experience of their collective stakeholders. So, what they ask of their consultants is much less than the industry standard; this allows time for professional development and, most importantly, time for a whole life.

From the base to the middle of the pyramid, Envision is intentional about their practices. They regularly and consistently work on conscious leadership in order to foster a conscious culture. In addition to having formal development (workshops, conferences, coaching, and leveraging conscious leadership practices), they also do self-study (mindfulness practice, reading, etc.). Every aspect of how they set up their business honors their purpose, fosters trust and connection, nourishes effective communication, and creates a supportive climate where they can fuse their work and personal lives.

At the top of the pyramid, Envision is intentional to support their people so they can thrive. Their benefits are purposeful based on what Envisioners need, not what will look good on paper. They offer excellent health insurance with mental health support; anyone can be in therapy for (currently) only a $20 co-pay—no deductible or coinsurance. In 2017, several Envisioners had babies; so they decided to start seeding the college funds of every Envisioner born into their family. They noticed most Envisioners also have pets, and pets are people's fur babies. And when an Envisioner's dog had cancer, they decided to offer and subsidize pet insurance. They also noticed people would be rushing out to get to a yoga class, so they started offering free yoga on-site.

Envision also offers a lot of family events and activities and volunteer work opportunities that help them build community and bring them closer together, such as Habitat for Humanity or Meals on Wheels. One of the things they do is called Balloons in a Box; they help create birthday parties (cards, decorations, etc.) with their families for other kids who aren't able to afford their own birthday parties. So the children of Envisioners are helping other kids. The key is that nothing is forced upon people!

Perhaps most inspiring is how they take care of their own. In October 2016, they found out they were a finalist for the Innovation Award for work they did with their client Exact Sciences. Exact Sciences is a company based in Madison, WI, that does colon cancer screening worldwide. They created a test that serves as an alternative to a colonoscopy. Envision worked with them to help them grow and open labs all over the world to help more people be screened; they were helping them in their work to eradicate colon cancer.

The day after Nancy Pautsch found out that they were a finalist for this worldwide award, they discovered that one of their key stakeholder value seekers (a.k.a. salespeople)—and they only had three at the time—was diagnosed with stage 4 colon cancer. Envision leadership didn't blink and supported him and his family; he passed away in June 2017. They didn't backfill his position while he was sick because they didn't want to send a message to anyone that he might not recover. And then they grieved like a family; it was really hard for them. This was a financial blow to the company; but Envision's executive leadership team said they wouldn't have done anything differently. They're still growing at a rate they feel good about, and their reputation is growing too.

We can learn a great deal from how Envision approaches supporting well-being and hopefully follow their lead. Remember, when people are **both** thriving in their well-being and engaged, the organization benefits!

How to *Show Up as a Leader* and Influence Change at This Part of the Pyramid

Employee well-being starts at the base of the pyramid. So, by the time you've reached the top, it's like the cherry on top and further enhances all of the good work that's already occurring. Here are some ways you can advocate for and help support well-being in a humane, holistic way within your organization:

- **Reexamine the programs you offer to support well-being.** Are you offering programs because employees are asking for them, or because some vendor, consultant, or health plan suggests they will reduce risk and health care costs? Leverage an outward mindset and offer programs and resources *for* and *with* people rather than "wellness or else" done *to* them. Make sure to take a holistic approach to support more than just physical health. Uncouple wellness from your health insurance premiums. And move far, far away from harmful weight-loss programs and competitions.

- **Advocate for effective health care cost-savings strategies.** Like it or not, all organizations are in the health care business if they offer benefits and health insurance. Look into the efforts and resources of Health Rosetta. Better yet, be intentional to partner with benefits consultants who are trained and certified by Health Rosetta. Take a cue from Rosen Hotels to make a real impact on employee health; reinvest your savings to help nurture the social determinants of health. Create additional support by leveraging health care consumerism and literacy initiatives.

- **Embrace *The Employee Health and Wellness Program Code of Conduct*.** We need to work together to draw boundaries between those who are providing effective, humane, and ethical services and those who continue to be stuck and dehumanized. Become familiar with *The Code of Conduct* and leverage the language in any contract you sign with a health and wellness provider. If a potential partner has not yet officially endorsed it, invite them to do so. Also, leverage critical thinking as you read about claims regarding health and the impact of various interventions; be wary of the red flags we mentioned—especially headlines and claims of causality from observational studies.

- **Rethink the role of workplace wellness professionals.** Well-trained wellness professionals can do so much more than "just run programs" and can play an important role in leadership and people development efforts. If you're a wellness professional, beware of your own self-limiting stories. Look for opportunities to build relationships and contribute to other initiatives for creating a thriving workplace; expand your knowledge and invite yourself to the table. If you are fortunate to have wellness expertise within your stakeholders, broaden your perspective; include them in discussions and efforts at the other parts of the pyramid.

CONCLUSION

Our world and workplaces have become increasingly dehumanized. We are living in a new reality (VUCA) where disruption is the norm. It's not going away, and our world is not going to get less complex; so we must call upon ourselves to show up differently and more effectively so we can be less reactive and triggered and more intentional and collaborative. We must shift away from applying outdated, machine-like logic to people and business.

The good news is that there is a "rehumanizing revolution" already underway that shows us that:

- Rehumanizing workplaces **can** be done.
- It doesn't have to start at the C-suite.
- We can build critical mass one person, one team at a time.

The "rehumanizing antidote" ultimately requires leveraging the Five Rehumanizing Principles:

1. ***Build a lighthouse***
2. ***Create fearless environments***
3. ***Wade in the messy middle***
4. ***Show up as a leader***
5. ***Find your tribe***

These are essential in supporting people and creating a safe space for them to do the work that is necessary to make the adaptive leaps our VUCA world demands. We need to do the essential work to upgrade our IOS so we can operate from a place of greater mental complexity. Doing so helps us make the shift:

- From controlling to compassion
- From strategy to purpose
- From participation to fulfillment
- From self-protection to self-reflection
- From guarded to connected
- From scarcity to abundance

We have a tremendous opportunity to transform our workplaces, find fulfillment, and be a fierce advocate for humanity. But where do you start? Use the Thriving Organization Pyramid as a guide for determining where efforts are needed within your organization in order to have strength and sustainability. If your base is strong (i.e., thriving organizational well-being), continue to nurture it while you focus improvement efforts further up the pyramid. Remembering that the well-being of employees really starts at the bottom of the pyramid (and quality health and well-being programs and resources are more like icing on the cake), make sure to provide resources **for** and **with** employees and avoid doing "wellness or else" **to** them. And ensure any provider of such services first pledges to do no harm and endorses *The Employee Health and Wellness Program Code of Conduct.*

However, if your base needs work, your employees' well-being will benefit much more from redeploying resources that might be currently spent on things like tracking portals, biometric screenings, health risk assessments, incentives, wearable devices, and behavior change challenges. This includes developing leaders at all levels within your organization, clarifying and aligning with your **WHY** (purpose), strengthening communication, and putting people back to the forefront. Then, over time, you can move to supporting well-being at the top of the pyramid.

Embrace VUCA 2.0

When you create the conditions for your organization and its people to thrive in the midst of this VUCA world, you essentially future-proof your workplace. This means starting with honoring the complexities of what it means to be human. It is nearly impossible to have thriving organizations if the people that comprise them are not able to thrive, be the best version of themselves, and *show up as leaders*. But this requires a radically different approach to leadership, people, and well-being.

Enter VUCA 2.0—what former CEO of Medtronic and bestselling author Bill George suggests we need for this unsteady world:[224]

- Vision. We need to move from *Volatile* to *Vision*. We do this by *building a lighthouse* to cut through the fog and clearly articulate a common vision for the organization and where it's headed. When there is clarity of the vision and purpose (**WHY**), it becomes much easier for people to see how they fit into the picture and find meaning and fulfillment in their work; we can then support people in clarifying their individual purpose or **WHY**.

- **Understanding.** We need to move from *Uncertainty* to *Understanding.* We do this by broadening our horizons and learning to truly listen to multiple perspectives. Accepting opportunities to be challenged and influenced by diverse opinions increases our ability to see more, build relationships, and adapt so we don't become stuck. This is how we *find our tribe.*

- **Courage.** We need to move from *Complexity* to *Courage.* Now more than ever it is critical that we have the courage to go against the grain and challenge the status quo. Bill George argues that leaders can't afford to keep their heads down, using traditional management techniques and avoiding criticism. And, as Brené Brown's research shows, it is impossible to have courage without being vulnerable. Being vulnerable and making bold moves is essential for us to thrive—and even survive. So we must *create fearless environments* and then embrace the discomfort to *wade in the messy middle.*

- **Adaptability.** We need to move from *Ambiguity* to *Adaptability.* Being flexible is critical; most long-range plans are obsolete by the time they are approved. We need to stay true to a clear **WHY** and be intentional about **HOW** we get there, but we need to be flexible and able to adapt to external circumstances. Our **WHATS**, on the other hand, need to have room to evolve, and we need to have multiple contingency plans.

Embracing the principles of VUCA 2.0 can help us to *show up as leaders* and create workplaces that inspire and foster humanity. We are at a critical juncture; we can cling to what is comfortable or *wade in the messy middle*, step into our greatness, *show up as leaders*, and start advocating for more human workplaces.

In their book *Leadership on the Line*, Ronald Heifetz and Marty Linsky suggest that the opportunity for leadership stands before us every day in various ways. And every day we must decide whether or not to put our contribution out there, or keep it to ourselves to avoid upsetting anyone. The reality is that we appear dangerous to people when we question their values, beliefs, or habits; we place ourselves on the line when we tell people what they *need* to hear rather than what they want to hear. "To lead is to live dangerously because when leadership counts, when you lead people through difficult change, you challenge what people hold dear—their daily habits, tools, loyalties, and ways of thinking—with nothing more to offer perhaps than a possibility."[225]

Going against the grain of "business as usual" requires a great amount of new learning, engaging ourselves and others in adjusting our unrealistic expectations, and promoting our resourcefulness. **If not you, then who?** At the end of the day, leadership is a **behavior**, not a title or job function. So we can choose to stay comfortable and wait for someone else "more qualified" to "fix" the problem, or we can embrace the discomfort, *wade in the messy middle*, and step into leading positive change.

Brené Brown says that "you shift a culture by creating a critical mass of courageous leaders." As you read the powerful words from the Hopi Elders of the Hopi Nation from Oraibi, AZ, think about how you want to show up: on the sidelines, or as a leader of hope, humanity, and the future?

. . .

You have been telling the people that this is the Eleventh Hour.

Now you must go back and tell the people that this is **The Hour**.
There are things to be considered:

Where are you living?
What are you doing?
What are your relationships?
Are you in right relation?
Where is your water?
Know your garden.
It is time to speak your Truth.
Create your community.
Be good to each other.
And **do not look outside yourself for the leader.**

This could be a good time!

There is a river flowing now very fast.
It is so great and swift that there are those who will be afraid.
They will try to hold on to the shore.
They will feel they are being torn apart, and they will suffer greatly.

Know the river has its destination.
The elders say **we must let go of the shore, push off into the middle of the river, keep our eyes open, and our heads above the water.**

See who is in there with you and celebrate.

At this time in history, we are to take nothing personally.
Least of all, ourselves.
For the moment that we do, our spiritual growth and journey comes to a halt.

The time of the lone wolf is over.
Gather yourselves!

Banish the word struggle from your attitude and vocabulary.

All that we do now must be done in a sacred manner and in celebration.

We are the ones we've been waiting for.[226]

. . .

We are not alone. Be in community. Build relationships. Be a courageous leader and fierce advocate for rehumanizing the workplace. Be a conduit for positive change so that we can restore hope, well-being, and performance to our organizations.

NOTES

1 McKinsey Global Institute, *Jobs Lost, Jobs Gained: Workforce Transitions in a Time of Automation*, December 2017, https://www.mckinsey.com/~/media/mckinsey/featured%20insights/Future%20of%20Organizations/What%20the%20future%20of%20work%20will%20mean%20for%20jobs%20skills%20and%20wages/MGI-Jobs-Lost-Jobs-Gained-Report-December-6-2017.ashx.

2 David Lee, "Why the Jobs of the Future Won't Feel Like Work," filmed July 2017 in Atlanta, GA, TED video, 10:07, https://www.ted.com/talks/david_lee_why_jobs_of_the_future_won_t_feel_like_work#t-207367.

3 Erica Keswin, *Bring Your Human to Work* (New York: McGraw-Hill, 2017).

4 Maritz Research, *Maritz Research Hospitality Group 2011 Employee Engagement Poll*, June 2011, http://www.maritzresearch.com/~/media/Files/MaritzDotCom/White%20Papers/ExcecutiveSummary_Research.pdf.

5 Jeffrey Pfeffer, *Dying for a Paycheck* (New York: Harper Collins, 2018).

6 Amy C. Edmondson, *The Fearless Organization* (Hoboken, NJ: Wiley, 2019).

7 Ibid.

8 Andy Swann, *The Human Workplace* (London: Kogan Page Limited, 2017).

9 Raj Sisodia, Timothy Henry, and Thomas Eckschmidt, *Conscious Capitalism Field Guide* (Boston: Harvard Business Review Press, 2018).

10 Simon Sinek, *Start with WHY* (New York: Portfolio/Penguin, 2009).

11 Sisodia, Henry, and Eckschmidt, *Conscious Capitalism Field Guide*.

12 Raj Sisodia, David Wolfe, and Jag Sheth, *Firms of Endearment*, 2nd ed. (Upper Saddle River, NJ: Pearson Education, 2014).

13 Ronald Heifetz and Marty Linsky, *Leadership on the Line* (Boston: Harvard Business Review Press, 2017).

14 Martin Luther King Jr., "Beyond Vietnam—a Time to Break Silence," Martin Luther King Jr. Center for Nonviolent Social Change, uploaded on July 6, 2015, YouTube video, 56:48, https://www.youtube.com/watch?v=AJhgXKGldUk.

15 The American Institute of Stress, "Workplace Stress," https://www.stress.org/workplace-stress/.

16 American Psychological Association, *Stress in America: The State of Our Nation*, November 2017, https://www.apa.org/news/press/releases/stress/2017/state-nation.pdf.

17 Daniel S. Hamermesh and Elena Stancanelli, *Long Workweeks and Strange Hours* (National Bureau of Economic Research, September 2014), https://www.nber.org/papers/w20449.pdf.

18 David Kelleher, "Survey: 81% of U.S. Employees Check Their Work Mail Outside Work Hours," *TechTalk*, May 20, 2013, https://techtalk.gfi.com/survey-81-of-u-s-employees-check-their-work-mail-outside-work-hours/.

19 Pfeffer, *Dying for a Paycheck*.

20 Gallup, "Gallup Daily: U.S. Employee Engagement," 2017, https://news.gallup.com/poll/180404/gallup-daily-employee-engagement.aspx.

21 Joel Goh, Jeffrey Pfeffer, and Stefanos Zenios, "Workplace Stressors and Health Outcomes: Health Policy for the Workplace," *Behavioral Science & Policy Association*, February 15, 2017, https://behavioralpolicy.org/articles/workplace-stressors-health-outcomes-health-policy-for-the-workplace/.

22 Pfeffer, *Dying for a Paycheck*.

23 Margaret Wheatley, *Who Do We Choose to Be? Facing Reality, Claiming Leadership, Restoring Sanity* (Oakland, CA: Berrett-Koehler, 2017).

24 Bob Chapman and Raj Sisodia, *Everybody Matters* (New York: Portfolio-Penguin, 2015).

25 Margaret Wheatley, *Finding Our Way: Leadership for an Uncertain Time* (San Francisco: Berrett-Koehler, 2015).

26 Ibid.

27 Kevin Cashman, *The Pause Principle* (San Francisco: Berrett-Koehler, 2012).

28 Laura Rediehs, "From Dehumanization to Rehumanization," Carnegie Council for Ethics in International Affairs, February 14, 2014, https://www.carnegiecouncil.org/publications/ethics_online/0090.

29 Margaret Wheatley and Myron Kellner-Rogers, "The Irresistible Future of Organizing," Margaret J. Wheatley, July/August 1996, https://www.margaretwheatley.com/articles/irresistiblefuture.html.

30 David S. Hilzenrath, "Misleading Claims about Safeway Wellness Incentives Shape Health-Care Bill," *Washington Post*, January 17, 2010, http://www.washingtonpost.com/wp-dyn/content/article/2010/01/15/AR2010011503319.html?noredirect=on.

31 Mary Agnes Cary, "Are Big Insurance Discounts for Healthy Behavior Unfair?", July 27, 2009, McClatchy DC Bureau, https://www.mcclatchydc.com/news/politics-government/article24548149.html.

32 Kevin Volpp, David Asch, Robert Galvin, and George Loewenstein, "Redesigning Employee Health Incentives—Lessons from Behavioral Economics," *New England Journal of Medicine*, August 4, 2011, https://www.ncbi.nlm.nih.gov/pmc/articles/PMC3696722/.

33 Al Lewis, Vik Khanna, and Shanna Montrose, "Workplace Wellness Produces No Savings," Health Affairs, November 25, 2014, https://www.healthaffairs.org/do/10.1377/hblog20141125.042926/full/#comment-1088570.

34 Willis Towers Watson, *2017 Global Benefits Attitudes Survey*, 2017, https://cdn2.hubspot.net/hubfs/2705714/(Research)%202017-global-benefits-attitudes-survey.pdf.

35 Adam Gaffney, "The West Virginia Teachers' Strike Is Over. But the Fight for Healthcare Isn't," *The Guardian*, March 7, 2018, https://www.theguardian.com/commentisfree/2018/mar/07/west-virginia-teachers-strike-healthcare.

36 Tom Rath and Jim Harter, *Wellbeing: The Five Essential Elements* (New York: Gallup Press, 2010).

37 Dan Witters and Sangeeta Agrawal, "Well-Being Enhances Benefits of Employee Engagement," Gallup, October 27, 2015, https://www.gallup.com/workplace/236483/enhances-benefits-employee-engagement.aspx.

38 Quoted in Rosie Ward, "From 'Dying for a Paycheck' to Building Thriving, Humanistic Workplaces: A Call for Courageous Leaders," Fusion 2.0 Conference, https://fusion2conference.com/dying-for-a-paycheck/.

39 Andy Swann, *The Human Workplace*.

40 Cy Wakeman, *Reality-Based Leadership* (San Francisco: Jossey-Bass, 2010).

41 R. A. Heifetz and D. L. Laurie, "The Work of Leadership," *Harvard Business Review*, December 2001, 131–141.

42 Ronald Heifetz and Marty Linsky, *Leadership on the Line*.

43 Ibid.

44 Rob Cross, Reb Rebele, and Adam Grant, "Collaborative Overload," *Harvard Business Review*, January–February 2016, https://hbr.org/2016/01/collaborative-overload.

45 Brené Brown, *The Gifts of Imperfection* (Center City, MN: Hazelden, 2010).

46 Mike Robbins, *Bring Your Whole Self to Work* (New York City: Hay House, 2018).

47 Amy C. Edmondson, *The Fearless Organization*.

48 John D. Adams, ed., *Transforming Work*, 2nd ed. (New York: Cosimo, 2018).

49 Robert Kegan and Lisa Laskow Lahey, *Immunity to Change* (Boston: Harvard Press, 2009).

50 Robert J. Anderson and William A. Adams, *Mastering Leadership* (Hoboken, NJ: Wiley, 2016).

51 Kegan and Lahey, *Immunity to Change*.

52 Anderson and Adams, *Mastering Leadership*.

53 Ibid.

54 David Rock, "SCARF: A Brain-Based Model for Collaborating with and Influencing Others, *NeuroLeadership Journal*, 2008, http://web.archive.org/web/20100705024057/http://www.your-brain-at-work.com:80/files/NLJ_SCARFUS.pdf.

55 Ibid.

56 C. G. Jung, *The Collected Works of C. G. Jung: Complete Digital Edition*, edited and translated by Gerhard Adler and R. F. C. Hull (New York: Princeton University Press, 2014).

57 Anderson and Adams, *Mastering Leadership*.

58 Viktor Frankl, *Man's Search for Meaning* (London: Hodder & Stoughton, 1946).

59 Richard Fry, "Millennials Are the Largest Generation in the U.S. Labor Force," Pew Research Center, April 11, 2018, http://www.pewresearch.org/fact-tank/2018/04/11/millennials-largest-generation-us-labor-force/.

60 Peter Economy, "The (Millennial) Workplace of the Future Is Almost Here—These 3 Things Are About to Change Big Time," *Inc.*, January 15, 2019, https://www.inc.com/peter-economy/the-millennial-workplace-of-future-is-almost-here-these-3-things-are-about-to-change-big-time.html.

61 Morley Winograd and Michael Hais, *How Millennials Could Upend Wall Street and Corporate America*, Brookings, May 28, 2014, https://www.brookings.edu/research/how-millennials-could-upend-wall-street-and-corporate-america/.

62 Josh Miller, "10 Things You Need to Know About Gen Z," *HR Magazine*, November/December 2018, 51–56.

63 Rasmus Hougaard and Jacqueline Carter, *The Mind of the Leader* (Boston: Harvard Business Review Press, 2018).

64 *Rewriting the Rules for the Digital Age: 2017 Deloitte Global Human Capital Trends* (Deloitte University Press, 2017), https://www2.deloitte.com/content/dam/Deloitte/global/Documents/About-Deloitte/central-europe/ce-global-human-capital-trends.pdf.

65 Deloitte Insights, *The Rise of the Social Enterprise: 2018 Deloitte Global Human Capital Trends*, 2018, https://www2.deloitte.com/insights/us/en/focus/human-capital-trends.html.

66 Raj Sisodia, David Wolfe, and Jag Sheth, *Firms of Endearment*.

67 Kegan and Lahey, *Immunity to Change*.

68 David Roth, "Five Blind Men," David Roth—Topic, uploaded on August 23, 2015, YouTube video, 5:26, https://www.youtube.com/watch?v=e-YtNU6OYjU.

69 Willis Harman, *Global Mind Change: The Promise of the 21st Century Paperback* (San Francisco: Berrett-Koehler, 1998).

70 Thomas S. Kuhn, *The Structure of Scientific Revolutions: 50th Anniversary Edition*, 4th ed (Chicago: University of Chicago Press, 2012).

71 Joel Arthur Barker, *Paradigms: The Business of Discovering the Future* (New York: HarperCollins, 1992).

72 Margaret Wheatley, *Who Do We Choose to Be?*

73 M. Scott Peck, *The Road Less Traveled: A New Psychology of Love, Traditional Values, and Spiritual Growth* (New York: Simon and Schuster, 1979).

74 Steven Shapin, *The Scientific Revolution*, 2nd ed. (Chicago: University of Chicago Press, 2008).

75 Fritjof Capra, *The Turning Point: Science, Society and The Rising Culture* (New York: Bantam Books, 1982).

76 Carolyn Merchant, "'The Violence of Impediments': Francis Bacon and the Origins of Experimentation," *Isis* 99 (2008), 731–60, https://warwick.ac.uk/fac/arts/history/students/modules/hi203/group2/bacon.pdf.

77 C. Stephen Byrum, *From the Neck Up: The Recovery and Sustaining of the Human Element in Modern Organizations* (Littleton, MA: Tapestry Press, 2006).

78 Charles S. Jacobs, *Management Rewired* (New York: Portfolio, 2009).

79 Heifetz and Linsky, *Leadership on the Line*.

80 Ibid.

81 Jacobs, *Management Rewired*; Daniel Pink, *Drive: The Surprising Truth about What Motivates Us* (New York: Riverhead Books, 2009); Alfie Kohn, *Punished by Rewards* (Boston: Houghton Mifflin, 1999); and E. L. Deci and R. Flaste, *Why We Do What We Do: Understanding Self-Motivation* (New York: Penguin Books, 1996).

82 Richard H. Thaler, "The Power of Nudges, for Good and Bad," *New York Times*, October 31, 2015, https://www.nytimes.com/2015/11/01/upshot/the-power-of-nudges-for-good-and-bad.html.

83 Pat Kane, "Playing Politics: Exposing the Flaws of Nudge Thinking," NewScientist, November 16, 2016, https://www.newscientist.com/article/mg23231002-200-playing-politics-exposing-the-flaws-of-nudge-thinking/.

84 Ron Friedman, *The Best Place to Work* (New York: Penguin Group, 2014).

85 Brené Brown, *The Gifts of Imperfection*.

86 Danielle Harlan, *The New Alpha* (New York: McGraw-Hill, 2017).

87 Brené Brown, *Dare to Lead* (New York: Random House, 2018).

88 Simon Sinek, "The New Rules of Leadership," How To Academy, uploaded on February 12, 2019, YouTube video, 1:30:54, https://www.youtube.com/watch?v=AankK-V0QF8.

89 Swann, *The Human Workplace*.

90 Ibid.

91 *The New Organization: Different by Design—Global Human Capital Trends 2016* (Deloitte University Press, 2016), https://www2.deloitte.com/content/dam/Deloitte/global/Documents/HumanCapital/gx-dup-global-human-capital-trends-2016.pdf.

92 Swann, *The Human Workplace*.

93 The Morning Star Company, http://www.morningstarco.com/.

94 Vikas Narula, "The Power of Connection—Bridging the Divide," TEDx Talks, uploaded on May 5, 2017, YouTube video, 18:13, https://www.youtube.com/watch?v=2qKmeu5NyoQ&t=603s.

95 Michael Simmons, "The No. 1 Predictor of Career Success According to Network Science," Accelerated Intelligence, August 10, 2015, https://medium.com/accelerated-intelligence/the-number-one-predictor-of-career-success-according-to-network-science.

96 Patricia Waldon, "Why Birds Fly in a V Formation," *Science*, January 15, 2014, https://www.sciencemag.org/news/2014/01/why-birds-fly-v-formation.

97 Frederic Laloux, *Reinventing Organizations* (Brussels: Nelson Parker, 2014).

98 Frederic Laloux, "The Keys to Self-Management. A Coherent Set of Structures and Practices to Get Rid of Bosses, Hierarchy and the Pyramid," Management Innovation eXchange, March 30, 2014, https://www.managementexchange.com/story/how-self-management-works-coherent-set-structures-and-practices-get-rid-bosses-hierarchy-and.

99 Laloux, *Reinventing Organizations*.

100 Ibid.

101 Laloux, "The Keys to Self-Management."

102 Laloux, *Reinventing Organizations*.

103 Sun Hydraulics, https://www.sunhydraulics.com/.

104 Laloux, *Reinventing Organizations*.

105 Swann, *The Human Workplace*.

106 Edgar Schein, "Organizational Culture," *American Psychologist* 45, no. 2, (1990), 109–19.

107 Schein, "Organizational Culture" and *Organizational Culture and Leadership* (San Francisco: Jossey-Bass, 1985).

108 Robert Richman, *The Culture Blueprint: A Guide to Building the High-Performance Workplace* (Culture Hackers, 2015).

109 The Arbinger Institute, *The Outward Mindset: Seeing Beyond Ourselves* (Oakland, CA: Berrett-Koehler, 2016).

110 Ibid.

111 Nate Boaz and Erica Ariel Fox, "Change Leader, Change Thyself," *McKinsey Quarterly*, March 2014, https://www.mckinsey.com/featured-insights/leadership/change-leader-change-thyself.

112 The Arbinger Institute, *The Outward Mindset*.

113 Nate Boaz and Erica Ariel Fox, "Change Leader, Change Thyself."

114 Joanna Barsh and Johanne Lavoie, "Lead at Your Best," *McKinsey Quarterly*, April 2014, https://www.mckinsey.com/featured-insights/leadership/lead-at-your-best.

115 Quoted in Rosie Ward, "3 Key Considerations for Bringing Humanity Back to the Workplace," LinkedIn, September 12, 2017, https://www.linkedin.com/pulse/3-key-considerations-bringing-humanity-back-workplace-ward-ph-d-.

116 Society for Human Resource Management, "SHRM Urges Employers to Consider Applicants with Criminal Histories," https://www.shrm.org/about-shrm/news-about-shrm/pages/shrm-urges-employers-to-consider-applicants-with-criminal-histories.aspx.

117 Society for Human Resource Management, "Ban the Box Laws by State and Municipality," https://www.shrm.org/resourcesandtools/hr-topics/talent-acquisition/pages/ban-the-box-turns-20-what-employers-need-to-know.aspx.

118 Society for Human Resource Management, "Hiring People with Criminal Histories."

119 Televerde, https://televerde.com/.

120 Edmondson, *The Fearless Organization*.

121 Brené Brown, *Dare to Lead*.

122 Ibid.

123 Rudyard Kipling, "Surgeons and the Soul," Telelib.com, http://www.telelib.com/authors/K/KiplingRudyard/prose/BookOfWords/surgeonssoul.html.

124 Anderson and Adams, *Mastering Leadership*.

125 David Rooke and William Torbert, "Organizational Transformation as a Function of CEO's Developmental Stage," *Organizational Development Journal* 16, no. 1 (1998), 11–28.

126 Simon Sinek and Diana Ransom, "Simon Sinek: How to Build a Company That People Want to Work For," *Inc.*, uploaded on June 27, 2016, YouTube video, 8:55, https://www.youtube.com/watch?v=INjECrw7YYs.

127 Bob Chapman and Raj Sisodia, *Everybody Matters*.

128 Mihnea Moldoveanu and Das Narayandas, "The Future of Leadership Development," *Harvard Business Review*, March–April 2019, 40–48.

129 Rasmus Hougaard and Jacqueline Carter, *The Mind of the Leader*.

130 Rebecca Shannonhouse, "Is Your Boss Making You Sick?" *Washington Post*, October 20, 2014, https://www.washingtonpost.com/national/health-science/is-your-boss-making-you-sick/2014/10/20/60cd5d44-2953-11e4-8593-da634b334390_story.html?noredirect=on&utm_campaign=buffer&utm_content=buffer4f314&utm_medium=social&utm_source=twitter.com&utm_term=.5e067c3c824e.

131 A. Nyberg, L. Alfredsson, T. Theorell, H. Westerlund, J. Vahtera, and M. Kivimäki, "Managerial Leadership and Ischaemic Heart Disease Among Employees: The Swedish WOLF Study," *Occupational & Environmental Medicine* 66, no.1 (August 18, 2009), https://oem.bmj.com/content/66/1/51.full.

132 James Campbell Quick, Thomas Wright, Joyce Adkins, Debra Nelson, and Jonathan Quick, *Preventive Stress Management in Organizations*, 2nd ed. (Washington, DC: American Psychological Association, 2012).

133 Joel Goh, Jeffrey Pfeffer, and Stefanos Zenios, "Workplace Stressors and Health Outcomes."

134 C. Jacobs, H. Pfaff, B. Lehner, E. Driller, A. Nitzsche, B. Stieler-Lorenz, J. Wasem, and J. Jung J, "The Influence of Transformational Leadership on Employee Well-Being: Results from a Survey of Companies in the Information and Communication Technology Sector in Germany," *Journal of Occupational & Environmental Medicine* 55, no. 7 (July 2013), 772–78, https://www.ncbi.nlm.nih.gov/pubmed/23836019.

135 Anderson and Adams, *Mastering Leadership*.

136 Kegan and Lahey, *Immunity to Change*.

137 Ibid.

138 Hougaard and Carter, *The Mind of the Leader*.

139 Wheatley, *Who Do We Choose to Be?*

140 Peter Drucker, "Managing Oneself," in The Drucker Lectures: Essential Lessons on Management, *Society and Economy*, ed. Rick Wartzman (New York: McGraw-Hill, 2010), 199–204.

141 Kevin Brennan, "Check Your Frame," Top 20 Training, March 5, 2018, https://top20training.com/check-your-frame/.

142 Jim Dethmer, Diana Chapman, and Kaley Warner Klemp, *The 15 Commitments of Conscious Leadership: A New Paradigm for Sustainable Success* (Amazon Digital Services, 2014).

143 Viktor Frankl, *Man's Search for Meaning*.

144 Kim Scott, *Radical Candor* (New York: St. Martin's Press, 2017).

145 Daniel Coyle, *The Culture Code* (New York: Bantam, 2018).

146 Rah Sisodia, "20130716_STU_Raj Sisodia Round Table," Barry-Wehmiller, uploaded on July 23, 2013, YouTube video, 10:03, https://www.trulyhumanleadership.com/?p=824.

147 Sinek, *Start with WHY*.

148 Ed Freeman, "Purpose Beyond Profit," Conscious Capitalism Arizona, August 1, 2013, https://ccarizona.org/purpose-beyond-profit-ed-freeman/.

149 David Koji, "An Inspiring Discussion with Simon Sinek about Learning Your 'Why,'" Entrepreneur, December 8, 2016, https://www.entrepreneur.com/article/284791.

150 Swann, *The Human Workplace*.

151 Wheatley, *Who Do We Choose to Be?*

152 Daniel Coyle, *The Culture Code*.

153 Cy Wakeman, *Reality-Based Leadership*.

154 Kristen Hadeed, *Permission to Screw Up* (New York: Portfolio/Penguin, 2017).

155 Aaron Hurst, *The Purpose Economy* (Boise, Idaho: Elevate, 2014).

156 Paul L. Marciano, *Carrots and Sticks Don't Work: Build a Culture of Employee Engagement with the Principles of RESPECT™* (New York: McGraw-Hill, 2010).

157 The Energy Project, https://theenergyproject.com/.

158 Naina Dhingra, Jonathan Emmett, and Mahin Samadani, "Employee Experience: Essential to Compete," McKinsey & Company, March 12, 2018, https://www.mckinsey.com/business-functions/organization/our-insights/the-organization-blog/employee-experience-essential-to-compete.

159 Tammy Perkins, "7 Ways to Deliver a Stellar Employee Experience," Glassdoor for Employers, October 9, 2018, https://www.glassdoor.com/employers/blog/7-ways-to-deliver-a-stellar-employee-experience/.

160 David Sturt and Todd Nordstrom, "Employee Experience vs. Engagement, and 3 Things You Should Start Thinking about Now," *Forbes*, May 18, 2018, https://www.forbes.com/sites/davidsturt/2018/05/18/employee-experience-vs-engagement-and-3-things-you-should-start-thinking-about-now/#e29348ca88f6.

161 Imperative, "2019 Workforce Purpose Index: Pathways to Fulfillment at Work," 2019, https://www.imperative.com/2019wpi.

162 Simon Sinek, David Mead, and Peter Docker, *Find Your WHY: A Practical Guide for Discovering Purpose for You and Your Team* (New York: Portfolio/Penguin, 2017).

163 Hougaard and Carter, *The Mind of the Leader.*

164 Victor Strecher, *Life on Purpose: How Living for What Matters Most Changes Everything* (New York: Harper One, 2016).

165 Imperative, "2019 Workforce Purpose Index: Pathways to Fulfillment at Work."

166 Amy Wrzesniewski and Jane E. Dutton, "Crafting a Job: Revisioning Employees as Active Crafters of Their Work," *Academy of Management Review* 26, no. 2 (2001), 179–201, https://spinup-000d1a-wp-offload-media.s3.amazonaws.com/faculty/wp-content/uploads/sites/6/2019/06/Craftingajob_Revisioningemployees_000.pdf.

167 J. M. Berg, A. Wrzesniewski, and J. E. Dutton, "Perceiving and Responding to Challenges in Job Crafting at Different Ranks: When Proactivity Requires Adaptivity," *Journal of Organizational Behavior* 31, no. 2–3 (2010), 158–86.

168 Amy Wrzesniewski, Juston Berg, and Jane Dutton, "Managing Yourself: Turn the Job You Have Into the Job You Want," *Harvard Business Review*, June 2010, https://hbr.org/2010/06/managing-yourself-turn-the-job-you-have-into-the-job-you-want.

169 Barry Schwartz, *Why We Work* (New York: TED Books/Simon and Schuster, 2015).

170 Brown, *Dare to Lead.*

171 Edmondson, *The Fearless Organization.*

172 Charles Duhigg, "What Google Learned from Its Quest to Build the Perfect Team," *New York Times Magazine*, February 28, 2016, https://www.nytimes.com/2016/02/28/magazine/what-google-learned-from-its-quest-to-build-the-perfect-team.html.

173 Julia Rozovsky, "The Five Keys to a Successful Google Team," Re:Work Blog, November 17, 2015, https://rework.withgoogle.com/blog/five-keys-to-a-successful-google-team/.

174 William Kahn, "Psychological Conditions of Personal Engagement and Disengagement at Work," *Academy of Management Journal* 33, no. 4 (1990), 692–724.

175 Edgar Schein, "How Can Organizations Learn Faster? The Challenge of Entering the Green Room," *Sloan Management Review* 34, no. 2 (1993), 85–92.

176 Edmondson, *The Fearless Organization.*

177 Coyle, *The Culture Code.*

178 Edmondson, *The Fearless Organization.*

179 Stephen M. R. Covey, *The Speed of Trust* (New York: Free Press, 2006).

180 Charles Feltman, *The Thin Book of Trust* (Bend, OR: Thin Book Publishing, 2009).

181 Stephen M. R. Covey, *The Speed of Trust.*

182 Brené Brown, *Braving the Wilderness: The Quest for True Belonging and the Courage to Stand Alone* (New York: Random House, 2017).

183 Covey, *The Speed of Trust.*

184 Center for Courage & Renewal, "Circle of Trust Touchstones," http://www.couragerenewal.org/touchstones/.

185 Julianne Holt-Lunstad, Timothy Smith, Mark Baker, Tyler Harris, and David Stephenson, "Loneliness and Social Isolation as Risk Factors for Mortality: A Meta-Analytic Review," *Perspectives on Psychological Science* 10, no. 2 (2015), 227–37, https://www.ahsw.org.uk/wp-content/uploads/2019/06/Perspectives-on-Psychological-Science-2015-Holt-Lunstad-227-37.pdf.

186 Brown, *The Gifts of Imperfection.*

187 Edgar Schein, "How Can Organizations Learn Faster?"

188 Kevin Cashman, *The Pause Principle.*

189 Ibid.

190 Wendy Lynch and Clydette de Groot, *Get to What Matters* (Steamboat Springs, CO: What Matters Press, 2017).

191 Miron Construction, "Our Company," https://miron-construction.com/our-company/.

192 Ibid.

193 Matthew Kelly, *The Dream Manager* (New York: Beacon Publishing, 2007).

194 Coyle, *The Culture Code.*

195 Kim Scott, *Radical Candor.*

196 Ibid.

197 WorkHuman Research Institute, *Bringing More Humanity to Recognition, Performance, and Life at Work*, 2017, https://www.globoforce.com/wp-content/uploads/2017/10/WHRI_2017SurveyReportA.pdf.

198 Wheatley, *Finding Our Way.*

199 Robert Kegan and Lisa Laskow Lahey, *An Everyone Culture: Becoming a Deliberately Developmental Organization* (Boston: Harvard Business Review Press, 2016).

200 Ibid.

201 Everett Rogers, *Diffusion of Innovations*, 5th ed. (New York: Free Press, 2003).

202 Hadeed, *Permission to Screw Up.*

203 Simon Sinek, foreword to *Permission to Screw Up*, by Kristen Hadeed.

204 Constitution of the World Health Organization, 1946, https://www.who.int/governance/eb/who_constitution_en.pdf.

205 David B. Morris, *Illness and Culture in the Postmodern Age* (London: University of California Press, 1998).

206 Ivan Illich, *Medical Nemesis: The Expropriation of Health* (New York: Pantheon, 1982).

207 Tia Ghose, "Otzi 'The Iceman' Had Heart Disease Genes," Live Science, July 30, 2014, https://www.livescience.com/47114-otzi-had-heart-disease-genes.html.

208 Centers for Disease Control and Prevention, "NCHHSTP Social Determinants of Health: Frequently Asked Questions," https://www.cdc.gov/nchhstp/socialdeterminants/faq.html.

209 Michael Marmot, *The Status Syndrome: How Social Standing Affects Our Health and Longevity* (New York: Henry Holt and Company, 2005).

210 Nortin M. Hadler, *The Last Well Person: How to Stay Well Despite the Health-Care System* (Montreal, QC, and Kingston, ON: McGill-Queen's University Press, 2009).

211 Zack Friedman, "78% of Workers Live Paycheck to Paycheck," *Forbes*, January 11, 2019, https://www.forbes.com/sites/zackfriedman/2019/01/11/live-paycheck-to-paycheck-government-shutdown/#4c29325a4f10.

212 Sarah O'Brien, "Fed Survey Shows 40 Percent of Adults Still Can't Cover a $400 Emergency Expense," CNBC, May 22, 2018, https://www.cnbc.com/2018/05/22/fed-survey-40-percent-of-adults-cant-cover-400-emergency-expense.html.

213 Susan McFarland, "U.N. Report: With 40M in Poverty, U.S. Most Unequal Developed nation," UPI, June 22, 2018, https://www.upi.com/UN-report-With-40M-in-poverty-US-most-unequal-developed-nation/8671529664548/.

214 Ibid.

215 Otis Webb Brawley, with Paul Goldberg, *How We Do Harm: A Doctor Breaks Ranks about Being Sick in America* (New York: St. Martin's Griffin, 2011).

216 Dave Chase, *The CEO's Guide to Restoring the American Dream: How to Deliver World Class Health Care to Your Employees at Half the Cost* (Bellingham, WA: Health Rosetta Media, 2017).

217 Health Rosetta, https://healthrosetta.org/.

218 T. Tylka, et al., "The Weight-Inclusive versus Weight-Normative Approach to Health: Evaluating the Evidence for Prioritizing Well-Being over Weight Loss," *Journal of Obesity*, July 23, 2014, https://www.hindawi.com/journals/jobe/2014/983495/.

219 Lily Ohara and Jane Taylor, "What's Wrong with the 'War on Obesity'? A Narrative Review of the Weight-Centered Health Paradigm and Development of the 3C Framework to Build Critical Competencies for a Paradigm Shift," *SAGE Open*, April–June 2018, 1–28.

220 J. Schaefer and A. Magnuson, "A Review of Interventions That Promote Eating by Internal Cues," *Journal of the Academy of Nutrition and Dietetics* 114 (2014), 734–60.

221 Linda Bacon and Lucy Aphramor, "Weight Science: Evaluating the Evidence for a Paradigm Shift," *Nutrition Journal* 10, no. 9 (2011), https://nutritionj.biomedcentral.com/articles/10.1186/1475-2891-10-9.

222 "The Health at Every Size Approach," Association for Size Diversity and Health, https://www.sizediversityandhealth.org/content.asp?id=76.

223 Salveo Partners, *Helping Health System Employees Foster Positive Self-Care Regardless of Size: Results of a Pilot Program*, August 3, 2018, https://salveopartners.com/hfeb-beaumont-whitepaper/.

224 Bill George, "A Strategy for Leadership in an Uncertain World," Harvard Business School, February 14, 2017, https://hbswk.hbs.edu/item/a-strategy-for-steady-leadership-in-an-unsteady-world.

225 Heifetz and Linsky, *Leadership on the Line*.

226 A prophecy from the Hopi Elders spoken at Oraibi, Arizona, June 8, 2000, as attributed in the book *Perseverance*, by Margaret Wheatley (Berrett-Koehler Publications, 2010).

Rosie Ward is an energetic, passionate, and compassionate leader, consultant, coach, and author who focuses on transformation from the inside out. Her mission started nearly twenty years ago when she experienced firsthand the ill effects of working in a toxic work environment and found her well-being eroding. Since then, she has worked tirelessly to find a solution, so this experience is no longer the norm. She is sought after to help rehumanize workplaces so that people are freed, fueled, and inspired to bring their best selves to work—and home—each day.

Rosie serves as CEO and cofounder of Salveo Partners, LLC, a professional consulting and training company focused on equipping organizations to find success while putting people back at the forefront of their business. They focus on leveraging *The Fusion* (the inextricable interconnectedness of organizational and employee well-being) to help transform workplaces and support people in integrating their personal and professional lives. Her first book, *How to Build a Thriving Culture at Work: Featuring the 7 Points of Transformation*, coauthored with Jon Robison, has served as a blueprint for hundreds of organizations to break past old, outdated paradigms and rehumanize their workplace.

Rosie is a fierce advocate for humanity. In addition to consulting with organizations of all sizes and industries, coaching leaders, and developing a growing community of Paradigm Pioneers, she serves on the leadership team for the Twin Cities chapter of Conscious Capitalism. A lifelong learner, she continues to seek growth opportunities so she can help others break past barriers, step into their greatness, and show up as leaders in all areas of their lives. In addition to having a PhD and numerous certifications, Rosie was trained by Dr. Brené Brown as a certified Dare to Lead™ facilitator. She is often referred to as a "PhD with a personality," and is known for challenging and inspiring people to think differently about what it takes to become the best version of themselves and for organizations to foster their growth and development. She currently lives in Minneapolis with her husband and son.

Jon Robison holds a doctorate in health education/exercise physiology and a master of science in human nutrition from Michigan State University. He has spent his career working to shift health promotion away from its traditional, biomedical, control-oriented focus, with a particular interest in *why people do what they do and don't do what they don't do.*

Jon has authored numerous articles and book chapters and is a frequent presenter at conferences throughout North America. He is coauthor of *The Spirit and Science of Holistic Health: More Than Broccoli, Jogging, and Bottled Water, More Than Yoga, Herbs, and Meditation*, a college textbook and a guidebook for practitioners who wish to incorporate holistic principles and practices into their work. This book provided the foundation for Kailo, one of the first truly holistic employee wellness programs. Kailo won prestigious awards in both Canada and the United States, and the creators lovingly claim Jon as its father.

Jon has been a national leader in the Health at Every Size® movement for more than two decades. He has implemented Health for Every Body®—a unique alternative to weight-loss programs at the worksite in over twenty cities across the United States in the past five years. His 2015 book, *How to Build a Thriving Culture at Work: Featuring The 7 Points of Transformation*, written with coconspirator Dr. Rosie Ward, gives organizations a realistic, step-by-step blueprint for transforming their cultures—"from the inside out." The book was selected by *Employee Benefit News* as one of the top reads for 2016.

Dr. Robison is cofounder of Salveo Partners—an expert consulting and professional development firm that guides organizations to create thriving workplace cultures, enhance organizational performance, and cultivate employee well-being. As a certified Intrinsic Coach®, Jon understands that behavior is the outward manifestation of thinking and feeling—and that behavior modification approaches that focus on extrinsic motivation rarely result in sustained change and, in fact, often inhibit intrinsic motivation.

Aside from his work, Jon's passions include his wife, Jerilyn; their son, Joshua; music; humor; and a twelve-pound living teddy bear named Ginger.

ELEVATE HUMANITY THROUGH BUSINESS.

Conscious Capitalism, Inc., supports a global community of business leaders dedicated to elevating humanity through business via their demonstration of purpose beyond profit, the cultivation of conscious leadership and culture throughout their entire ecosystem, and their focus on long-termism by prioritizing stakeholder orientation instead of shareholder primacy. We provide mid-market executives with innovative learning exchanges, transformational storytelling training, and inspiring conference experiences all designed to level-up their business operations and collectively demonstrate capitalism as a powerful force for good when practiced consciously.

We invite you, either as an individual or as a business, to join us and contribute your voice. Learn more about the global movement at www.consciouscapitalism.org.

CPSIA information can be obtained
at www.ICGtesting.com
Printed in the USA
LVHW061925240320
651011LV00007B/272